Praise for
UNSAVORY TRUTH

"What happens when one of the country's great nutrition investigators follows the money in food and science? You get this riveting, provocatively-written book, which deftly explores how the processed food industry has deepened our dependence on its products by sponsoring and manipulating food research for decades. This book should be read by anyone who has been seduced by the words, 'New study shows . . .' which is all of us."

—MICHAEL MOSS,
author of *Salt Sugar Fat*

"Marion Nestle is a truth-teller in a world awash with nutrition lies of one kind or another. In this scintillating and eye-opening book, Nestle reveals how much of our confusion about food in modern times has been spread by the food industry itself, which passes off marketing as science and funds 'research' designed to show that its products are harmless. *Unsavory Truth* is essential reading for anyone in search of hard facts about what to eat."

—BEE WILSON,
author of *First Bite* and *Consider the Fork*

Also by Marion Nestle

Soda Politics

Eat Drink Vote

Why Calories Count (with Malden C. Nesheim)

Feed Your Pet Right (with Malden C. Nesheim)

Pet Food Politics

What to Eat

Safe Food

Food Politics

Nutrition in Clinical Practice

UNSAVORY TRUTH

*How Food Companies Skew
the Science of What We Eat*

Marion Nestle

BASIC BOOKS
New York

Basic Books
Hachette Book Group
1290 Avenue of the Americas, New York, NY 10104
www.basicbooks.com

Printed in the United States of America
First Edition: October 2018
Published by Basic Books, an imprint of Perseus Books, LLC, a subsidiary of Hachette Book Group, Inc. The Basic Books name and logo is a trademark of the Hachette Book Group.

The Hachette Speakers Bureau provides a wide range of authors for speaking events. To find out more, go to www.hachettespeakersbureau.com or call (866) 376-6591.

The publisher is not responsible for websites (or their content) that are not owned by the publisher.

Print book interior design by Linda Mark.
Image on title page: Spencer Jones/Getty Images

Names: Nestle, Marion, author.
Title: Unsavory truth : how food companies skew the science of what we eat / Marion Nestle.
Description: First edition. | New York : Basic Books, [2018] | Includes bibliographical references and index.
Identifiers: LCCN 2018015889 | ISBN 9781541697119 (hardcover) | ISBN 9781541617315 (ebook)
Subjects: LCSH: Food—Research—Moral and ethical aspects—United States. | Food—Marketing—Moral and ethical aspects—United States. | Food industry and trade—United States. | Nutrition policy—United States.
Classification: LCC TX360.U6 N475 2018 | DDC 664.00973—dc23
LC record available at https://lccn.loc.gov/2018015889
ISBNs: 978-1-5416-9711-9 (hardcover); 978-1-5416-1731-5 (ebook)

LSC-C

10 9 8 7 6 5 4 3 2 1

To Charles, Rebecca, and Mal, of course

Contents

The Food Industry and Nutrition

I LOVE NUTRITION SCIENCE. ON MY FIRST TEACHING JOB, I WAS assigned to teach a nutrition course and it was like falling in love. To this day, I love the intellectual challenge of figuring out what we eat, why we eat what we do, and how diets affect our health. It is not easy to study these questions in the context of everything else that influences health, not least our genetics, cultural upbringing, lifestyle, income, and education. I am also endlessly fascinated by the way food choices relate to so many of the most challenging problems in society—health is only the most obvious. What we eat is linked to matters of poverty, inequality, race and class, immigration, social and political conflict, environmental degradation, climate change, and much else. Food is a lens through which to examine all those concerns. I love the complexity of food issues and the passion people bring to every one of them. But I do not love the way the food industry has added an unnecessary complication: engaging nutrition professionals in marketing objectives, sometimes against the interests of public health.

Unsavory Truth is about how food, beverage, and supplement companies (collectively, *food* companies) fund nutrition researchers and practitioners and their professional associations, with the ultimate goal of promoting sales. This book appears at a time when scandals created by such funding make front-page news. Let me plunge right in with an unexpected—and highly surreal—example of why the topics in this book should matter to all of us.

You may recall that during the especially contentious US presidential race of 2016, hackers linked to the Russian government stole a trove of electronic messages from Democratic Party officials and posted them on the WikiLeaks website. They also stole emails from people working on Hillary Clinton's campaign and posted them on a new website, DC Leaks. International intrigue like this ought to seem light-years removed from food-industry funding of nutrition professionals except for one truly bizarre coincidence: the cache on DC Leaks included messages exchanged between an adviser to the Clinton campaign, Capricia Marshall, and Michael Goltzman, a vice president of the Coca-Cola Company. While working with Clinton, Marshall was also consulting for Coca-Cola and billing the company $7,000 a month for her services.[1]

The Coca-Cola emails may have been collateral damage from Russian interference in the American election, but to me they were a gift. They bear directly on the major themes of this book, not least because I turn up in them. The hacked emails included a January 2016 message from the director of an Australian agency doing public relations for Coca-Cola with notes taken at a lecture I had just presented to the Sydney chapter of the Nutrition Society of Australia. I was then a visiting scholar at the University of Sydney affiliated with the bias-in-research group of Professor Lisa Bero, whose studies of corporate influence on research appear frequently in this book. The emailed notes on my lecture—quite nicely done, actually—name some of the people attending my talk, review its content, and advise Coca-Cola to monitor my future presentations, research, and presence on social media and also to keep tabs on Professor Bero's work.[2]

I vaguely remember someone telling me that a representative from Coca-Cola was at my talk but thought nothing of it. My 2015 book about the soft-drink industry, *Soda Politics: Taking on Big Soda (and Winning)*, had just been published, and I assumed that someone from that industry was in the audience at every talk I gave. The stolen emails demonstrate Coca-Cola's intense interest in the activities of individuals anywhere in the world who might question the health effects of its products.

The emails also reveal this particular company's pressures on reporters—and their editors—who write about such topics. In 2015, Candice Choi, a reporter for the Associated Press (AP), was investigating Coca-Cola's recruitment of dietitians to promote sodas on social media. This company's public relations staff had been working with dietitians for years to get them "to place sponsored content that promotes how our beverages can fit within a healthy, balanced diet." Because the staff expected Choi's article "to have a cynical, negative perspective," they "reached out to the AP's editors to formally register concerns about the story," promising to "continue to urge them not to run with the story."[3] In this instance, the pressures did not succeed. As published, Choi's article described the ways food companies worked "behind the scenes to cast their products in a positive light, often with the help of third parties who are seen as trusted authorities." She quoted a company spokesman's defense of this strategy: "We have a network of dietitians we work with. . . . Every big brand works with bloggers or has paid talent."[4] Really? Thanks to the emails, we now know something about how this system works.

The emails show how Coca-Cola operates to influence reporters who write about such topics. Coca-Cola staff were on a first-name basis with Mike Esterl, a reporter for the *Wall Street Journal*. They had learned about a study demonstrating the benefits of soda taxes and wanted to make sure that "Mike understood the source of the study and that it had not been published or peer reviewed yet."[5] Another message said, "FYI—please note we have been engaging Candice Choi AP reporter since April on this story and there have been numerous engagements—both verbal and written."[6]

This same email also refers to the cozy relationship between Coca-Cola's then chief scientific officer, Rhona Applebaum (whom we will also meet again), and university scientists conducting research funded by the company. Coca-Cola staff wrote that they had confirmation from Choi that her story would include an email exchange in which Applebaum referred to the group of university researchers she works with regularly as the "Cartel" and another in which Applebaum referred to critics of Coca-Cola as "trolls." Choi's published article (in which I am quoted) made two points: industry-funded research typically promotes the sponsor's interests, and some researchers make a living doing research funded by food companies and trade associations. She noted that one such group "regularly delivered favorable conclusions for funders—or as they call them, clients."[7]

Other messages referred to Coca-Cola's lobbying to influence federal nutrition advice. The public relations team worried that the academic advisory committee responsible for reviewing the research for the 2015 *Dietary Guidelines for Americans* had proposed "eliminating sugar-sweetened beverages from schools, taxing them, and restricting advertising of foods and beverages with 'high' sodium or added sugars for all populations." The public relations team suggested that the company "should be prepared for this report to be cited frequently by activists" and should "work together to balance coverage."[8] Coca-Cola's director of government relations later assured colleagues that his team had been working closely with Congress and federal agencies "to ensure that policy recommendation on a soda tax is not included in the final guidelines."[9] These efforts succeeded; the word "tax" does not appear anywhere in the 2015 dietary guidelines.[10]

Overall, the hacked emails offer a rare glimpse into how this beverage company—simply in the normal course of doing business— attempted to influence nutritionists, nutrition research, journalists covering this research, and dietary advice to the public. Other food companies do this too when they can.[11] The difference? Coca-Cola got caught.

This was not the first time Coca-Cola got caught, and therein lies the genesis of this book. In August 2015, while *Soda Politics* was at the printer, the *New York Times* ran a front-page story on Coca-Cola's funding of university researchers who had created a group called the Global Energy Balance Network (GEBN). The GEBN's purpose was to convince the public—against much evidence to the contrary— that physical activity is superior to dieting (and to avoiding Coca-Cola, of course) as a means of controlling body weight.[12] Because I was quoted in that story, reporters called me for further comment. They could hardly believe that a company as prominent as Coca-Cola would fund research so obviously self-serving, that researchers at respected universities would accept funds from Coca-Cola for this purpose, or that universities would allow faculty to do so. It seemed clear that if reporters had no idea such practices existed, I had another book to write.

As it happened, I was ready to take this on. I wrote my first article about such matters in 2001.[13] By August 2015, I was well into what turned out to be a year-long project to collect industry-funded studies that produced results favorable to the sponsor's interests. In March 2015, I began to post summaries of such studies on the blog I have written since 2007 at my website FoodPolitics.com. I continued these postings until March 2016. I will get to the results of this exercise later on, but for now let me just summarize a couple of examples, the first from scientists associated with the GEBN.

Coca-Cola had given these investigators research grants to examine the effects of physical activity on energy balance and body fat. The GEBN scientists reported that the people they studied could balance calorie intake by taking just 7,116 steps per day, "an amount achievable by most adults."[14] This study may appear to be basic research on exercise physiology, but it implies that physical activity—and not all that much—is all you need to control your weight, regardless of how much Coca-Cola you drink.

Coca-Cola is by no means alone in sponsoring marketing research masquerading as basic science. Here is another example. Late in 2017, the *Journal of the American Heart Association* published the results of a clinical trial concluding that incorporating dark chocolate and almonds in your diet may reduce your risk of coronary heart disease.[15] I love that. But can you guess who paid for this study? The Hershey Company and the Almond Board of California were its funders. They also paid seven of the nine authors for their participation; the other two were employees of the funders.

But what if the findings of such studies are true? If exercise, chocolate, and almonds are good for health, what is wrong with funding research to prove it? This is a serious question that deserves a serious answer. Hence: this book. Let me state for the record that financial ties with food companies are not necessarily corrupting; it is quite possible to do industry-funded research and retain independence and integrity. But food-company funding often does exert undue influence, and it invariably *appears* to do so. Even a hint of industry funding is all it takes to reduce trust among some segments of the public. Nutrition professionals have long recognized the reputational hazards of accepting sponsorship from food companies but for the most part have considered the benefits—in money, resources, and contacts—to be well worth the risk. From the food industry's standpoint, "capturing" nutrition scientists and practitioners is a well-established strategy for influencing dietary advice and public policy.[16]

Food companies must believe they need such strategies to survive in today's fiercely competitive marketplace. The US food supply provides about four thousand calories a day per capita (which includes everyone from tiny babies to sumo wrestlers), adding up to roughly twice average need. But Wall Street expects publicly traded corporations to do more than make profits; it expects them to increase shareholder value every quarter.[17] Competition forces food companies to work hard to convince customers to buy their products rather than those of competitors, to eat more in general, and to choose products that are more profitable. But by far the most profitable products are highly processed "junk" foods and beverages, high in calories but low in nutritional value. Enlisting nutrition professionals to declare such products harmless makes good business sense. So does engaging them in promoting healthier foods as "superfoods," a marketing term with no nutritional significance.

As a nutrition professor, I deal every day with people's bafflement about food choices. In 2006, I wrote *What to Eat* in the hope of reducing some of the confusion and encouraging readers to enjoy food—one of life's greatest pleasures. Basic dietary advice is so constant and simple that the journalist Michael Pollan can summarize it in seven words: "Eat food. Not too much. Mostly plants."[18] Advice like this, alas, does not sell food products. Influencing nutrition professionals does.

Much of what we know about corporate influence comes from studies of the tobacco, chemical, and pharmaceutical industries. Most relevant to the food industry is the way pharmaceutical companies induce physicians to prescribe more expensive and sometimes unnecessary brand-name drugs and commission research to demonstrate that their drugs are safer and more effective than generics or those of competitors. Decades ago, medical professionals recognized the distorted effects of drug-company practices, measured the distortions, and took steps to counter them. Medical journals required authors to disclose financial ties to drug companies that might profit from the results of their studies. Medical schools banned drug companies from marketing to students. In 2010, Congress required drug companies to disclose payments to physicians. Nothing close to that level of concern, scrutiny, or action applies to food-company efforts to engage nutrition professionals.[19]

Perhaps because food-industry practices are less easily measured, nutrition professionals have lagged in recognizing and dealing with the reputational and other hazards of such partnerships. Research on these hazards is relatively new, but the few studies that have been published suggest close parallels with drug-industry effects. Like drug-industry influence, food-industry influence is a *systemic* problem as well as a matter of personal ethics.[20] Food companies also distort research to focus on topics useful for product development or marketing, influence investigators to put favorable spins on equivocal results, and encourage nutrition professionals to offer favorable opinions about sponsors' products or to remain silent about unfavorable effects. When nutrition professionals partner with food companies, they can appear to be more interested in promoting industry marketing objectives than in furthering public health.

Let me make clear that I do not find these issues easy to talk about. One reason is that the effects of industry funding seem to occur at an unconscious level, so much below the radar of conscious thought that the influence is not recognized. Another is that revealing financial relationships with food companies is so personally embarrassing that nobody wants to talk about them. My own situation illustrates these difficulties.

As should already be evident, I am in this story as well as writing about it, and I have my own issues dealing with food companies, professionally as well as personally. On the professional side, I work with colleagues who accept such funding and resent the slightest suggestion that doing so might influence their work. Journal editors seem leery of publishing pieces on industry-induced conflicts. I have had more than my share of publication difficulties writing about these topics: multiple rounds of peer review, rejection of commentaries I had been invited to submit, and, in one especially painful instance, a retraction.[21]

Yet I cannot easily avoid engaging with food, beverage, and supplement companies. They send me product samples. They sponsor the meetings I attend, the societies I belong to, and the journals I read. They send me newsletters, books, press materials, teaching materials, and gifts, both small (pens, squeeze toys, flashlights, jump drives) and large (would you believe a full-size punching bag resembling a can of soda?). I occasionally advise food companies or answer their questions, and I speak at meetings they sponsor. As I explained in my book *Food Politics*, these kinds of interactions are commonplace among academic nutritionists; it is only questioning them that is unusual.

As a nutrition professor, I need to know what food companies are doing, and I find interactions with them informative, if occasionally awkward. I was well along in writing this book when Daniel

Lubetzky, the charismatic owner of the KIND fruit-and-nut snack-bar company, asked me to help select the board of his new nonprofit foundation, Feed the Truth (FTT). He had pledged $25 million over ten years to FTT to "improve public health by making truth, transparency and integrity the foremost values in today's food system."[22] FTT would sponsor investigative research and education programs to expose food companies' efforts to distort research and oppose public health efforts. I could not possibly refuse.

But the AP's Choi, ever on the case, wrote about my role, "The irony of such a group being established by a snack bar CEO is not lost on Marion Nestle, a professor of food studies at New York University who is helping nominate the board. She said she usually keeps industry at arm's length, but found Lubetzky 'very persuasive' and felt Feed the Truth could raise awareness about corporate influence in nutrition research."[23] Choi's article then noted that FTT had paid my travel expenses to a meeting in Washington, DC. Choi deserves high marks for asking about payments received, but I did not particularly relish having this reimbursement disclosed in the *Washington Post*.

Let me put that reimbursement in context. Over the years, I have had to develop a management policy for dealing with payments and gifts from food companies—what I can and cannot accept—to try to minimize their influence and to remind me to be vigilant about avoiding unconscious influence. Under this policy, I accept reimbursements for travel, lodging, and meal expenses, but I do not personally accept honoraria, consulting fees, or any other direct payments. Instead, I ask food companies to make an equivalent donation to the Marion Nestle Food Studies Collection at the New York University (NYU) library or, now that I am officially retired from NYU, to my department's student-travel fund. If the payments come directly to me, I endorse the checks over to one or the other (and declare all of this on tax forms).

As we will see, much evidence demonstrates that payments for travel, hotel, meals, meeting registrations, and small gifts are all it takes to influence the research results and prescription practices of physicians.[24] I have no reason to think I am unusually immune from the influence of payments that go to a library collection or scholarship fund from which I derive reputational benefit. Imperfect as my policy may be, it requires me to think carefully about every interaction with a food company that involves payments or gifts.

Another example: in 2017, I was invited to speak at a scientific symposium in Switzerland organized by Nestlé (to which I am not related), a company long accused of evading or violating ethical and legal codes for marketing breast-milk substitutes and weaning foods.[25] I accepted because I was curious to learn more about the company's science enterprise and wanted the opportunity to share my views with an audience to which I do not usually have access. But critics of Nestlé's actions judged the risk of the company's using me for its own ends and the damage to my reputation as so great that they urged me to refuse the invitation. Having the policy forced me to think long and hard about the potential consequences of my decision to speak at this symposium.

I am well aware that I am in an unusually fortuitous position to be able to hold such a policy, make such decisions, and write books about such topics. I have never had to depend on grant funding. During my three decades at NYU, I was privileged—and believe me, I know exactly how privileged—to hold a tenured, "hard-money" full professorship that paid my entire salary and provided a research stipend, telephone, computer, and first-class library, all I need for the kind of research I do.

In writing this book, I also faced one other difficult decision: what *not* to include. To limit its scope, I chose to focus on the consumption side of food-industry influence—the companies making foods and beverages that people typically eat. Even here, I chose to exclude several categories: alcoholic beverages, dietary supplements, and artificial sweeteners. The alcohol industry's similarity to the tobacco industry in manipulating research and policy is already well established.[26]

In *Food Politics*, I wrote extensively about the paucity of evidence for the value of dietary supplements for anyone who eats enough of a reasonably varied diet. The supplement industry funds many studies that demonstrate health benefits from taking one supplement or another, but studies funded independently usually do not—and sometimes suggest that taking nutrients in pill form can be harmful. Despite this evidence, half of American adults take supplements in the belief that they compensate for poor diets.[27] This industry is highly skilled at getting the research it needs to exploit anxieties about dietary inadequacy. Caveat emptor.

As for artificial sweeteners, the companies that make and use them often fund studies to prove that these substances, singly and together, are safe and effective for weight loss, but research funded by nonindustry sources questions such results.[28] While waiting for further studies to determine the safety or efficacy of these chemicals, I follow a personal food rule: never eat anything artificial.

Furthermore, to keep this book from being twice its current length, it will say nothing or little about companies involved in production agriculture—genetically modified foods, agrochemicals, or organic foods. The efforts of these industries to influence research, opinion, and policy also have been thoroughly investigated and documented.[29] But even without these deliberate omissions, we still have plenty to talk about.

Unsavory Truth is about the conflicts of interest induced by food-industry interactions with nutrition professionals and the systemic effects of those conflicts on public policy and public health. For our purposes, such conflicts can occur when researchers or nutritionists whose primary interest is to produce new science or offer advice about nutrition and health end up distorting—or appearing to distort—their findings or opinions as a result of their financial ties to food companies.

In public health terms, industry-induced conflicts constitute a "wicked" problem, one with no easy solution beyond not taking the money.[30] But in the real world of nutrition research and practice, not taking the money is easier said than done, especially by those who are more dependent than I am on external funding for their research and salaries. Even so, I think it would be healthier for all of us if nutrition professionals—practitioners as well as researchers—grappled much harder with the risks and consequences of food-company sponsorship and set firm policies to minimize these problems.

But what about you? The real question here is how you—as a reader, eater, and citizen—can recognize and protect yourself against the onslaught of misleading information and advice that results from food-company manipulation of nutrition research and practice. Everyone eats. Food matters. All of us need and deserve sound nutrition advice aimed at promoting public health—not corporate commercial interests. How do we make that happen? Read on.

A Cautionary Tale:
Drug Company Influence

A MAJOR SOURCE OF CONCERN ABOUT THE EFFECTS OF FOOD-industry sponsorship is what we know about the consequences of funding by other industries, particularly those involved with to-bacco, chemicals, and pharmaceutical drugs. Decades of books, reports, reviews, and commentaries describe how these industries in-fluence research and opinion. One search, just for studies or reviews of the effects of industry funding since the 1970s, identified about eight thousand items. Of these, only a handful were about funding by food companies (food-industry funding is a relatively new area of interest). But regardless of the industry, these studies come to similar conclusions. All industries making products of questionable health benefit exert influence by diligent adherence to strategies—collec-tively referred to as the "playbook"—first established to great effect by tobacco companies and recently described in detail as a set of political and legal tactics to influence policy and shape public per-ceptions and to obtain research that helps with such efforts.[1]

As early as the 1950s, tobacco-industry executives were well aware of evidence linking cigarette smoking to lung cancer. Nevertheless, they embarked on campaigns to cast doubt on that science and to deny that cigarettes were harmful. The playbook required executives to repeatedly deflect attention from diseases caused by cigarettes, to neutralize criticism, and to undercut calls for regulation. The playbook demanded endless repetition of carefully crafted statements: cigarette smoking is a matter of personal responsibility, government attempts to regulate tobacco are manifestations of a "nanny" state, restrictions on smoking infringe on freedom, and research reporting harm from smoking is "junk science." Let us credit the tobacco industry for producing the model now followed by other industries, the food industry among them.[2] Whatever the industry, the playbook requires repeated and relentless use of this set of strategies:

- Cast doubt on the science
- Fund research to produce desired results
- Offer gifts and consulting arrangements
- Use front groups
- Promote self-regulation
- Promote personal responsibility as the fundamental issue
- Use the courts to challenge critics and unfavorable regulations

For our purposes, the closest example of the playbook in action is its use by the pharmaceutical ("drug") industry. This industry's adoption of the playbook was so successful that by the early 1990s medical ethicists were dismayed to observe that nearly all medical specialties and subspecialties were rife with conflicts of interest.[3] Today, the conflicts created by drug-industry practices have been thoroughly recognized and thoroughly documented. Most relevant is the way this industry—pejoratively, "Big Pharma"—induces physicians to prescribe brand-name drugs and funds research to demonstrate the superiority of brand-name drugs over generics. Also relevant are the increasingly insistent demands to curb this industry's most egregious practices. Current drug-industry policies and regulations may be less than fully effective, but they demonstrate that the medical profession has long recognized the risks of this industry's influence and has taken steps to prevent or mitigate those risks.

I personally encountered the playbook actions of Big Pharma in 2005 when the American Diabetes Association invited me to speak about dietary aspects of that disease at its annual meeting. In browsing through the program book, I was surprised to see so few sessions dealing with nutrition issues. I could find only one other—a session on sugars and health organized by Oldways Preservation & Exchange Trust (a group we will meet again) that was sponsored by Coca-Cola. The session description included this statement: "Diets based on demonizing any one food, including sweetness and sugars, are diet plans that are doomed to fail; the issue is portion control."[4] Yes, it is, but this session seemed designed to reassure diabetes specialists that their patients could drink Coca-Cola with impunity.

In my talk, I showed a slide illustrating a recently approved injectable diabetes drug with the brand name Byetta (exenatide), extracted from Gila monsters. Injections? Gila monsters? Surely eating vegetables and losing a few pounds would be a better approach to preventing type 2 diabetes. But members of the audience chided me for questioning the value of a drug that could help patients control blood-sugar levels. This too surprised me. I assumed that this audience knew as well as I did that losing weight—often just a few pounds—can reverse symptoms of type 2 diabetes in many patients.[5]

But then I went to the exhibition hall. Acres of exhibit space were packed to the walls with booths marketing one drug after another. I trekked the aisles collecting the free swag—the "brand-reminder" items distributed at every booth. These ranged from small things like pens, prescription pads, and squeeze toys to more expensive ones like lab coats, stethoscopes, medical bags, and textbooks. As I will soon explain, it is well established that even small gifts induce doctors to prescribe the donor company's specific products.

Drug companies spend fortunes on brand-reminder items, but they spend even greater fortunes on personal visits from representatives, continuing-education courses, meals, and vacations—all aimed at influencing prescription practices. As early as the 1970s, critics were writing books about drug-company spending to "reach, persuade, cajole, pamper, outwit, and sell" to doctors. Most of the money went for detailers—the men (and later women) who visited doctors' offices to explain the benefits of their employer's drugs and to drop off gifts. Even then, community and hospital pharmacists could tell when detailers had visited by the sudden increase in prescriptions for specific brands of drugs. Drug advertisements in the American Medical Association's journal accounted for half its income, perhaps explaining why this group was not complaining about drug-industry marketing practices.[6]

The most obvious explanation for the size and extent of the literature on drug-industry practices is that this industry's interactions with physicians are easily *measured*: by the monetary value of the gifts and payments, of course, but also by their effects on recipients' prescription practices, votes on drug-advisory committees, and research results. Other effects are also measurable but with more difficulty: unnecessary treatment of patients, higher health care costs, and loss of trust in the medical profession. By analogy, all these findings are relevant to the less well studied influence of food companies. For any industry, the starting point for analysis of funding influence is what psychologists have learned about how gifts affect human behavior.

The Psychology of Gifts

You might think, as I did before researching this book, that gifts are no big deal. You give presents and you receive them (happily or not), you thank the donor, and that is the end of it. But psychologists who study the effects of drug-industry gifts to physicians—and many have—remind us that doctors are human and that much of what humans think and feel occurs subconsciously. All of us, including doctors, respond to gifts in predictable ways. But—and this is critical—our responses are usually unintentional, unconscious, and unrecognized. No doctor intends to be beholden to a drug company, yet even a small gift is enough to change prescription practices in the donor's favor. Larger gifts have even greater influence. Despite this evidence, recipients—human as we are—believe that gifts and payments from drug companies have no influence.[7]

These conclusions derive from experimental studies in psychology, neurobiology, and behavioral economics; these demonstrate that even recipients with honest intentions respond predictably to gifts and payments but are unaware of doing so. Drug companies do not "buy" physicians. Physicians do not "sell out" to drug companies. The influence is far more subtle, making it exceptionally difficult to prevent or manage—or even to discuss. If recipients do not believe they are influenced by gifts and payments, they see no reason to refuse them.[8] It is not that doctors are necessarily corrupt; it is the system that is corrupting.

Pharmaceutical companies are in the business of selling drugs. They want doctors to prescribe their brands rather than those of competitors, generics, or over-the-counter products, even when those alternatives might be better tested, more effective, and less costly. They pay physicians to consult for them, speak on their behalf, and serve on their committees or boards, and they offer free registrations at conferences (often at resorts), travel expenses, and meals. Figure 2.1 satirizes the way the system works.

Ethically minded physicians, concerned about the effects of these practices on health care costs, risks to patients, and trust in the profession, demanded regulation. They lobbied Congress to require public disclosure of drug-industry gifts and financial ties to doctors. Despite industry opposition, Congress finally agreed and passed the Physician Payments Sunshine Act as part of the Affordable Care Act in 2010. The result is the Open Payments website, where you can easily discover that in 2016, 1,479 pharmaceutical companies spent $8.19 billion on payments of one kind or another to 631,000 physicians and 1,146 teaching hospitals. About half the total expenditures went for research, leaving the remaining half for reaching physicians in other ways.[9]

FIGURE 2.1. Drug company gifts—small branded items, consulting fees, conference registrations, and meals—induce physicians to prescribe the donor's specific products rather than less expensive and sometimes safer and more effective alternatives. ©Steve Kelley Editorial Cartoon, used with the permission of Steve Kelley and Creators Syndicate. All rights reserved.

The results of drug-industry spending are well established. By the early 1990s, researchers could already show that a free trip to an industry-sponsored conference doubled the prescription rate for the sponsor's product. In 2000, a review of more than five hundred studies found that industry gifts, meals, travel funds, and detailers' visits correlated strongly with prescription of brand-name drugs rather than less expensive or more effective alternatives.[10]

Open Payments makes such studies easier to do and more accurate. In 2015, researchers found that nearly half of all US physicians accepted payments from industry, adding up to $2.4 billion. A study of statin prescriptions the following year yielded a formula: for every $1,000 received from drug companies, the prescribing rate for brand-name statins increased by 0.1 percent; payments for educational training led to a 4.8 percent increase. Investigators concerned about the health crisis caused by overuse of opioids found that from 2013 to 2015, one in twelve American doctors received payments—more than $46 million—from drug companies selling these drugs.[11]

One especially troubling observation is how little it takes to exert this influence. Brand-reminder pens and prescription pads induce changes in prescription rates, as do drug samples. Visits from detailers are particularly effective, which is why many teaching hospitals now ban them. Payments for speaking or consulting also work splendidly. So do meals; these are now the most frequent kind of drug-industry gift, with a median value of $138 each (one hopes wine is included). But even meals costing as little as $13 correlate closely with higher prescription rates—and for months afterward. Investigative journalists at ProPublica used Open Payments data to demonstrate a dose-response relationship between the size of drug-company payments and prescribing practices. Overall, the link between drug-industry gifts and prescription practices is so firmly established that it is considered beyond debate.[12]

Equally disturbing is the widespread willingness to accept such gifts. In 2009, nearly 84 percent of physicians reported receiving gifts or payments from drug companies; cardiologists were especially welcoming targets. Yet when asked, 90 percent of physicians who accept drug-industry funding deny its effects and say they base their prescribing habits solely on clinical knowledge and experience. Research shows otherwise. Recipients remain loyal to a donor's products long after receiving payments, and the larger the gifts, the more recipients are likely to oppose measures to prevent such influence.[13] No wonder drug companies spend billions to reach doctors.

Why do doctors allow this? This too has been researched. Recall that doctors are human and the influence of gifts is not always conscious; doctors believe they *deserve* such gifts. They went to school for years, sacrificed to get where they are, work hard, and may still be paying off student loans. They see themselves as entitled to the gifts, rational in their prescribing practices, and invulnerable to drug-industry influence. Reminding them of the sacrifices they have made actually increases their willingness to accept such gifts.[14] None of this would matter if the gifts had no influence, but they do. Financial ties to drug companies not only affect doctors' prescription practices but also influence their opinions on drug advisory committees and the conclusions of their research.

Influencing Drug Advisory Committees

If medical experts who serve on advisory committees have financial ties to products under consideration, are they more likely to recommend questionable drugs, brand-name drugs rather than generics, and wider use of drugs as treatment options? Yes, they are. By law, experts who serve on federal advisory committees are not supposed to be in thrall to special interests. Those with links to companies making products under review are precluded from serving on such committees, except when the agencies waive that rule—which they frequently have done.[15]

The US Food and Drug Administration (FDA) is responsible for approving drugs. It uses about fifty committees to obtain advice from independent experts about scientific, technical, and policy matters. Many laws, regulations, and guidance documents govern potential conflicts, real and apparent, among candidates for positions on those committees. Committee members are considered "special government employees" who may not participate in matters that have direct effects on their financial interests: stock and bond holdings, consulting arrangements, grants, contracts, or employment. But because the FDA insists that it cannot find enough candidates who are not tied to industry, the laws permit waivers to candidates who have such ties, and the FDA still often grants them.[16]

Because so much money is involved in drug-approval decisions and because some brand-name drugs are ineffective or harmful or increase health care costs, the FDA's policies have long troubled critics. The Open Payments website makes it possible to investigate the FDA's committee system. Studies of votes on drug approvals find striking results: committee members with financial ties to the makers of drugs under scrutiny are far more likely to vote for approvals than are members without such ties, and some drug approvals would not have occurred if the committees had excluded the votes of members with ties to manufacturers. But the FDA ignores such evidence. In 2017 the FDA announced how it would respond to critics' complaints: it intended to grant *more* waivers to committee members with financial ties to industry, not fewer.[17] Statements like these make the FDA appear to be "captured" by the drug industry.

Investigators concerned about industry capture have also looked at committees issuing practice guidelines. Their studies show that members of such committees frequently receive gifts, speaker fees, and other payments from drug companies likely to be affected by their guidelines. One investigation found that 84 percent of authors of guidelines issued by the National Comprehensive Cancer Network receive such payments. Another reported that 62 percent of the members of an international consensus committee writing gastroenterology clinical practice guidelines had at least one financial tie to a relevant drug company; in this case, the experts with such conflicts recused themselves from discussions of six of the eight recommendations—a step in the right direction.[18]

The standard explanation for these high percentages is the impossibility of finding independent experts to serve on guideline committees. I have some doubts about this, and I also have trouble believing that recusals are sufficiently protective. In my experience, committee members want to hear each other's opinions and can be influenced by them even when the recused individuals are physically absent from discussions of the matter at hand.

Beyond direct financial ties to committee members, drug companies have other ways of influencing decisions. One is to pay for the formation of patient-advocacy front groups to press for approval. A database established by Kaiser Health News found that fourteen pharmaceutical companies collectively donated $116 million to 594 such groups in 2015.[19] In 2018, a US Senate report called for more transparency on this issue, noting that the five leading producers of opioid drugs contributed nearly $9 million to third-party advocacy groups from 2012 to 2017. Such groups, the report charged, "have, in fact, amplified and reinforced messages favoring increased opioid use."[20]

My favorite example is the FDA's approval in 2015 of flibanserin, the "female Viagra," marketed as treating what critics believe is a nondisease: "acquired, generalized hypoactive sexual desire disorder in premenopausal women."[21] On the basis of the drug's minimal benefits and well-documented risks, FDA committees twice rejected the drug. On the third try, the maker of flibanserin, Sprout Pharmaceuticals, organized a front group, Even the Score, positioned as a grassroots feminist organization campaigning on behalf of the right of women to take this drug. The advisory committee voted for approval based on the group's ostensibly independent advocacy. In what I see as another example of the FDA's corporate capture, it accepted the committee's decision even though it listed the drug's hazards in its approval announcement and required a boxed warning label and three further studies. The *Washington Post* attributed the decision to Sprout's "clever, aggressive public relations campaign" and termed it "bad news for rational drug approval."[22]

Drug companies also fund patient-advocacy groups to buy silence. Funded groups rarely call for controls on drug prices, for example. Donations to such groups can be considerable; in 2015, drug companies contributed $26.7 million to the American Diabetes Association. But in this particular case, the association broke ranks and called on the federal government to negotiate with drug companies to reduce prices for Medicare patients, something that Congress, under pressure from Big Pharma, does not allow the government to do.[23]

When it comes to industry funding, as we will see throughout this book, the issues are never simply black or white; they are usually more complicated shades of grey.

Influencing Research

Drug companies have strong economic incentives to convince the FDA, doctors, and the public that their products do wonders for health, cause no harmful side effects, and are better than alternative remedies. In addition to funding clinical trials designed to prove safety and effectiveness, the companies fund "seeding trials"—studies aimed at marketing drugs to physicians. They pay ghostwriters to produce articles signed by authors who appear to be independent but are anything but. They withhold the results of studies that do not favor their products. They engage in selective reporting of trial outcomes.[24]

The most thoroughly investigated effect is the way industry-funded research almost invariably favors the sponsor's commercial interests. Sheldon Krimsky, a Tufts University professor who studies industry manipulation of science, dates the discovery of this "funding effect" to the mid-1980s, when social scientists realized that if they knew who paid for a study, they could predict its results. One funding-effect investigation from the late 1990s looked at studies on the safety of calcium channel blockers for reducing blood pressure. Nearly all authors (96 percent) who concluded that the drugs were effective reported financial ties to their manufacturers; only 37 percent of authors who doubted their effectiveness had such ties. In 2003, a systematic review of more than one thousand biomedical research studies came to similar conclusions; investigators with industry affiliations were nearly four times more likely to come up with pro-industry conclusions than those without such ties.[25]

Since the mid-1990s, Lisa Bero's research group, now at the University of Sydney, has produced evidence that industry-funded studies generally favor the sponsor's interests. Other groups have confirmed this work, and new confirmations appear regularly. Their findings: research sponsored by drug companies generally favors newer—and more expensive—drug treatments. Research funded by a drug company alone is likely to be more biased than research sponsored by a drug company plus any other sponsor. If the results of studies sponsored by drug companies produce unfavorable results, they are less likely to be published. With respect to drug studies, the idea that industry funding distorts the outcomes of research seems beyond dispute.[26]

But how does this happen? Recall: recipients of industry funding do not recognize its influence and typically deny it. For approval, a drug company only has to prove that its products are reasonably effective and safe; it does not have to compare the drug to generics or competitive products. Although preliminary research might have eliminated less effective drugs, that is not enough to explain the consistency of the funding effect.

A more realistic explanation is the ease of designing research to obtain a desired result, whether consciously or unconsciously. All it takes is to leave out appropriate comparisons and put a positive spin on results that do not show an effect. Bero's group has demonstrated that five industries, pharma among them, selectively fund research that supports industry objectives, manipulate research questions to obtain desired results, and suppress research with unfavorable results. Funding source, Krimsky suggests, may not be definitive evidence of bias, but it should strongly suggest the possibility of bias. Intentionally or not, drug-industry funding drives the research agenda, confuses the science, and fuels public distrust. At issue is what to do about it. A recent study suggests that journal editors cannot be counted on to pay much attention to research bias; half the editors of leading US medical journals received payments from drug and medical-device companies.[27]

Managing Drug Industry Influence

The influence of drug-industry gifts and payments is so measurably blatant that it cannot be ignored. But what to do? If you view doctors' financial relationships with industry as flat-out corruption, then obvious solutions are education programs about conflicts of interest, restrictions on gift size, codes of ethics, and disclosure of industry contacts. These help, but the issues are invariably more complicated. When industry influence is unconscious, unrecognized, or denied, these methods cannot be effective. Indeed, their imposition can result in perverse effects, causing recipients to believe even more strongly in their personal immunity to any influence. For this reason, some experts on this topic argue that there is only one way to deal with the conflicts of interest induced by industry gifts and payments: ban all such gifts and payments.[28]

For decades, medical leaders have tried to encourage policies in that direction. In 1984, Arnold Relman, then editor of the *New England Journal of Medicine*, broke new ground by requiring authors to declare conflicts of interest. A year later, he called on physicians to remove themselves from the medical marketplace and put the interests of patients first. And a decade later, the American Medical Association, finally taking up this issue, observed that drug-industry gifts were creating three hazards: influencing physicians, giving the appearance of impropriety, and increasing drug costs to patients. It argued for a new policy: physicians should accept only gifts that directly benefit patients and are of minimal value.[29] But as we have seen, even small gifts exert influence.

With no evident improvement in drug-industry practices, Congress became concerned about the integrity of federally supported research. In 1995, it established standards to ensure that research design, conduct, and reporting would not be biased by conflicting interests resulting from financial ties to corporations. Congress required recipients of research grants to disclose such ties, which it specified as salaries, consulting fees, honoraria, stocks, patents, copyrights, or royalties. Congress stated that conflicted researchers should, if necessary, modify their research plans, end their participation, or divest their conflicted holdings.[30] It applied these guidelines to all research, including nutrition research.

In 2009, the Pharmaceutical Research and Manufacturers of America (PhRMA), the industry's trade association, issued a code for interacting with health care professionals, an action that appeared to be designed to head off federal regulation. In deciding what drug company representatives—the detailers—could and could not give to physicians, PhRMA proposed that the gifts ought to benefit patients or contribute to medical education.[31] Table 2.1 summarizes some of its guidelines. These are revelatory about now-forbidden practices that were common prior to 2009 and about potential loopholes, such as the meaning of "modest."

Despite these guidelines, Congress passed the Physician Payments Sunshine Act the following year. Some of the pressure for its passage

TABLE 2.1. The Pharmaceutical Industry's 2009 Guidelines for What Companies May and May Not Give to Physicians (Selected Examples)

ITEM	ALLOWED	NOT ALLOWED
Stethoscopes, pens, clipboards, prescription pads		✓
Gift certificates for books		✓
Brochures for patients		✓
Golf balls, sports bags		✓
Continuing-education meetings at resorts or golf facilities		✓
Tickets to sports events, concerts, shows		✓
Gasoline		✓
Restaurant meals; meals for spouses		✓
Educational materials: anatomical models, brochures, patient self-assessment tools, medicine starter kits	✓ if < $100	
Meals or pizza to accompany presentations or at medical-education conferences	✓ if modest	
Meals with company business executives	✓ if modest	

came from medical professionals such as Jerome Kassirer, who had just stepped down as editor of the *New England Journal of Medicine*. In his words, "Deans of medical schools and training program directors must do a better job of addressing conflict of interest. Where professionalism is concerned, they must teach that there is no free lunch. No free dinner. Or textbooks. Or even a ballpoint pen."[32]

In 2013, a task force sponsored by the Pew Charitable Trusts recommended best practices for physicians engaged in medical education. These included a requirement for disclosure of industry ties but also outright bans on accepting industry funding for speaking, writing, or education; for gifts or meals; or for consulting and advising relationships. More recently, Robert Steinbrook, an editor at large for *JAMA Internal Medicine*, pointed out the "inherent tensions between the profits of health care companies, the independence of physicians and the integrity of our work, and the affordability of medical care." He noted, "If drug and device manufacturers were to stop sending money to physicians for promotional speaking, meals, and other activities without clear medical justifications and invest more in independent bona fide research on safety, effectiveness, and affordability, our patients and the health care system would be better off."[33]

Despite evidence that drug companies readily find ways around restrictions on gifts and payments, they and their beneficiaries continue to deny its influence and oppose regulation. In 2016, nearly one hundred US national and state medical societies supported a Senate bill, the Protect Continuing Physician Education and Patient Care Act, that would exempt medical drug and device makers from having to report payments made to doctors for continuing medical education, medical journals, or textbooks.[34] With powerful forces lobbying to continue business as usual, the medical profession still has a long way to go to address industry-induced conflicts of interest, even when those conflicts—and the harm they cause—are thoroughly documented.

Dealing with the effects of industry funding on food and nutrition professionals is even more difficult, in part because the effects are far more difficult to measure. As we see next, only a few studies to date have examined the influence of food companies on nutrition research.

The Unusual Complexity
of Nutrition Research

T HE EFFECTS OF FUNDING BY DRUG COMPANIES, AS WE HAVE just seen, are measurable. Drug studies also are easier to design. To find out whether a drug is safe and effective, you give people one medication—a single product—and see what it does in comparison to giving nothing or to taking an alternative drug. Food is more complicated. We eat an enormous variety of foods, and diets also vary enormously—from day to day and from one person to another. Everything else we do also varies. Humans make terrible experimental animals. We cannot be locked in cages and fed controlled diets, at least not long enough to learn anything useful. All of this forces studies of diet and health to be largely observational rather than experimental and, therefore, exceptionally vulnerable to biases in design and interpretation.

These complexities also make the effects of industry funding more difficult to research. Studies of food-industry influence are more recent, fewer in number, and more complicated to interpret than studies of drug-industry effects. Much of my particular fascination with nutrition research lies is its inherent complexity. Adding to that complexity are matters pertaining to the distinction between nutrition research and food science, the cost of nutrition research involving human subjects, and the particular difficulties of measuring the effects of food-company sponsorship.

Nutrition Research Differs from Food Science

A bit of history helps explain this distinction. Since at least the time of Hippocrates, scientists have attempted to study how food keeps us warm and alive.[1] But the involvement of the food industry in these kinds of studies dates only to the early 1900s, when scientists began to identify vitamins, the thirteen distinctly different substances that must be obtained from food. They also began to identify minerals needed in extremely small amounts. The vitamin discoveries, which took place from 1913 (vitamin A) to 1948 (vitamin B_{12}), thrilled researchers eager to discover which foods contained them and what they did in the body. Food and drug companies were equally thrilled; they could sell vitamins and minerals not only to improve the quality of animal feed or food products but also as supplements. In those heady days of nutrient discovery, research partnerships between scientists and food or drug companies made perfect sense.

Following World War II, American companies such as General Foods, Kraft, and Quaker Oats built research facilities and recruited scientists to work in them, as did Nestlé and Unilever in Europe. Science directors of food companies had large budgets with enough discretionary funds to conduct basic research along with studies aimed at product development. Unilever scientists, for example, studied fundamental properties of fats and oils that might or might not apply to margarines. But by the mid-1980s, in response to shareholder pressures for higher and more immediate returns on investment, American food companies shifted their research enterprises to focus more directly on commercial goals. As companies merged and consolidated and as short-term financial objectives became ever more pressing, most food companies in the United States closed their in-house research facilities and contracted out their research needs to university scientists. Today, Nestlé (in Switzerland) and Unilever (in the Netherlands) are unique in maintaining large research operations that still do basic research, although they too partner with researchers at universities.[2]

In the United States, the Morrill Act of 1862 set the stage for future collaborations between university scientists and food companies. This act gave land to states to establish colleges of agriculture for promoting "the liberal and practical education of the industrial classes in the several pursuits and professions in life." The new "land-grant" colleges created departments of animal, poultry, and dairy sciences and recruited faculty to conduct research explicitly aimed at helping expand animal agriculture in their states. In New York State, where I live, Cornell is the designated land-grant university; it established animal-science departments in 1902. Its dairy department, for example, recruited faculty to teach courses about dairy chemistry and microbiology but also about the processing and manufacture of dairy products. This university created its own dairy business to train students, and the current department still manages a dairy herd and produces Cornell ice cream, yogurt, and cheese.[3]

Food processing hardly existed in the early twentieth century but quickly became important to New York's economy. In 1956, in response to a request from the New York State Canners and Freezers Association, Cornell's dairy department set up a Food Science and Technology program to support the state's food processors. Eventually, these units were combined into today's Department of Food Science. This department's stated mission is to prepare students for leadership roles in the food industry, academia, and government; to expand information about the properties of foods and beverages; and to transfer this new information to food systems.[4] The purpose of food science is to support the food industry by training students for jobs in that industry and by conducting research to support industry goals and practices. Because food science developed as an arm of the food industry, the missions of food scientists and industry sponsors are closely aligned, minimizing possibilities for conflicts of interest.

In contrast, the development of nutrition departments took a decidedly different path. To again use Cornell as an example: its faculty interested in the human diet were dispersed among programs in nutrition and home economics; other faculty were interested in the nutritional value of animal feed. In 1974, Cornell established its present Division of Nutritional Sciences by uniting these faculty. The division's missions are to generate knowledge through scientific research; to educate and mentor the next generation of scholars, researchers, nutrition professionals, and responsible citizens; to improve nutrition and human health; and to inform nutrition policy and practice through public engagement.[5] These goals differ from those of food science. The purpose of nutrition science is to improve public health. But because not all food products promote health, the goals of nutrition science are not necessarily aligned with those of food companies—creating the possibility of conflicted relationships.

The way I look at it, food science *is* the food industry. Cornell's food science students take classes in the PepsiCo Auditorium. But as with everything else about food and nutrition, the distinctions are more complicated and the boundaries more porous. Faculty in either department can be working on similar problems. Many food scientists now investigate matters of human physiology and health, thereby raising the possibility of conflicts of interest in their field as well. But to understand why researchers in either field might welcome food-industry funding, it helps to appreciate what it costs to study diet and health in human subjects.

Human Nutrition Research Is Expensive

If researchers welcome industry funding, it is surely because government and foundation grants are scarce. Because observational studies are especially subject to misinterpretation, scientists consider the gold standard of experimental nutrition research to be randomized, controlled clinical trials. These examine the effects of consuming certain diets, foods, or nutrients on one or more measures of health. Such trials cost fortunes. I learned this during the years I was involved with the Women's Healthy Eating and Living (WHEL) study, a randomized, controlled clinical trial to find out whether women who survived breast cancer would have fewer recurrences if they ate more fruits and vegetables.[6] This project began in 1993 as a result of a grant from John and Christie Walton (of the Walmart family), who had a personal interest in diet and cancer prevention. Their foundation gave $5 million to cancer researcher John Pierce and his team at the University of California, San Diego, to pay for a feasibility study and the start-up costs of what turned out to be a lengthy investigation.

When the feasibility results showed that women who enrolled in the study would follow its protocols, Pierce applied to the National Cancer Institute (NCI) for funding for a multicenter trial to measure the dietary intake, health, and survival of three thousand women who had been treated for breast cancer—for an average of seven years. Eventually, the NCI granted $17 million to cover the study's costs from 1997 to 2002 and, later, an additional $15 million for expenses through 2007. No, these are not misprints. The NCI grants really did add up to $32 million on top of the Walton Foundation's $5 million. But, Pierce reminded me, those costs need to be viewed in context: "At the time, it was approximately the same as a single piece of innovative technological equipment in the hospital."[7]

The funding paid for staff at seven locations in several states, equipment and supplies, laboratory tests, office visits, the storage of tissue and blood samples (*very* expensive), meetings, and juicers and other incentives for participation. It also paid my travel expenses to San Diego for about ten years, first for the initial planning meetings and later for my participation in the trial's data-management committee. In the end, the WHEL results were disappointing. The study found no overall survival benefit from eating extra servings of fruits and vegetables, although one subgroup of women who were physically active survived longer. Nevertheless, WHEL investigators were able to publish 110 scientific reports about how to conduct such trials and on the health benefits of dietary improvements.[8]

Funding for the WHEL trial came from a wealthy foundation and a government agency. Companies producing fruits or vegetables do not have that kind of money, nor would they—or any other food company—want to invest in a study so costly, lengthy (fourteen years from concept to completion), and unpredictable in outcome. Instead, food companies have more pragmatic interests.

I occasionally receive letters from the California Table Grape Commission's research director soliciting proposals for "$35,000 grants toward research on any relevant health issue in which grape consumption may have a beneficial impact."[9] A similar announcement for $30,000 grants comes from Yogurt in Nutrition for "research on the health benefits associated with yogurt consumption."[10] The California Strawberry Commission's request for proposals is even more explicit: "The primary goal of the CSC nutrition research program is to establish the scientific evidence to support a vascular health claim under EFSA [European Food Safety Authority] or FDA criteria."[11] The wording of these requests indicates that these groups are not asking open-ended, basic research questions about the health effects of specific foods. Instead, they are asking for studies designed specifically to establish their products' benefits as a basis for health claims. As we will see, such research is so useful for marketing purposes that a great many companies and trade associations eagerly invest in these kinds of studies.

Funding Effects Are Complicated

I have argued so far that food science is mainly, though not exclusively, about finding technical solutions to problems related to food products, whereas nutrition science is mainly about the effects of nutrients, foods, and diets on human physiology and health. But marketing research has a decidedly different purpose: to create and sell food products. Food companies have always funded research aimed at product development but are now even more interested in research to demonstrate the health benefits of their products or to discredit evidence to the contrary.

This kind of research is easy to spot. Whenever I see a study suggesting that a single food (such as pork, oats, or pears), eating pattern (having breakfast), or product (beef, diet sodas, or chocolate) improves health, I look to see who paid for it. This is possible because most professional journals now require scientific articles to include special sections where authors must disclose who paid for their study and whatever financial arrangements they might have with the funder or a similar company.

Some years ago, I began posting particularly entertaining examples of sponsored research with self-serving results on my website, FoodPolitics.com. By March 2015, I was running across so many such studies that I began posting summaries of them, five at a time. I found these studies in publications I read routinely, and colleagues who knew I was collecting them sent me others. Although I pleaded with readers to tell me about industry-funded studies with conclusions contrary to sponsors' interests, hardly anyone did. I continued posting these research summaries for an entire year. By then, I had collected 168 studies sponsored by food companies or conducted by investigators with financial ties to food companies. Of these, 156 reported results favoring the sponsor's interests; only 12 did not.

This was a casual collection, a "convenience" sample. Because I was not collecting the studies in any systematic way, the results permit only one scientific conclusion: it is much easier to find industry-funded studies with results favorable to the sponsor's interests than those with unfavorable results. Still, the collection illustrates some useful points. The most obvious: many different kinds of companies fund research potentially useful for marketing purposes. My haphazard collection included research sponsored by the makers and sellers of, among other products, artificial sweeteners, breakfast cereals, chewing gum, canned foods, chocolate, coffee, corn, dairy foods, dietary supplements, garlic, infant formula, lentils, nuts, orange juice, potatoes, soft drinks, soy products, and sugar.

Industry contributions to the research ranged from minimal (providing supplements or other products to be tested in the study), to more significant (paying partial or total costs). Many investigators who disclosed industry funding of their research stated that they had no conflicts of interest. Apparently, they did not view such funding as conflicting. When studies found no statistically significant results, industry-funded researchers tended to interpret the results as favorable to the sponsor. In my collection, favorable spins were especially noticeable in studies sponsored by supplement companies.

These results, casually obtained as they were, are reasonably consistent with the more scientific results of systematic studies. "Systematic" means attempts to ensure scientific validity by setting criteria for analysis in advance, casting a wide net for studies likely to meet the criteria, evaluating each study on the basis of those criteria, and using validated methods of meta-analysis to summarize and interpret the evidence from the studies chosen for evaluation. "Meta-analysis" is the term used to describe a process of combining the results of multiple studies of the same phenomenon to increase the statistical power of their conclusions.

Gary Sacks and his colleagues at Deakin University in Melbourne, for example, used systematic methods to find out how much nutrition research is funded by food companies or conducted by researchers with financial ties to such companies. They examined every peer-reviewed research article published in the fifteen most-cited nutrition journals in 2014. Their as yet unpublished results show that of more than four thousand studies, the great majority were funded by government agencies or foundations. Only 14 percent disclosed food-company funding or financial ties. But of that cohort, more than 60 percent reported results favorable to the sponsor, whereas only 3 percent came to unfavorable conclusions (the rest were not applicable to the sponsor's interests).[12] Funding effects appear in nutrition research as well as drug research.

But in contrast to the thousands of examinations of drug-industry funding published over the years, only a few studies have examined the effects of food-industry funding on the outcome of research on nutrition and health. By August 2018, I had identified precisely *eleven* published studies, although from doing journal peer reviews I know that others were in the pipeline.

And while I was working on this book, Professor Ralph Walton, now retired from his position as chair of the Department of Psychiatry at Northeast Ohio Universities College of Medicine, sent me what is surely the first attempt at such studies: a never-published review of research on the safety of the artificial sweetener aspartame that he had prepared for a televised interview with Mike Wallace in 1996. Walton had seen that the conclusions of studies on the safety of aspartame were highly contradictory and wondered whether study outcome correlated with funding source. It did. NutraSweet, the maker of aspartame, funded seventy-four studies; *all* concluded that the sweetener was safe. But among ninety-two independently funded studies, eighty-four—more than 90 percent—questioned its safety.[13]

The first published funding-effect study of nutrition research appeared only in 2003—decades after the earliest studies of drug-industry effects. I can think of several explanations for the delay. Food is more complicated than drugs, and research on it is more difficult. But beyond that, we must eat to live, and food companies make products we love to eat. It hardly seems possible that food companies would need to be as deliberately manipulative as drug or cigarette companies. But the few studies to date suggest close parallels.

I say "suggest" because this research is difficult to discuss in any coherent way. The few studies vary in funding sources, degree of funding, and whether authors had financial ties to the funder. They examine the effects of widely different products, and they differ in the health outcomes measured, in the methods of examination and analysis, and in their findings. In Table 3.1, I have summarized the differing elements to emphasize how difficult it is to draw simple conclusions from just eleven studies.

Credit for the first published study of food-industry influence goes to investigators at Teachers College, Columbia University. They were interested in whether funding source had anything to do with conclusions about the safety and effectiveness of Olestra,

TABLE 3.1. Studies Examining Food-Industry Influence on Nutritional Health Research, 2003–2018

YEAR	PRODUCT	HEALTH OUTCOME	METHOD	CONCLUSION
2003[1]	Olestra	Safety and efficacy	Correlation	Industry-funded studies favored sponsor
2007[2]	Sugar-sweetened beverages	Multiple risks	Correlation	Industry-funded studies found fewer risks
2007[3]	Sugar-sweetened beverages	Weight gain	Meta-analysis	Industry-funded studies found smaller effects
2009[4]	Calcium supplements	Bone density in children	Correlation	Industry-funded clinical trials more likely to favor sponsor, but not significantly
2012[5]	Dairy foods	Obesity	Correlation	No difference in funding effect, although industry-funded research questions favored sponsor
2013[6]	Sugar-sweetened beverages	Weight gain	Systematic review of systematic reviews	Sponsored authors' results favored sponsor
2013[7]	Probiotics, prebiotics, or both added to infant formula*	Beneficial microflora, infections	Systematic review	No difference by funding source but industry-funded trials more likely to recommend sponsor's product
2014[8]	Sugar-sweetened beverages	Weight gain	Meta-analysis	Industry-funded studies found only weak effects
2016[9]	Sugar-sweetened beverages	Obesity and type 2 diabetes	Correlation	Sponsored authors' results favored sponsor
2016[10]	Artificial sweeteners	Weight loss	Systematic review of reviews	Industry-funded studies and sponsored authors favored sponsor
2018[11]	Sugar-sweetened beverages	Adverse health effects	Systematic review	Industry-funded research underestimates adverse effects

NOTE: Source notes are located in the "Notes to Tables" on pages 287–290.

Probiotics are beneficial microbes; prebiotics are nondigestible substances that promote microbial growth.

a no-calorie fat substitute created by Procter & Gamble (P&G). I had a special interest in this study. In 1998, I had written an account of P&G's $500 million, twenty-five-year campaign to convince the FDA to approve Olestra as an ingredient in snack foods, despite concerns about its tolerability, interference with vitamin A absorption, and ability to help people lose weight.[14]

The Columbia investigators examined sixty-seven articles of various types: research reports, reviews, commentaries, and letters. Of those arguing for the safety and utility of Olestra, 80 percent were sponsored by P&G or other food companies. But among articles expressing doubts, 89 percent were funded by nonindustry groups. Among studies by authors who reported employment or consulting affiliations with P&G, every single one favored Olestra. If you have never heard of Olestra, it is because it did poorly on the market, and few products still contain it; in 2010, *Time* ranked it as one of the world's fifty worst inventions.[15]

By the early 2000s, weight gain and obesity had become widely recognized as national public health problems. In looking for causes, researchers singled out soft drinks for their high sugar content and lack of nutritional value. They began to examine links between sugar-sweetened beverages and increased risks for obesity, especially among children.[16] To counter these findings, Coca-Cola and the American Beverage Association began funding their own studies. This made it possible to compare study outcome by funding source.

Six of the eleven funding-effect studies deal with the effects of sugar-sweetened beverages (SSBs). The first appeared in 2007. Its authors reviewed more than two hundred studies of the effects of sugary drinks on health. Studies funded by industry were eight times more likely to produce favorable conclusions than those funded by nonindustry sources. That same year, a systematic review and meta-analysis of eighty-eight studies linked sugary drinks to higher calorie intake and related health risks, but studies funded by food companies reported smaller effects than those funded by nonindustry sources. Three other studies confirm these findings.[17] A fourth, published in 2016, concluded, "This industry seems to be manipulating contemporary scientific processes to create controversy and advance their business interests at the expense of the public's health."[18] The most recent, which observed systematic underreporting of adverse health effects in industry-funded studies, argues that such research "hindered the pursuit of scientific truth about the health effects of SSBs, and may have harmed public health."[19]

My interpretation: these results are generally consistent with what we know about the effects of drug-industry funding, but with a bit less certainty. In 2016, Lisa Bero and her colleagues attempted to resolve the uncertainty by performing a systematic analysis of every study they could find on nutrition-funding effects. Of an initial pool of 775 studies, only 12 met their criteria for inclusion. Their cautious analysis: "Although industry-sponsored studies were more likely to have favorable conclusions than non-industry sponsored studies, the difference was not significant," meaning that this result could have occurred by chance.[20]

What are we to make of this? Reviews of reviews, no matter how systematic, have inherent sources of error. The small number of studies lacks the statistical power of the hundreds or thousands of studies examining drug-company influence. The Bero group's review included the studies listed in Table 3.1 except for the three published in 2016 or later, which appeared after its analysis. But this review also included four studies omitted from Table 3.1. One dealt with genetically modified foods, not health.[21] The other three also did not look at health outcomes. Instead, they examined the effects of funding source on the quality of the science. This is a separate issue worth its own discussion, not least because those three studies, all finding no effect of industry funding on scientific quality, were either sponsored by a food-industry front group or conducted by authors with ties to that group or to food companies.

The front-group funder was the North American branch of the International Life Sciences Institute (ILSI), an organization that turns up often in this book. ILSI describes itself as an independent scientific think tank, but it was created and is largely funded by the food industry. This makes it, by definition, a front group. But you might not realize this from reading the study authors' disclosure statement, which describes ILSI as "a public, nonprofit scientific foundation that provides . . . a neutral forum for government, academic, and industry scientists to discuss and resolve scientific issues of common concern for the well-being of the general public."[22]

ILSI keeps a relatively low public profile but seems never to miss an opportunity to defend the interests of its four hundred or so corporate sponsors. Its 2016 annual report takes four pages and fifteen columns to list industry supporters of its national and international branches; these contribute two-thirds of this group's nearly $18 million in annual revenues (the rest comes from government or private grants or contributions). ILSI's board of trustees is about half industry and half academia, all unpaid volunteers. Critics describe ILSI as a "two-level" organization. On the surface, it engages in legitimate scientific activities. But deep down, it provides funders with "global lobbying services . . . structured in a way which ensures that the funding corporations have majority membership in all its major decision-making committees."[23]

ILSI has a vested interest in defending the scientific quality of industry-funded research. So do investigators with financial ties to food companies. One of the other two studies finding no funding-source effect on scientific quality looked at randomized controlled clinical trials reported in top-tier medical journals. Its senior author, David Allison, disclosed that he "has received grants, honoraria, donations, royalties, and consulting fees from numerous publishers, food, beverage, pharmaceutical companies, and other commercial and nonprofit entities with interests in obesity and randomized controlled trials." The second study, also with Allison as senior author, found that industry-funded clinical trials had *higher* scores for the quality of science reporting than those funded by nonindustry sources.[24] These studies of scientific quality prove the rule; the conclusions of studies by investigators with industry ties generally tend to favor the sponsor's interests.

This rule especially holds in these instances because that last study is the only one of which I am aware suggesting that the

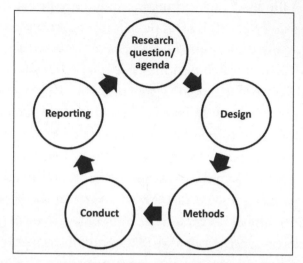

FIGURE 3.1. Biases can be introduced into the research process at any stage. Because biases can be unconscious and unintentional and are typically unrecognized, scientists must make special efforts to protect against them at every stage. Adapted from Odierna DH, Forsyth SR, White J, Bero LA, "The cycle of bias in health research," *Accountability Res.* 2013, 20(2):127–141. Used with permission, courtesy of Lisa Bero.

scientific quality of industry-funded studies is better than that of studies funded by nonindustry sources. How well the studies are conducted is not the issue. Here again, the concerns about nutrition research are more complicated.

Bero and her colleagues explain that investigators can introduce biases—consciously or unconsciously—at every stage of the research process, as shown in Figure 3.1.[25] The Bero group examined where funding biases are most likely to appear in research on obesity interventions. Their analysis finds food-industry funding to have little effect on how well the studies are conducted. Instead, the funding effects are more likely to show up in the way the research question is asked and the results interpreted. Obesity trials funded by industry tend to focus on the role of specific nutrients, whereas trials funded by independent sources ask broader and more complicated questions about dietary behavior. This discrepancy, they noted, "could limit the public health relevance of rigorous evidence available for systematic reviews and dietary guidelines."[26]

Research funded by food companies has an especially high probability of bias. For example, the requests noted earlier for proposals from the grape, yogurt, and strawberry trade associations *expect* that studies will yield evidence of health benefits; otherwise, the associations will not fund them. Bero's group notes the ways researchers can skew studies to demonstrate benefits. They can focus on single nutrients, ingredients, or foods rather than on interactions or overall diets. They can compare the effects of single foods by contrasting diets that include them to diets that lack them. They can design trials without randomization, blinding, or appropriate comparisons. They can focus on obvious or irrelevant effects. And they can give a positive spin to results that show no effect or fail to publish unfavorable results.[27]

Martijn Katan, a lipid researcher in Amsterdam, points out that food companies have no reason to look for unfavorable effects of their products and much prefer studies that allow them to adjust product dosages to increase the probability of finding benefits or of keeping adverse effects below statistical significance. He also emphasizes that industry funding can influence investigators to overlook unfavorable data, downplay negative results, or avoid publishing them out of reluctance to displease a sponsor.[28] Because all of this can happen unconsciously, investigators need to make special efforts to control for such bias. Some do. Others do not.

The ethicist Jonathan Marks notes that biases in industry-funded research are so embedded in the process that inappropriate framing of research questions and spinning of results are predictable. But investigators can favor industry in other ways—explaining obesity as a matter of individual responsibility (rather than as a result of the food environment), emphasizing physical inactivity rather than diet as its cause, or focusing on supplements rather than diets as solutions to health problems.[29] Even though not all industry-funded research favors the funder, we can understand why the funding is associated with research outcome. Food companies want to sell products. Researchers want to get grants. Industry funding is by no means the only reason for caution in interpreting research, but it is a big one. The next chapters explain why.

How Sweet It Is: Sugar and Candy as Health Foods

IF YOUR COMPANY PRODUCES SUGAR OR PRODUCTS MADE WITH it, you have a public relations problem. Sugars are today's food enemy number 1, toxic by some reports. How much is safe? None, claims science journalist Gary Taubes; sugar is responsible for obesity, type 2 diabetes, heart disease, stroke, gout, and Alzheimer's disease. Without going nearly that far, the American Heart Association advises six teaspoons as the upper daily limit for women and children. Men are bigger; they get to have nine. Public health recommendations are slightly more generous. The World Health Organization and the US dietary guidelines both advise limiting sugars to 10 percent of daily calories, which works out to about twelve teaspoons a day on average.[1] All these recommendations refer to *added* sugars. Nobody is or should be concerned about the sugars naturally present in whole fruits and vegetables; the amounts are low, and the sugars are accompanied by vitamins, minerals, and fiber. In contrast, added sugars provide calories devoid of other nutrients.

If you sell sugary products, what to do? Invoke the playbook, of course. Cast doubt on science linking sugars to poor health. Resist regulation, fund front groups, manage the media—and be sure to fund your own research. In 2014, the Union of Concerned Scientists (UCS) summarized the sugar industry's tactics for undermining policy: attack the science, spread misinformation, deploy industry scientists, and influence academics.[2]

As we now know from the discovery of decades-old documents from a bankrupt sugar company, this industry was engaged in casting doubt on inconvenient science as early as the 1960s. Then, the Sugar Research Foundation, the forerunner of today's Sugar Association, was spending 10 percent of its research budget on studies to counter research suggesting an association between sugar and the risk of heart disease. To distract dental professionals from suggesting limits on sugar to prevent tooth decay, the foundation lobbied the National Institute of Dental Research to fund studies on anything except sugar: plaque removal, vaccines, fluoride treatments, mouth bacteria, or tooth brushing. This effort succeeded; the 1971 National Caries Program promoted the alternative methods to reduce tooth decay but said nothing about the need to reduce exposure to sugary foods and drinks.[3]

Today's Sugar Association wants to convince you that "sugar" refers only to crystals refined from beets and cane—sucrose, in biochemical terms. Soon after my book *Food Politics* came out in 2002, I did a radio interview in which I mentioned that soft drinks contain sugar and water but are otherwise nutritionally useless. I soon received a certified letter from a lawyer for the Sugar Association accusing me of making "numerous false, misleading, disparaging, and defamatory statements about sugar." What had I said? "As commonly known by experts in the field of nutrition, soft drinks have contained virtually no sugar (sucrose) in more than 20 years. The misuse of the word 'sugar' to indicate other caloric sweeteners is not only inaccurate, but it is a grave disservice to the thousands of family farmers who grow sugar cane and sugar beets."[4]

This lawyer had to be kidding. By "other caloric sweeteners," the Sugar Association means high-fructose corn syrup (HFCS)— the sweetener that must not be named, apparently. In biochemical terms, sucrose and HFCS are not much different; both contain glucose and fructose sugars. Sucrose is glucose and fructose stuck together (50 percent each), but the two are quickly separated by intestinal enzymes. HFCS is about 45 percent glucose and 55 percent fructose, already separated. Both end up in the body as "free" (meaning separated) glucose and fructose. At that stage, their source is irrelevant.

Until corn started to be grown for ethanol fuels, HFCS was much cheaper than sucrose, so food processors put it in every food or drink they could, beginning in the early 1980s, just as the prevalence of obesity was rising rapidly. The increasing use of HFCS occurred in parallel with increasing obesity—an association, not necessarily a cause. "High-fructose" sounds ominous, given that excess fructose ends up as fat in the liver. HFCS came to be viewed as a cheap and potentially harmful ingredient, best avoided. In reality, both sucrose and HFCS are sugars. Both are best consumed in small amounts.

As I see it, the most critical difference between sucrose and HFCS is their representation by different—and warring—trade associations. The Sugar Association represents the producers and processors of sucrose from sugar cane and sugar beets; it wants no part of HFCS. The Corn Refiners Association (CRA) represents the industry that processes corn into HFCS; it wants you to think of HFCS as "corn sugar." As part of this fight for market share, sugar producers sued the CRA to prevent it from applying the word "sugar" to HFCS.[5] The Union of Concerned Scientists' report I referred to earlier reproduced documents released during this lawsuit. They include an email from the president of the Sugar Association calling for research to prove that sucrose is healthier than HFCS: "Question the existing science. Call for more science that compares sucrose to free fructose and free glucose. The majority of science on this issue compares . . . apples to apples."[6]

The Corn Refiners Association, in contrast, wants to position HFCS as equivalent to sucrose. I learned this when I inadvertently got caught up in a CRA advertising campaign. In 2010, an executive at Ogilvy Public Relations asked if I would meet with his client, CRA president Audrae Erickson. Shortly after our meeting, my statements about the approximate biochemical equivalence of sucrose and HFCS appeared on the CRA's website. I asked to have them removed. Erickson's response? Take us to court.[7]

I was not about to do that, but I later learned more about how the CRA operated from a *New York Times* account of the legal battles between the two trade associations. Reporter Eric Lipton based his investigation on emails and other documents, which he posted online in categories; one was titled "Using Marion Nestle."[8] The emails in that section refer to my criticism of a study done by investigators at Princeton University reporting that rats fed HFCS gained more weight than those fed sucrose. Because the study had not provided data on the rats' calorie intake, I did not think its conclusion was justified, and I said so on my blog. My post solved a problem for the CRA; their emails stated, "Agreed, we cannot look too orchestrated. Nestle piece works best for us on Princeton study" and "We've already sent the Nestle piece out to reporters (which I think has been relatively successful)."[9]

Other emails referred to tests of the sugar composition of drinks sweetened with HFCS done by investigators at the University of Southern California (USC). Their tests showed the average fructose content to be higher than 55 percent, with some drinks containing as much as 65 percent.[10] But Rick Berman, head of the Center for Consumer Freedom, assured the CRA, "If the results contradict USC, we can publish them, or maybe even reach out to Marion Nestle & give her the exclusive so she can be a conduit to media. If for any reason the results confirm USC, we can just bury the data."[11]

The Center for Consumer Freedom? Use me as a conduit? Bury the data?

Berman and his center are infamous for their aggressive public relations campaigns on behalf of clients whose identities they keep deeply secret, never revealed. According to Lipton's account, the CRA board had paid Berman $3.5 million for his services and had authorized spending up to $100,000 to hire him to find out whether the sugar industry was behind anti-HFCS science, as indeed it was.[12] But the CRA was determined to hide its connection to Berman's center: "As you know, our sponsorship of this campaign remains confidential. We are funding Berman & Co. directly, not the Center for Consumer Freedom which is running the ads. If asked, please feel free to state the following: 'The Corn Refiners Association is not funding the Center for Consumer Freedom.'"[13]

The emails also showed that the CRA was funding research conducted by James Rippe, who runs an institute devoted to producing studies requested by food companies. The CRA paid Rippe about $10 million over a four-year period for his studies. These, unsurprisingly, showed no special health effects of consuming HFCS. Rippe disclosed the CRA's funding, but the emails demonstrate that the CRA also paid him a $41,000-a-month retainer to write editorials disputing claims that HFCS might be riskier than sugar. Rippe told the CRA, "The point of doing this would be [to] show that fructose at normally consumed levels, whether it comes from High Fructose Corn Syrup or sucrose, does not lead to any metabolic abnormalities."[14] Indeed, one of his articles cautions against attributing adverse health consequences to fructose, and two others find the effects of sugars on health to be minimal and clinically insignificant.[15]

As you might guess by now, I have no argument with Rippe's conclusions. I doubt that the slightly higher amount of fructose in HFCS makes much of a difference to health. Whether small differences in fructose content do make a metabolic difference is a legitimate scientific question. Calling for research to prove that sugars are safe is not. This distinction may seem subtle, but designing studies to prove a foregone conclusion falls into the category of marketing research, not basic science. The Corn Refiners Association's demand for such studies introduces a strong possibility of bias, particularly because investigators with no financial ties to industry have associated fructose from any source with increased risks for type 2 diabetes and cardiovascular disease.[16] What are the real effects of fructose on human metabolism? We would find out a lot sooner if trade-association agendas were not involved.

One more example: John Sievenpiper, a scientist who reports having financial ties to Coca-Cola, PepsiCo, Dr. Pepper Snapple Group, Tate & Lyle, the Canadian Sugar Institute, and other such organizations, writes that a causal relationship between sugars and chronic disease is unproven, that other dietary factors and physical inactivity are equally related to weight gain and obesity, and that the "pox on sugar is overwrought."[17] His studies do not always exonerate sugar from harm, however. He was senior author of a meta-analysis that linked fructose to an increased risk of gout, and he also led an independently funded study suggesting that sugar-sweetened beverages modestly raise the risk of hypertension.[18] Sievenpiper has been quoted as arguing that although industry funding could influence conclusions drawn from research, "that does not necessarily mean that it affects the actual results" and that any problems are "easily overcome by systematic reviews and meta-analyses that pool the totality of the evidence . . . as these are based on the data and not the authors' conclusions."[19] But industry funding is often associated with research outcome, and systematic reviews also can be biased.[20] If nothing else, industry funding biases the research agenda—the questions asked—as studies funded by the honey, candy, and chocolate industries seem to indicate.

Honey Research

Sievenpiper is correct in arguing that industry-funded studies do not inevitably produce outcomes desired by their funders. Consider honey, the sweet substance produced by bees from the nectar in flowers. The sugars in honey are mostly glucose (22 to 35 percent) and fructose (28 to 41 percent), with smaller percentages of others. In 2008, honey producers created the National Honey Board, an industry-funded, US

Department of Agriculture (USDA)–managed marketing program aimed at expanding the market share of honey through research, advertising, and education. The board collected nearly $8 million from honey producers in 2016 for these purposes, through an assessment of 1.5 cents per pound of honey produced.[21]

Wouldn't it be terrific for honey marketing—and its market share—if scientists could prove that honey is healthier than either sucrose or HFCS? The Honey Board partnered with the USDA to determine whether eating honey causes less of a rise in blood sugar than eating similar amounts of sucrose or HFCS; if so, honey would be a better choice for people with diabetes. No such luck. The study found no difference. This should have been predictable; honey contains glucose and fructose just like sugar and HFCS. But the Honey Board must have thought it was worth a try to prove otherwise, and it engaged the USDA in this dubious enterprise. The authors, to their credit, made no attempt to spin the results. To manage blood-sugar levels, they said, eating less sugar is far more effective than trying to find one that is "more neutral in terms of its health effects."[22]

Candy Research

Candy is a big industry in the United States. It generated about $35 billion in retail sales in 2017, two-thirds of that from chocolate.[23] The candy industry would like to expand this market. But to do that, consumers would have to eat more—and they might if they thought they could get away with it. In her investigation of the candy-industry research I mentioned in Chapter 1, Associated Press reporter Candice Choi noted that such research "carries the weight of academic authority, becomes a part of scientific literature and generates headlines."[24] The studies she referred to concluded that eating candy has no effect on the weight or health of children. Their pleased funder was the National Confectioners Association (NCA), the candy industry's principal trade association, in partnership with the USDA.[25]

The authors based their conclusions on parental reports of what children ate in one twenty-four-hour period, a method infamous for its imprecision. Although the authors cautioned readers that the data might not reflect typical intakes and "cause and effect associations cannot be drawn," they certainly were drawn, and immediately. The NCA press release announced, "New study shows children and adolescents who eat candy are less overweight or obese."[26]

Choi's article quoted me: "Unlike other research, industry-funded studies are designed and produced to be useful in marketing. The hypotheses are market driven. . . . The only thing that moves sales . . . is health claims." This got a response from the editor of the trade magazine *Candy Industry*: "When I read the above quote from Marion Nestle, nutrition professor at New York University, I almost spewed my morning coffee." He insisted that the confectionery industry does not rely on health claims to spur sales: "Merchandising, promotions, advertising, clever media campaigns and innovative/convenient/tasty products do much more. Another thing, candy makers are not selling nutrition. They are selling sweetness, taste, comfort, indulgence, a permissible treat."[27] Fine, but then why fund studies like this?

Choi observed that the authors of the study had written more than two dozen papers funded by food companies since 2009. Two, Carol O'Neil and Theresa Nicklas, are professors. The third is Victor Fulgoni, senior vice president of Nutrition Impact, a consulting firm that helps food companies "develop and communicate aggressive, science-based claims about their products and services."[28] His business, like that of Rippe, is to help food companies obtain FDA-approved health claims and achieve other marketing objectives. Choi had obtained emails showing that Nicklas had billed Nutrition Impact $11,500 for work on three manuscripts in 2011.

Choi's article quotes Fulgoni: "Industry-funded studies show favorable results because companies invest in projects with the 'best chance of success'" and "any type of funding creates bias or pressure to deliver results." Perhaps, but industry funding demonstrably increases the chance of bias, especially when funders are closely involved in the research, as was the NCA. Although the authors said the funders had no role in the design, analysis, or writing of the manuscript, the emails suggest otherwise. In one, Fulgoni writes O'Neil, "You'll note I took most but not (all) their comments." About a similar study of candy consumption in adults, Fulgoni wrote, "I have finally waded through the comments from NCA. Attached is my attempt to edit based on their feedback."[29]

More recently, some of these authors published yet another study arguing that kids can eat candy without increasing their risk of obesity or cardiovascular disease. This one, however, was funded by groups with no apparent interest in the outcome: the National Institutes of Health (NIH), the USDA, and the American Heart Association.[30] The authors declared no conflicts of interest, apparently in the belief that the NCA's previous funding of their candy studies was irrelevant. I think it is highly relevant and should have been disclosed.

Other investigators funded by the NCA also conclude that candy is only a modest contributor to dietary intake of calories, fat, and sugars and shows no association to the risk of obesity or cardiovascular risk factors.[31] These authors disclose that the NCA "developed the research question, though did not contribute to the design of the study, analysis, interpretation of data, or drafting of the manuscript." They also disclose that the NCA "reviewed the manuscript prior to submission and provided minor editorial suggestions for consideration by the authors who retained the authority to accept or reject them."[32] Minor? This is an unusually high level of involvement from a research sponsor, suggesting an even greater chance of bias in the study results.

The NCA is not alone in funding research on candy consumption. Soremartec Italia, a producer of cocoa powder, chocolate, and sugar candy, sponsored a study concluding that "the substitution of free sugars for complex carbohydrates had no effect on blood pressure or body weight and an unclear effect on blood lipid profile."[33] Three of its four authors report having received payments from Soremartec for "seminars, congress presentations, and didactic activities." However well conducted they may be, these studies have troubling implications. Candy is not a health food. It is a treat best consumed occasionally and in small amounts.

Chocolate Research

Everyone (well, almost) loves chocolate. Wouldn't it be dreamy if chocolate, rather than being a guilty indulgence, made us healthier? I love wishful-thinking hypotheses. How about this one: the number of Nobel Prizes in a country correlates with its overall chocolate consumption?[34] Correlation does not mean causation (sadly, in this case), but that does not stop chocolate marketers from sponsoring research to promote chocolate as a health food. The Hershey Company, for example, participated in a study suggesting that chocolate can "inhibit naturally occurring deactivation of the brain during mundane and less interesting tasks" (translation: it can keep you alert when you are bored). Hershey's provided the chocolate for the study, but the researchers also thanked Hershey's staff for "guidance and support throughout this project and for their careful review of this manuscript prior to submission."[35] Their study elicited an unusually honest headline: "Step aside energy drinks: Chocolate has a stimulating effect on human brains, says Hershey-backed study."[36] I categorize reports like these as "nutrifluff," my term for sensational findings based on preliminary research on the benefits of single foods removed from their dietary context.[37]

But Mars, Incorporated, is the company most invested in promoting the benefits of components of chocolate, and it produces special products for this purpose under the brand CocoaVia. In 1982, Mars established a chocolate research center in Brazil.[38] Its scientists were particularly interested in cocoa flavanols, plant chemicals with antioxidant, anti-inflammatory, and other heart-healthy effects. Through the 1980s and 1990s, Mars's scientists produced studies suggesting such benefits.

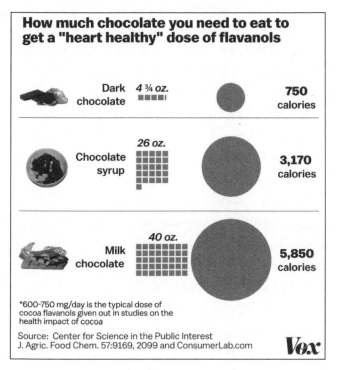

How much chocolate you need to eat to get a "heart healthy" dose of flavanols

Dark chocolate	4 ¾ oz.	750 calories
Chocolate syrup	26 oz.	3,170 calories
Milk chocolate	40 oz.	5,850 calories

*600-750 mg/day is the typical dose of cocoa flavanols given out in studies on the health impact of cocoa

Source: Center for Science in the Public Interest
J. Agric. Food Chem. 57:9169, 2099 and ConsumerLab.com

Vox

FIGURE 4.1. Chocolate companies fund research to show that cocoa flavanols have health benefits, but it takes nearly five ounces even of dark chocolate (which has the most flavanols) to obtain a useful dose. This much chocolate also provides 750 calories, however—more than a third of the daily calorie standard for an average person. Reproduced from *Vox*, Oct 16, 2017. Figure by Javier Zarracina. Vox Media, Inc., used with permission.

Unfortunately, cocoa flavanols come with complications. They taste bitter (dark chocolate contains more of them). They are present in cocoa in such small amounts that you would have to eat at least a quarter of a pound a day and often much more to achieve the recommended dose, as shown in Figure 4.1. The calories, saturated fat, and sugars in chocolate might cancel out any benefits. Worse, flavanols are destroyed by traditional chocolate processing. The losses may explain why a Hershey-funded clinical trial failed to find neuropsychological or cardiovascular benefits from eating dark chocolate when compared to a placebo.[39]

But to return to CocoaVia: Mars developed a process to preserve the cocoa flavanols during processing. It combined the rescued flavanols with cholesterol-lowering plant sterols and used them as an ingredient in its CocoaVia chocolate bars and chocolate-covered almonds. By 2002, the company decided that it had enough research to promote CocoaVia candies as heart-healthy. As the *New York Times* put it, Mars was on a "corporate quest to transform chocolate into a healthy indulgence."[40] Mars marketed the candy bars—recommending two a day, no less—as a means of increasing blood flow, lowering blood pressure, and reducing the risk of heart disease.

Unfortunately for Mars, the FDA takes a dim view of using unproven health claims in marketing campaigns. In 2006 it sent a letter warning the company that statements like "promotes a healthy heart" and "now you can have real chocolate pleasure with real heart health benefits" were false, misleading, and easily misunderstood as promoting chocolate as a health food. The FDA considered Mars's advertisements—"Cocoa Via Chocolate Bars contain natural plant extracts that have been proven to reduce bad cholesterol (LDL) by up to 8%"—to be claims that its candies were cholesterol-lowering drugs. If Mars wanted to make drug claims like these, it would have to conduct clinical trials to prove that eating CocoaVia chocolate bars really does reduce cholesterol and prevent heart disease.[41]

Rather than run the hefty financial—and scientific—risks of such an attempt, Mars gave up on candy bars and began marketing CocoaVia in pills and powder as dietary supplements, a shift that allowed the company to take advantage of the more lenient marketing claims permitted by the Dietary Supplement Health and Education Act (DSHEA) of 1994. This act allowed companies to make "structure/function" claims stating that a dietary supplement might be useful for supporting some structure or function of the body. Under DSHEA, Mars labels can claim that CocoaVia supplements "promote a healthy heart by supporting healthy blood flow," but not that they prevent heart disease—a subtle distinction easily missed by anyone who is not a lawyer or lobbyist.

To convince people to take CocoaVia supplements, Mars funds lots of research. In 2015, it funded studies demonstrating that cocoa flavanols are well tolerated in healthy men and women, support healthy cognitive function in aging, reverse cardiovascular risk in the healthy elderly, and improve biomarkers of cardiovascular risk.[42] Lest the "eat more chocolate" implications of these studies be missed, Mars issued a press release: "Cocoa flavanols lower blood pressure and increase blood vessel function in healthy people."[43] The company followed this announcement with a full-page ad in the *New York Times* quoting a dietitian: flavanols "support healthy blood flow . . . which allows oxygen and nutrients to get to your heart more easily."[44]

Perhaps because of conflicting results about possible benefits and the implication that chocolate is good for you, the advertising industry's self-regulatory National Advertising Division (NAD) urged Mars to revise its claims for healthy blood flow and CocoaVia's ability to help "firefighters, or anyone, maintain who they are for years to come." The NAD said the company's support for such claims relied on evidence from studies largely commissioned by Mars, many of which were flawed by small sample sizes and unrepresentative populations.[45]

Mars ought to know better. It has funded more than 150 studies and holds about a hundred patents related to cocoa flavanols, but it has even more ambitious research plans. In 2014, it announced a partnership with the US National Heart, Lung, and Blood Institute (NHLBI) to conduct a clinical trial of the effects of cocoa flavanols, alone or in combination with vitamin supplements, on the risk of heart disease and cancer in eighteen thousand men and women over the age of sixty. This Cocoa Supplement and Multivitamin Outcomes Study (COSMOS) has evolved since then and now lists Brigham and Women's Hospital in Boston as the sponsor and Mars as a "collaborator" along with the Fred Hutchinson Cancer Research Center in Seattle and Pfizer. The NHLBI seems no longer to be involved.[46]

In mid-2017, the study was still recruiting participants, and results were not expected before 2020. Crossfit, Inc., a commercial strength and conditioning exercise program, acquired a copy of the recruitment letter. It explains to potential participants that COSMOS "will study the role of cocoa extract (including flavanols and other natural compounds in the cocoa bean) and multivitamins in improving health. . . . Studies have found that cocoa extract may reduce the risk of heart disease and age-related cognitive decline."[47] The letter is signed by Harvard University investigators at Brigham and Women's Hospital and the Hutchinson Cancer Center; it does not mention Mars.

Despite not yet having evidence from this trial for the benefits of flavanol supplements, this research conveys the impression that chocolate, especially dark chocolate, is good for you. Indeed, an investigative report on marketing chocolate as a health food in the *Guardian* (which quotes my "nutrifluff" definition) begins by noting that "chocolate has been touted as a treatment for agitation, anaemia, angina and asthma. It has been said to awaken appetite and act as an aphrodisiac." It continues, "You may have noticed we're still [only] on the letter A."[48]

If the chocolate industry did not fund this research, investigators might be working on other projects better aligned with public health. Chocolate is delicious, but it is candy. Mars must think that demonstrating health benefits is worth the research investment. It must expect that better evidence for what CocoaVia supplements can do for health will lead to increased supplement sales. By implication—without Mars having to say a word—claims for the benefits of flavanol supplements ought to do wonders for sales of M&M's and Snickers bars.

But in response to the *Guardian* and to an earlier investigative report about this research by Julia Belluz in *Vox*, Mars says it has changed its strategy. It no longer intends its flavanol studies to create a "chocolate health halo." Chocolate, Mars said, "should not be considered a health food."[49]

Mars is a privately held company and has recently taken some unusually consumer-friendly actions. It discloses genetically modified ingredients on M&M's labels, supports the FDA's proposals for voluntary sodium reduction and labeling of added sugars, promises to label its candies as "everyday" or "occasional" options and to stop using artificial dyes, and is so critical of the industry-funded ILSI for sponsoring efforts to attack the dietary guidelines and other such positions that it withdrew from this group in 2018.[50]

Mars cares about public perception. In September 2016, I received an email request from the Mars's Corporate Reputation Team to participate in a survey: "We need your insight to help us assess our external relationships and corporate standing—how you view us, our strengths and what we need to improve."[51] My suggestion: stop funding research encouraging the public to believe that chocolate candy is a health food.

Selling Meat and Dairy Foods

M ANY PEOPLE PREFER NOT TO EAT MEAT OR DAIRY FOODS FOR reasons of religion, ethics, animal welfare, environmental protection, personal preference—or, of course, health. Vegetarians tend to live healthier lives and display less obesity, heart disease, and type 2 diabetes than people who eat beef and other red meats (chiefly pork and lamb). Some of the evidence for such benefits comes from investigators committed to vegetarian or vegan lifestyles, and some of their research is published in journal supplements sponsored by Loma Linda University, a Seventh-Day Adventist institution in California. Because Adventists are vegetarians, some more strictly adherent than others, investigators can correlate variations in vegetarian practices with long-term health effects.[1]

Researchers who believe in the benefits of vegetarian diets are subject to intellectual or ideological biases that can influence their research. Such biases are common to all scientists and are inherent in scientific hypotheses. Scientists are—or should be—trained to control for potential biases in study design and interpretation. In the case of vegetarian diets, the preponderance of evidence from all sources supports health benefits. Dietary guidelines promote plant-based diets. The flip side is that diets high in animal products must be less healthful. But which products and how much less? The answers are not simple; they depend on what else nonvegetarians eat, drink, and do. Some studies find that vegetarians live longer than nonvegetarians, but others do not.[2]

As I discussed in *Food Politics*, the meat and dairy industries are so powerful that US dietary guidelines cannot advise Americans to eat less of their products. The 2015 guidelines use euphemisms: "Choose lean meats," or, for dairy, "choose fat-free or low-fat." The meat advice is based on "strong" evidence that eating less beef, pork, and lamb, and especially processed meats like bacon and sausage, helps reduce the risk of heart disease and on "moderate" evidence for a reduced risk of obesity, type 2 diabetes, and certain cancers. I put the judgments in quotes because the evidence is mainly correlational; meat-eating is consistently associated with disease risk, but whether it causes disease or is just a marker for other causal factors has been difficult to demonstrate.

We evolved to eat meat, but today meat-eating tracks with other unhealthful dietary and lifestyle practices. Modern meat contains residues of antibiotics and hormones used to promote animal growth. It is processed with potentially carcinogenic nitrites and other chemicals. Its industrial production causes environmental damage. The "lean" recommendation suggests that fat, especially saturated fat, is a concern. The 2015 US guidelines recommend no more than twenty-six ounces of meat a week, or three to four ounces a day. Many proponents of vegetarian diets go further; they believe that meat—and, sometimes, dairy foods—are so bad for health, the environment, and the animals themselves that nobody should ever eat these foods.[3] For the meat and dairy industries, paying for research to counter such views is an essential marketing strategy, one that the USDA aids and abets through its generic marketing, promotion, and research programs—the "checkoffs."

Checkoff-Funded Research: Meat

The explicit purpose of checkoff programs is to increase demand for commodity agricultural products. Producers pay fees per weight of product; these fees go into a common fund distributed to national and state programs. The USDA oversees and administers the programs, sets guidelines, approves board members, and monitors advertising, budgets, and contracts—as well as the research. The checkoff boards reimburse the USDA for the expenses it incurs. In theory, the boards advertise, educate, and do research; they are not supposed to lobby. In practice, the lines sometimes blur.[4]

The meat checkoffs include the American Lamb Board, the Cattlemen's Beef Board, and the National Pork Board. Early in 2018, the National Cattlemen's Beef Association (NCBA), which has a contract with the Cattlemen's Beef Board for research grants "to enhance the profit potential for beef/beef products," requested preproposals for research to support "health outcomes associated with aspects of physical and mental strength and wellbeing." The NCBA was particularly seeking research proposals to demonstrate that beef improves physical function, supports heart health, reduces inflammation, and preserves cognitive function in the elderly.[5] Positioning meat as a health food seems like a new tactic. Historically, the meat industry's main research concern has been to counter suggestions that beef, pork, lamb, and processed meats increase the risk of cancer or heart disease.

The idea that red meat is linked to cancer risk emerged shortly after World War II when the physician Denis Burkitt (famous for describing the cancer now known as Burkitt's lymphoma) observed that people consuming high-meat Western diets exhibited more cancers of the colon and rectum. Cigarette smoking and obesity are well-established risk factors for certain cancers; population studies suggest that meat is too. People who eat the most meat display about a 20 percent higher risk of colon and rectal cancers, but they also seem to be at higher risk for cancers of the esophagus, liver, lung, and pancreas.[6]

The reasons for these associations are not fully understood. Scientists suspect that certain components of meat naturally present or created during cooking or processing—salts, iron, nitrates, or nitrites—are potential carcinogens. On this basis, the World Health Organization (WHO) classifies red meat as "probably carcinogenic to humans" and processed meats as unambiguously "carcinogenic to humans."[7] These findings, says WHO, support public health recommendations to limit meat consumption.

You don't like this conclusion? Start by casting doubt on the science. The NCBA says, "The available scientific evidence simply does not support a causal relationship between red or processed meat and any type of cancer."[8] As evidence, it cites studies funded through contracts with the Cattlemen's Beef Board that not only find no association between red and processed meats and prostate cancer (which is not usually linked to meat) but also exonerate high-temperature cooking methods and several suspected carcinogens.[9]

Beyond checkoffs, the meat industry supports its own research. The North American Meat Institute funded a study concluding that children who eat processed lunch meats have *healthier* diets; they get more fruit, whole grains, protein foods, calcium, potassium, and vitamin C, but less sugar.[10] An investigator who reports financial ties to several meat groups says, "Targeting certain foods and beverages, including chocolate milk, processed meats, added sugars, . . . as villains in the nutrition wars is not a science-based strategy and may need to be countered on the political front if appointed scientific review committees continue to take this approach."[11] Science funded by the meat industry argues that meat is nutritious, necessary, and safe. Independently funded scientists advise eating less meat. Take your pick.

If anything, arguments about saturated fat as a risk factor for heart disease are even more contentious. Meat and dairy foods are the highest sources of saturated fatty acids (SFAs) in American diets. Milk fats—and therefore cheese—can be as high as 75 percent SFAs. The proportion in beef fat is about 40 percent, whereas the SFAs in avocados and olives are about 13 percent, less but still significant. Is the high proportion of SFAs from meat and dairy foods harmful? The meat and dairy industries fund studies to counter this idea; they typically find SFAs so benign that you would expect to be healthier if you ate *more* saturated fat. These industries want evidence that SFAs do not raise blood cholesterol levels or increase the risk of heart disease.

Studies funded by the meat industry yield predictable results. One concludes that eating more red meat than is recommended has no effect on blood cholesterol levels; its senior author discloses support from the beef and pork checkoff programs, among other food-industry groups. Another suggests that advice to reduce intake of SFAs may cause undesirable reductions in protein intake; it is published in a journal supplement sponsored by the beef checkoff, among others, and two of its six authors report receiving research or consulting funds from that program.[12] But the American Heart Association argues otherwise; its scientists observe substantial health benefits when SFAs are replaced by unsaturated fats.[13]

Researchers' financial ties to meat or dairy groups complicate debates about the effects of SFAs. For decades, the preponderance of research has shown that SFAs raise blood cholesterol levels when substituted for unsaturated fatty acids. In 2015, Harvard investigators demonstrated this again. But the senior author of that study, Frank Hu, reports receiving funding from trade associations for avocados and walnuts, sources of "healthy" fats. He also was senior author on a previous article in the *BMJ* (formerly the *British Medical Journal*) stating that dietary advice should continue to focus on replacing total saturated fat with healthier energy sources.[14] A letter to the *BMJ* complained that four of Hu's coauthors worked for Unilever, a company that produces margarines low in SFAs, raising "an unacceptable risk of bias, with previous research demonstrating that industry funded studies produce more favourable results than independent research."[15]

Point taken, although some industry-funded studies of SFAs do yield contrary results. The beef checkoff and the NCBA jointly funded a comparison of the effects of consuming low-carbohydrate, high-protein (beef) diets containing either 8 percent SFAs or 15 percent SFAs. After three weeks, the higher-SFA diet led to significantly increased levels of blood cholesterol and cardiovascular risk, consistent with research dating back to the 1950s.[16]

As I see these arguments, focusing on saturated fat rather than the foods and diets that contain it makes no sense. In chemical terms, fats (fatty acids, actually) are hydrocarbons distinguished by how much hydrogen is linked to their carbon atoms. If hydrogens are missing, the carbons link to each other with double bonds; their potential links to hydrogen are unfilled and, therefore, "unsaturated." The fats in foods are always—no exceptions—mixtures of fatty acids that are saturated (fully hydrogenated), monounsaturated (one double bond), or polyunsaturated (more than one double bond). Only the proportions of the three types differ. All three have the same digestibility and number of calories.

On balance, evidence supports the idea that substituting SFAs for unsaturated fats raises blood cholesterol levels and coronary risk. But once the studies start dealing with foods and diets, the results become far more complicated and difficult to interpret. That so much of this research is funded by industry only adds to the confusion, a problem especially acute when dealing with studies funded by dairy-industry groups.

Checkoff-Funded Research: Dairy

The dairy checkoffs are the National Dairy Promotion and Research Board and the Fluid Milk Processors Promotion Program. These programs generate about $200 million annually in fees and are best known for the milk-mustache "Got milk?" campaign.[17] A similar dairy program in Canada funds research to promote "the efficiency and sustainability of Canadian dairy farms, grow markets, and supply high-quality, safe and nutritious dairy products to Canadians."[18]

Michele Simon is currently the executive director of the Plant Based Food Association, a trade group for companies producing replacements for animal products. In 2014, she wrote *Whitewashed*, a report unsurprisingly critical of the USDA's promotion of dairy

FIGURE 5.1. Michele Simon's June 2014 report *Whitewashed: How Industry and Government Promote Dairy Junk Foods* argues that the government should stop helping the dairy industry sell junk foods through USDA-managed checkoff programs. Used with permission, courtesy of Michele Simon.

products (Figure 5.1). Simon made three intriguing observations: nearly half the US milk supply goes for cheese and frozen desserts; chocolate- and strawberry-flavored milks (with sugar added) account for 70 percent of milk sales in schools; and more than 10 percent of all US sugar goes into the production of dairy products. Checkoff funds, she said, should not be used to promote "dairy junk foods" that conflict with dietary guidelines. Her report also called for better USDA oversight to make certain that checkoff funds were not used for lobbying.[19]

Whitewashed did not say much about the role of checkoff programs in dairy research, which is too bad, but it could have done so because the programs actively engage in research to demonstrate the health benefits of dairy foods. When I wrote *What to Eat* in 2006, it took me three chapters to explain the research arguments about issues related to dairy foods. From my reading of the research, I concluded that dairy foods are just like other foods. I still hold that opinion. If you do not like dairy foods, cannot tolerate their lactose, are allergic to their proteins, or do not want to eat them for any reason, you do not have to. Plenty of other foods provide the same nutrients. If you like dairy foods (as I do), that is fine too—but watch out for calories and added sugars.

That said, the most troubling problem with dairy research is that so much of it is funded by the dairy industry. I know of only one study that has looked at dairy-funding effects, in this case on studies of obesity. It found no relationship between funding and study outcome, but the authors said they had a hard time locating studies that were *not* sponsored by dairy trade groups.[20]

I enjoy my conversations and debates with Greg Miller, the chief scientific officer of the National Dairy Council (NDC), who routinely sends me studies demonstrating the benefits of dairy products. The NDC is the marketing arm of the dairy checkoffs; it offers grants for research proposals to find health benefits for dairy foods.

The NDC says it funds research based on principles of scientific integrity, transparency, and public-private partnerships, as set forth by ILSI, the industry-funded entity mentioned often in this book. An NDC report lists hundreds of the studies it funds in three categories: nutrition, product development, and sustainability. In the nutrition category alone, I counted 119 studies completed or in progress from 2010 to 2016. Public health studies investigate the benefits of dairy products—particularly full-fat varieties—for cardiovascular, bone, metabolic, and childhood health. Studies aimed at consumer benefits examine how dairy foods improve muscle health, sports performance, digestive health, and cognition. The NDC also has other research priorities aimed at demonstrating the benefits of whey ingredients and milk fractions. It funds a few projects on sustainability—on methane emissions, for example.[21]

I knew that the dairy industry funded a great deal of nutrition research because one-third of the studies in my year-long collection were funded by dairy groups or conducted by investigators with ties to those groups. These studies typically concluded that dairy foods are beneficial or harmless, even when they suggest that "the possibility that milk intake is simply a marker of diets higher in nutritional quality cannot be ruled out."[22] "Harmless" allows a positive spin. A dairy-funded study with a neutral result elicited this press headline: dairy "does not increase heart attack or stroke risk."[23] In general, dairy-funded studies routinely find that dairy foods protect against stroke and coronary heart disease, help manage type 2 diabetes, reduce metabolic abnormalities, improve intake of vitamins and minerals, reduce the risk of allergies in children, and restore fluid balance after exercise more effectively than electrolyte solutions.[24] A consortium of dairy trade associations from Canada, Australia, the Netherlands, and Denmark sponsored a study concluding that dairy fats have no effect on "a large array of cardiometabolic variables"[25] These are impressive accomplishments for just one food.

To be fair, dairy-funded studies occasionally show no benefit. The Danish Dairy Research Foundation helped support a study of more than ninety-seven thousand people to find out whether milk-drinking reduced risks for obesity and type 2 diabetes. It did not. Independently funded studies also sometimes show negative effects, such as an association of dairy food consumption with reproductive difficulties in otherwise healthy premenopausal women.[26]

The dairy industry works especially hard to demonstrate the health benefits of specific products—cheese, for example. Cheese is high in SFAs, but not as high as butter; in comparison, cheese appears healthier. This may explain why a systematic review and meta-analysis of randomized controlled trials, written by authors with financial ties to dairy industry groups, concludes that eating hard cheese reduces blood cholesterol levels—as compared to eating butter.[27]

Another dairy consortium funded a study with this conclusion: diets containing high-fat cheese are *less* risky than low-fat, high-carbohydrate diets.[28] Letters to the editor about this study complained that the experimental diets appeared to be designed to reach the desired conclusion. The high-SFA diets were unusually high in dietary fiber and enriched with polyunsaturated fats, both of which reduce blood cholesterol levels; the low-fat diet had been enriched with SFAs likely to raise cholesterol levels. The authors replied by defending their methods and insisting that "the sponsors had no influence on the execution of the study, analysis and interpretation of the data, or the final manuscript."[29] Perhaps, but funding effects may occur unconsciously.

Yogurt companies in particular want us to believe that the living bacteria ("probiotics") in yogurt confer special health benefits. This idea dates to the early twentieth century when the Russian scientist Élie Metchnikoff attributed the ostensibly long life of Bulgarians to their yogurt consumption. I say "ostensibly" because claims of their longevity—and yogurt-eating—did not hold up to scrutiny. Nevertheless, the idea stuck. Yogurt-funded studies show that yogurt is associated with another wide array of benefits: reduced risk of metabolic syndrome, type 2 diabetes, weight gain, and obesity; higher bone density in older adults; and better digestibility by people intolerant to the lactose sugar in milk.[30] "Associated with" indicates correlation, not causation. This matters because some yogurt-funded studies do not show benefits. The drug company Sanofi-Aventis, which makes and sells probiotics, helped fund a study asking whether habitual yogurt consumption made people feel better about their health. It did not.[31]

During the year I was collecting industry-funded research on my blog, I received an anonymous comment referring to a study of dairy foods and type 2 diabetes. The comment came from an employee of the California Dairy Research Foundation, the study's sponsor. The unidentified writer said, "We take exception to the fact that you have judged our paper simply by its funding source rather than its content. . . . We used all of the highest quality of academic research available to draw these conclusions. This is the same process that a nonindustry academic would have gone through in order to produce this type of paper." The writer must not have read the entire post, which ended with my statement that industry funding does not inevitably bias a study, although it does suggest that the research question and interpretation require more than the usual level of scrutiny.[32]

As mentioned earlier, the scientific quality of industry-funded studies is not usually at issue. Most biases turn up in the research question (comparing cheese and butter) or in the interpretation (interpreting a neutral result as positive). But sometimes an industry-funded study is so egregiously self-serving that it gives all such studies a bad name. Try this: chocolate milk alleviates symptoms of concussions in high school football players. No, I am not making this up.

The University of Maryland's Chocolate Milk Scandal

In December 2015, the University of Maryland issued a press release announcing that "Fifth Quarter Fresh, a new, high-protein chocolate milk, helped high school football players improve their cognitive and motor function over the course of a season, even after experiencing concussions." The study had been conducted by Jae Kun Shim, a professor of kinesiology, who had followed 474 football players from several high schools in western Maryland throughout the fall 2014 season. The press release quoted professor Shim: "High school football players, regardless of concussions, who drank Fifth Quarter Fresh chocolate milk during the season, showed positive results overall . . . specifically in the areas of verbal and visual memory."[33]

This was stunning news. Concussions are a deep concern in sports these days, increasingly recognized as causing not only short-term cognitive deficits but also permanent brain damage. Based on this evidence, pediatricians are now urging school boards to discontinue football programs.[34] The press release quoted Clayton Wilcox, superintendent of the local public schools: "There is nothing more important than protecting our student-athletes. . . . Now that we understand the findings of this study, we are determined to provide Fifth Quarter Fresh to all of our athletes." Wilcox told a reporter from *Stat News* that he planned to buy $25,000 worth of the milk because "a lot of kids just don't drink milk anymore," and Fifth Quarter has "really stumbled across that secret sauce."[35]

The press release got plenty of press attention, although surely not what the university wanted. Health News Review (HNR), an outfit that evaluates press releases on their clarity and accuracy, ranked this one as "highly unsatisfactory." Its evaluation began: "Got facts? They are almost absent from this boastful release touting vague neurological benefits of a specific chocolate milk." HNR noted that the press release said nothing about the measures that improved, the level of improvement, the study itself, or the composition of the drink. Its conclusion: the press release "may further the health haloing of a beverage that drop per drop has more calories and nearly as much sugar as Coca-Cola."[36]

Indeed it does. Fifth Quarter Fresh contained only four ingredients: fat-free milk, sugar, cocoa powder, and vitamins. Its fourteen-ounce bottle provided forty-two grams of sugars—more than ten teaspoons—making this drink nothing more than heavily sweetened chocolate skim milk with a vitamin supplement. You could easily make this at home. But as late as 2017 the company's website (no longer available) boasted that the drink contains milk from "super, natural" cows, is free of chemicals and preservatives, and "combines the best of protein drinks with an outstanding formula for rehydration, including unsurpassed levels of calcium plus Vitamins A and D" and twenty grams of protein.

An HNR reviewer asked the university to explain and reported, "What I heard astounded me. I couldn't find any journal article because there wasn't one. . . . There wasn't even an unpublished report they could send me."[37] The Baltimore press also was "shocked and confused by the University of Maryland's decision to put out a press release about the study, which has not yet been peer-reviewed, published in a journal, or even written in full."[38] The *Baltimore Business Journal* obtained a summary of the study and a PowerPoint presentation but could not release them publicly. *New York Magazine* provided a link to the PowerPoint presentation—the *only* source of information about what the study actually involved.[39]

Reporters noted that the study seemed badly designed. It did not compare the effects of Fifth Quarter Fresh to other brands of chocolate milk or to any other sweetened drink; it relied on athletic departments rather than trained investigators to administer the test and provide the milk to players; and it was based on cognitive tests of questionable validity. Also, Shim had not required waivers from players or permission from parents for participation, and he did not disclose his funding source or financial ties.

In response to the press uproar, the university appointed a committee to investigate; its report appeared in March 2016.[40] The report dealt mostly with the failure of the university and Shim to observe established research protocols and ethics but also revealed some juicy details. The parent company of Fifth Quarter Fresh had provided support for salaries and research materials, and a Pennsylvania dairy group had contributed $200,000 to Shim. The committee was dismayed by the widespread ignorance of basic principles of research ethics it found among university personnel. Shim, for example, had not considered the funding to be a conflict of interest because the money went to his research, not to him personally.

The committee advised the university to make sure that future press releases disclosed funding sources and dealt only with work that had been published. The university, it said, should require all research faculty, staff, and graduate students to undergo mandatory, in-person training on the principles of conflicts of interest in research and the need for disclosure. It advised the university to return all research and gift funds received from the dairy groups and to remove all press releases related to this incident from its website. The university complied and returned nearly $230,000.[41]

Even so, Julia Belluz of Vox judged the university as "incredibly irresponsible" in "behaving like a marketing machine for a dairy company."[42] HNR criticized the committee for not dealing adequately with the university's failure to be more transparent with the media. The AP's Candice Choi dug deeper and obtained emails between Fifth Quarter and the investigator that explained their hurry to publish the press release. Fifth Quarter wanted the study results out in time to coincide with the opening of the film *Concussion*, an exposé of the National Football League's decades of inaction in dealing with head trauma.[43] I can only imagine what this "study" could have done for sales of Fifth Quarter Fresh.

The moral: universities run grave reputational risks if they do not hold industry-sponsored research and research investigators to high standards of ethical conduct. Sometimes, as in this case, "it's everything wrong with modern-day science-by-press-release in one anecdote."[44] Universities earn respect when they hold everyone—students, professors, administrators, and even public relations staff—to high ethical standards.

6

Research on Healthy Foods: Marketing, Not Necessarily Science

R EGARDLESS OF WHO ISSUES THEM, GUIDELINES FOR HEALTH promotion and disease prevention universally recommend diets that are largely plant-based, meaning that they include plenty of fruits, vegetables, grains, beans, and nuts. The US dietary guidelines also recommend foods in the "protein" category. Grains, beans, and nuts are good sources of protein, but the guidelines use "protein" to mean low-fat dairy, lean meats, and fish. Recommended eating patterns include all these foods, relatively unprocessed, but with minimal addition of salt and sugars. Such patterns provide nutrients and energy in proportions that meet physiological needs but also minimize the risk of obesity, type 2 diabetes, and other chronic diseases. One more definition: "Patterns" refers to diets as a whole, not to single foods. No one food makes a diet healthful. The healthiest diets include a wide variety of foods in each of the recommended categories in amounts that balance calories.

In their largely unprocessed forms, foods from the earth, trees, or animals are healthful by definition. So why, you might ask, would the producers of foods such as cranberries, pears, avocadoes, or walnuts fund research aimed at proving that these particular foods—rather than fruits, vegetables, or nuts in general—have special health benefits? Marketing, of course. Every food producer wants to expand sales. Health claims sell. The FDA requires research to support health claims and greatly prefers studies that involve human subjects rather than animals.

All of this explains why Royal Hawaiian Macadamia Nut, Inc. petitioned the FDA in 2015 to allow it to say in advertisements that daily consumption of macadamias—along with eating a healthy diet—may reduce the risk of heart disease. The eighty-one-page petition cited several studies done in humans, one of them funded by the Hershey Company, which sells chocolate-covered macadamias.[1] The FDA ruled that it would permit a qualified health claim for macadamia nuts with this precise wording: "Supportive but not conclusive research shows that eating 1.5 ounces per day of macadamia nuts, as part of a diet low in saturated fat and cholesterol and not resulting in increased intake of saturated fat or calories may reduce the risk of coronary heart disease."[2] Can a statement this cumbersome help sell macadamia nuts? Definitely, with a little help from the press: "Go nuts, folks! FDA declares macadamia nuts heart healthy."[3]

Legitimate scientific questions can be asked about specific foods—their nutrient content or digestibility, for example—but most such issues were addressed ages ago. Foods are not drugs. To ask whether one single food has special health benefits defies common sense. We do not eat just one food. We eat many different foods in combinations that differ from day to day; varying our food intake takes care of nutrient needs. But when marketing imperatives are at work, sellers want research to claim that their products are "superfoods," a nutritionally meaningless term. "Superfoods" is an advertising concept.

But what is wrong with promoting the benefits of healthful foods? Wouldn't we be better off eating more of them? Yes, we would, but many industry-funded studies are misleading, which is why the FDA requires so many qualifications in the claims it allows. This kind of research is designed to produce results implying that people who eat this one food will be healthier and can forget about everything else in their diets. Research aimed at marketing raises questions about biases in design and interpretation, may create reputational risks for investigators, and reflects poorly on the integrity of nutrition science. It also raises questions about the role of government agencies in promoting single-food research and about their failure to do a better job of regulating marketers' claims about health benefits based on that research. To illustrate why such concerns matter, consider some of the marketing issues related to three healthy foods: blueberries, pecans, and pomegranates.

Maine Wild Blueberries: A "Nutrient-Rich SuperFruit"

The trade association Wild Blueberries of North America wants you to understand that frozen, fresh Wild Blueberries (always capitalized) are better for you than unfrozen, fresh supermarket highbush berries: "Jam-packed with a variety of natural phytochemicals such as anthocyanin, Wild Blueberries have twice the antioxidant capacity per serving of regular blueberries. A growing body of research is establishing Wild Blueberries as a potential ally to protect against diseases such as cancer, heart disease, diabetes and Alzheimer's."[4] This is an impressive range of health benefits for a tiny fruit consumed in small amounts even by people who can find them, but selling them as an antioxidant powerhouse has done wonders for the Maine wild-blueberry industry.

For years, I have had a potted highbush blueberry plant on my twelfth-floor Manhattan terrace, satisfyingly productive in years when I can manage to fend off the hordes of voracious finches. Unlike the easy-to-get-at highbush varieties, the wild ones grow close to the ground on sandy soils left behind by receding glaciers and are more difficult to harvest. In Maine, these blueberries are an important agricultural commodity. Since 1945, Maine blueberry growers have supported research—then and now focused on production practices—at the state's university. As techniques improved, blueberry growers produced more berries. These needed to be sold.

The Maine Wild Blueberry Commission consulted with marketing specialists. In 1992, a consultant advised focusing on taste as a means of differentiating wild from cultivated blueberries. But the consultant then read an article in a USDA magazine extolling the virtues of plant antioxidant pigments in "boosting the immune system, reducing inflammation and allergies, [and] detoxifying contaminants and pollutants."[5] The article said that USDA investigators had invented an assay for antioxidants demonstrating that blueberries have the highest levels of any fruit tested (kale was highest among vegetables). The consultant advised the commission to focus on antioxidants. From 1997 to 2000, half the Maine Wild Blueberry Commission's marketing resources went into repositioning blueberries as a health icon. The strategy worked. Maine's wild-blueberry industry flourished—at least for a while. Recent overproduction and competition from Canadian fruit have dropped prices below profitability.[6]

I love blueberries, wild and cultivated, but they are a fruit like any other. Their antioxidants may counteract the damaging actions of oxidizing agents (free radicals) in the body, but studies of how well antioxidants protect against disease yield results that are annoyingly inconsistent. When tested, antioxidant supplements have not been shown to reduce disease risk and sometimes have been shown to cause harm.[7] The USDA no longer publishes data on food antioxidant levels "due to mounting evidence that the values indicating antioxidant capacity have no relevance to the effects of specific bioactive compounds, including polyphenols on human health."[8] The US National Center for Complementary and Integrative Health at NIH judges antioxidants as having no special benefits.[9] People who eat more fruits and vegetables have less risk of chronic disease, but nobody really knows whether this is because of antioxidants, other food components, or other lifestyle choices.

Blueberries, like every other fruit and vegetable, have a unique combination of antioxidants. But so what? It is best not to expect miracles—like this especially wishful-thinking headline: "Blueberries associated with reduced risk of erectile dysfunction." Two of the authors of this study reported receiving funding from the US Highbush Blueberry Council "for a separate project unrelated to this publication."[10]

Pecans: A New Federal Marketing Order

In April 2016, I received an email from Jeff Worn, vice president of the South Georgia Pecan Company, asking if we could have a conversation about health claims for these nuts. I love pecans, particularly in pralines, but I am not a fan of health claims for foods; health claims are about marketing, not science. I told Worn that if he wanted to promote pecans as a superfood, I would be no help at all. He replied that his request was about education, not marketing. Most Americans, he said, think of pecans as something in pralines, ice cream, or pie, but, he said, pecans are "actually much more than that. They have a ton of nutritional value in the antioxidants they contain. . . . Plus the fats in Pecans are good fats, but the general public thinks more fat in a product means love handles and that's just not true with Pecans."[11]

Antioxidants again. But I could see his point about the healthy fats in pecans, and we began an email correspondence. He explained that his industry was in the process of obtaining a federal marketing order (FMO) from the USDA. FMOs are the USDA's way of helping producers of what it calls "specialty crops" (translation: fruits, vegetables, and nuts for human consumption, as opposed to industrial corn and soybeans fed to animals). The FMO for pecans applies to pecan growers in fifteen states; it authorizes the pecan industry to collect data, recommend quality standards, regulate packages and containers, and conduct research and promotional activities. It also establishes an American Pecan Council

TABLE 6.1. USDA Marketing Programs for Fruits, Vegetables, and Nuts ("Specialty Crops"), 2018

Research & promotion (checkoff) programs

Hass Avocado Board	National Processed Raspberry Council
Mushroom Council	National Watermelon Promotion Board
National Mango Board	Popcorn Board
National Peanut Board	United States Potato Board
National Potato Promotion Board	US Highbush Blueberry Council

Marketing orders

Almonds	Olives
Apricots	Onions
Avocados	Pears
Cherries, sweet	Pecans
Cherries, tart	Pistachios
Citrus	Plums/Prunes
Cranberries	Potatoes
Dates	Raisins
Grapes	Spearmint oil
Hazelnuts	Tomatoes
Kiwifruit	Walnuts

SOURCES: US Department of Agriculture, Agricultural Marketing Service, "Research and promotion," www.ams.usda.gov/rules-regulations/research-promotion; US Department of Agriculture, Agricultural Marketing Service, "Marketing orders and agreements," www.ams.usda.gov/rules-regulations/moa.

to work with the USDA to decide how the funds will be used and to oversee these activities.

I did not know much about FMOs and asked Tufts University professor Parke Wilde, my go-to person for information about checkoff programs, to help me understand how checkoffs and FMOs differ. He explained that both are run by the USDA's Agricultural Marketing Service and both collect mandatory fees from all producers for marketing, promotion, and research. Their most obvious difference is geographical; checkoffs are national, but FMOs are regional (most of the other differences have to do with their enabling legislation, scope of activities, and vulnerability to legal challenges). Table 6.1 lists the specialty crops covered by checkoffs and FMOs in 2017.

Worn said he was working with researchers at the University of Georgia to do clinical studies on the health benefits of pecans and wanted my thoughts on what his group should or should not say about the nutritional benefits of pecans for marketing purposes. I thought his comment "It's about education" sounded like marketing. Pecan growers want to sell more pecans. I want people to understand that *all* whole foods have nutritional value—all relatively unprocessed fruits, vegetables, grains, beans, meats, dairy, and, yes, nuts. But I could understand his emailed response: "I do want people to buy more Pecans. It's what pays the bills, but it's more than that to me. I am a facts based person. . . . I just have a desire to dig deeper and bring something to the consumer that isn't all about money."

I go through all this, with his permission, because he is especially thoughtful about the role of research in food marketing. I told him that I do not need more information about the nutritional benefits of pecans. I already know that people who habitually eat nuts tend to be healthier than people who do not. This is true whether the nuts are pecans, macadamias, walnuts, almonds, or any other. But nut-eaters may differ in other ways from non-nut-eaters. What kind of research would it take to demonstrate that eating pecans— as compared to any other nut—produced measurable improvements in health? Such studies would be impossibly difficult and expensive. Do the nutritional differences between one nut and another merit funding a clinical trial to find out? I think not, but I can understand that nut producers might disagree.

Worn sent me the protocol for a study of the effects of a pecan-rich diet on biomarkers of risk for cardiovascular disease and diabetes in overweight people. The investigators presented the preliminary results of this study at the 2016 annual meeting of the American Society for Nutrition. Their poster presentation associated eating pecans with "reductions in fasting insulin, glucose, blood lipids, systolic blood pressure, and inflammation, and longer lag time for LDL [low-density lipoprotein] oxidation . . . although none of these changes were statistically significant."[12] This conclusion put a positive spin on neutral (not statistically significant) results, as is typical of industry-funded research. The poster did not disclose the study's funder, but the protocol did: the National Pecan Shellers Association.

POM Wonderful: A $35 Million Research Investment

Early in 2008, I received a polite letter from Matt Tupper, president of POM Wonderful, a company making pomegranate juice and supplements. The company is owned by the billionaire couple Lynda and Stewart Resnick, owners of the largest farm in the United States. Their $4.5 billion, privately held company also owns Fiji Water as well as 180,000 acres (twenty-one square miles) of almond, pistachio, and citrus orchards in California alone, among them 18,000 acres of pomegranates.[13] Tupper wrote that he admired my work but was disappointed to see a quotation from me in an article he had just read: "Pomegranates are no better than any other fruit. They're just brilliantly marketed. . . . Spend $20 million researching just about any fruit . . . and you'd discover that it, too, provides unique and miraculous-sounding benefits."[14] Tupper's letter explained that "the medical research funded by Pom is not simply a tool to market more pomegranates. . . . Rather, the fundamental goal of Pom's research program is to develop a scientifically sound understanding about how and why the pomegranate impacts human health." He said the company believed that pomegranates are superior to other fruits and vegetables because they are "uniquely endowed with a myriad of potent antioxidant compounds and therefore sit at the top of the nutritional pile." Ah yes, antioxidants.

Since at least 2001, POM Wonderful had been investing in studies designed to show that daily intake of eight ounces of pomegranate juice or a supplement of pomegranate polyphenol extract would produce higher levels of antioxidants in the body and would therefore reduce risks for cardiovascular disease, type 2 diabetes, prostate cancer, and erectile dysfunction (the holy grail, apparently). It claimed these benefits in its advertisements.[15] In 2011, I wrote a column for

FIGURE 6.1. This POM Wonderful advertisement appeared the day after a district court judge ruled that POM's health claims were not scientifically substantiated. The judge's statement is slightly out of context; the full statement read, "Pomegranate juice is a natural fruit product with health promoting characteristics. The safety of pomegranate juice is not in doubt."

the *San Francisco Chronicle* explaining why nutrition research, particularly research funded by industry, requires careful interpretation. I said that whenever I see studies claiming benefits for a single food, I want to know three things: whether the results are biologically plausible; whether the study controlled for other dietary, behavioral, or lifestyle factors that could have influenced its result; and who sponsored it. I used pomegranates as an example, noting that one of its major producers was sponsoring research to hype its benefits. I agreed that pomegranates might have high antioxidant activity but asked, "Compared with what? Its maker does not say."[16]

In response, a vice president of clinical development at POM wrote me another polite letter stating, "POM Wonderful prides itself in supporting extensive scientific and medical research, well in excess of any other food company. With over 60 publications in peer-reviewed scientific journals, our commitment to understanding the health benefits of the pomegranate speaks for itself. . . . Comparing the health benefits of our product to other juices is not a key objective of our extensive research program." Instead, he said, POM intended the research "to unlock the secrets of a particularly healthy fruit."[17]

POM held nothing back in advertising those secrets. Its ads said POM had clinical studies proving that the juice and supplements "reduce the risk of, and treat heart disease, including by decreasing arterial plaque, lowering blood pressure, and improving blood flow to the heart." The company advertised that POM products reduce the risk of prostate cancer "by prolonging prostate-specific antigen doubling time." Even better, POM juice "prevents, reduces the risk of, and treats, erectile dysfunction." Drink POM juice, and you can even "cheat death" (see Figure 6.1).[18]

Under the FDA's arcane rules for health claims, POM was advertising its juice and supplements as drugs, not food. Understanding the distinction requires a bit of history. Until the early 1990s, the FDA did not permit foods or supplements to be marketed with statements that they could prevent, mitigate, or treat a disease; only drugs do these things. If marketers wanted to make drug claims, they had to prove safety and efficacy. Food companies knew that clinical trials would be impossibly expensive and unlikely to prove much. Instead, they lobbied for the right to "inform the public" about health benefits.

When Congress passed the Nutrition Labeling and Education Act of 1990, it instructed the FDA to allow food manufacturers to make health claims that were supported by "substantial scientific agreement" among experts. The FDA's regulations responding to this act permitted food labels to claim, for example, that fruits and vegetables—as a group—reduce the risk of cancer and heart disease. It also allowed a few other disease claims.[19] Subsequent claims that a food prevents or treats disease needed FDA approval, but POM had not made such requests.

I call the FDA's rules arcane because POM's marketers could simply have said that pomegranate juice "supports" healthy heart, prostate, or sexual function. This would have been a structure/function claim authorized by the dietary supplement act, which the FDA also permits for foods. POM's lawyers surely must have known the legal distinction between "prevents disease" and "supports health," but the company insisted that its research merited claims that POM products can prevent specific diseases and symptoms.

The FDA disagreed. Early in 2010, the agency warned POM that its advertisements were positioning the juice and supplements as drugs and were therefore illegal under current provisions of the laws that govern the FDA's activities.[20] In September, the Federal Trade Commission (FTC), which regulates advertising and usually follows FDA guidance in such matters, told POM that it had to stop making unproven claims in its advertisements. The FTC did not view POM-sponsored research as adequate evidence for the claims.

POM's response? It sued. The company argued that the FTC's actions "detrimentally impacted POM's freedom of speech now, the value of its research program now, and are violating its First and Fifth Amendment rights."[21] Really? I find it hard to believe that America's Founding Fathers introduced the First and Fifth Amendments to protect the rights of POM Wonderful to make unsubstantiated health claims. The court, apparently, had the same concern. It upheld the FTC's complaint that POM's heart disease and cancer claims were false and unsubstantiated. It agreed with the FTC that POM's research was insufficiently compelling, particularly because many of POM's studies were uncontrolled or unblinded (study subjects knew what they were drinking or taking). Furthermore, "the erectile dysfunction claims were false and unsubstantiated because the study on which the company relied did not show that POM Juice was any more effective than a placebo."[22]

POM-sponsored research provides additional examples of how easy it is to design studies to give desired results. According to information in the court decision, POM had invested more than $35 million in nearly one hundred studies at forty-four different institutions. At least seventy of its studies were published in peer-reviewed journals. Among other benefits, these demonstrated—using appropriate scientific methods—that pomegranate juice has antioxidant activity and acts as an antioxidant in the body. No surprise there. All fruits and vegetables have antioxidants (they help fend off invaders). POM's research did not compare the effects of the antioxidants in pomegranates to those in any other fruit. Whether a particular fruit has more antioxidants depends on which particular antioxidants you look for, but what difference does it make? Plant foods as a whole promote health. The particular role of antioxidants in health continues to be difficult to sort out.

POM, however, deserves credit for chutzpah. The day after the judge's decision, the company placed a full-page ad in the *New York Times* declaring, "FTC v. POM: You be the judge." The ad included selected quotations from the judge's decision. Here is one: "Competent and reliable scientific evidence shows that pomegranate juice provides a benefit to promoting erectile health and erectile function (page 198)." This statement is indeed on page 198, but the ad omitted the sentence that follows: "There is insufficient competent and reliable scientific evidence to show that pomegranate juice prevents or reduces the risk of erectile dysfunction or has been clinically proven to do so."[23] The company also put out-of-context quotations from the decision in other advertisements, such as the one shown in Figure 6.1.

POM Wonderful is privately held and does not have to disclose sales figures, but they are estimated at $100 million a year for the juice and supplements. Lynda Resnick once explained, "People needed pomegranate juice in their lives (even if they didn't know it yet), and I knew they would pay what it was worth."[24] POM's price premium is impressive. In 2018, a twenty-four-ounce bottle of POM cost $8.99 at my local Manhattan grocery store, but thirty-two ounces of Tropicana orange juice sold for $3.99. *Time* carried a full-page ad that read, "Refresh your memory: learn about this preliminary research on pomegranate polyphenol antioxidants and memory and cognition."

These, the ad admits, "are early scientific findings on cognitive health and the impact of pomegranate juice on the human brain has not yet been adequately studied. Clinical research is needed to help establish causation."[25] Is such research worth doing? For marketing, apparently so. For science? It depends on the research question.

I end this saga by quoting the conclusion of the one POM-funded study I ran across in my year-long collection: "While pomegranate extract supplementation may reduce blood pressure and increase the antioxidant activity in hemodialysis patients, it does not improve other markers of cardiovascular risk, physical function, or muscle strength."[26] The no-benefit results suggest that this study must have been designed with appropriate controls, which it was. But "may reduce blood pressure" gives the results a positive spin; the investigators observed no reduction when they corrected the results for baseline blood pressure.

Using Science to Market Healthy Foods

Health claims based on research, regardless of how well conducted, help sell foods and food products. When the FDA attempted to block the more far-fetched claims, food companies sued the agency on First Amendment grounds. In 2003, after losing several of these cases one after another, the FDA gave up fighting them and eased its standards.[27] Thereafter, it would accept a much broader range of evidence for health claims, would no longer insist on "substantial scientific agreement," and would only challenge claims—like those of POM Wonderful—that most flagrantly violated the law. This decision encouraged the marketers of whole foods like those shown in Table 6.2 to sponsor research to support health claims for their products.

The studies summarized in the table differ in type; they include reviews, animal experiments, and human trials. I simplified their conclusions to suggest how marketers might use their results in health claims. In fairness, some of these studies qualify their conclusions

TABLE 6.2. Industry-Funded Studies of Food Plants with Results Useful for Health Claims (Selected Examples), 2015–2018

FOOD	HEALTH BENEFIT REPORTED	INDUSTRY SPONSOR OR COSPONSOR
Almonds	Reduced body fat and blood pressure[1]	Almond Board of California
Avocados	Improved cognitive health[2]	Hass Avocado Board
Bananas	Improved metabolic recovery from exercise[3]	Dole Foods
Cashews	Decreased blood cholesterol[4]	Kraft Heinz
Cranberries	Reduced urinary tract infections[5]	Ocean Spray Cranberries
Garlic, aged	Improved immune system, reduced severity of colds and flu[6]	Wakunaga of America
Grapes, Concord	Improved cognitive function, driving ability[7]	Welch Foods
Mangos	Improved microbiome and tolerance to high-fat diets[8]	National Mango Board
Peanuts	Improved metabolic and blood-vessel functions[9]	The Peanut Institute
Potatoes	Lack of harmful effects on metabolism[10]	Alliance for Potato Research and Education
Raisins	Improved blood sugar and blood pressure[11]	California Marketing Raisin Board
Raspberries	Reduced risk of chronic disease[12]	National Processed Raspberry Council
Soy snacks	Improved satiety, diet quality, mood, cognition[13]	DuPont Nutrition & Health
Vegetables and fruits, canned	Improved nutrient intakes, diet quality[14]	Canned Food Alliance
Walnuts	Improved diet quality, blood cholesterol, blood vessels[15]	California Walnut Commission
Whole grains	Improved nutrient intakes, body weight[16]	General Mills

NOTE: Source notes are located in the "Notes to Tables" on pages 287–290.

more carefully. For example, the Hass avocado study says, "Avocados *could be* an effective dietary strategy for cognitive health in the aging population" (my emphasis). But even without convincing evidence, the FDA accepts health claims using the word "support," as authorized for dietary supplements. On the basis of this study, avocados can be—and are—marketed for their ability to support cognitive heath in the elderly. Wouldn't it be terrific if protecting cognitive health were that easy and delicious?

One question is why investigators would do this kind of research. John Sievenpiper, an investigator who sometimes partners with food companies, explained to a reporter, "It's very hard to fund randomized trials properly. . . . You have to engage the food industry to get those trials done. . . . [We] see it as our role to try to influence [companies] and produce healthier foods and promote healthier foods."[28]

A more critical question is what to make of all this. If I may overgeneralize, the quality of single-food marketing studies does not always hold up to scrutiny. For example, a nutritional biochemist criticized the raisin study noted in the table for its misuse of statistics and for comparing raisins to processed snack foods: "With the design used you can't really say that raisins were '*good*' for the participants, just not as bad as the junk snacks."[29] Even when done well, studies so clearly aimed at marketing skew the research agenda. If food companies were not funding marketing studies, investigators might be working on more important biological problems. All these foods are highly nutritious and well worth eating for their taste and texture— as well as for their health benefits. Is one fruit, vegetable, or nut better for you than another? The answer, as I keep saying, depends on everything else you eat or do. People who habitually eat largely plant-based diets are healthier. Variety in food intake and calorie balance are fundamental principles of healthful diets.

Again to be fair, not all studies funded by plant trade associations come out the way they are supposed to. The California Strawberry Commission, for example, sponsored a study to see whether eating forty grams of dried strawberry powder a day—equivalent to a pound of strawberries—would counteract the effects on blood lipids of eating a high-fat diet. It did not.[30] I do not want to even think about strawberry powder. But does this result mean we should not be eating strawberries? Of course not. All fruits, vegetables, and nuts have vitamins, minerals, fiber, antioxidants, and other components that collectively promote health. If we are fortunate enough to have choices, we can eat the ones we like.

Coca-Cola: A Case Study in Itself

IT MAY NOT SEEM FAIR TO DEVOTE AN ENTIRE CHAPTER TO THE Coca-Cola Company, but its attempts to influence research have been so deliberate, so comprehensive, and so thoroughly exposed—by reporters who obtained emails through open-records requests and by the company itself on its website—that they demand our attention. Coca-Cola has long supported university-based research by channeling funds through ILSI and the American Beverage Association (ABA), but its direct funding of health research appears to be relatively recent. Coca-Cola staff published research reviews about hydration in the early 2000s, but the company did not get seriously involved in health research until 2004. That year, it established the Beverage Institute for Health and Wellness expressly to raise awareness of the importance of "active, healthy lifestyles" and of beverages as effective delivery systems for hydration. By 2008, research papers by government and university scientists were disclosing Coca-Cola sponsorship.[1]

In 2012, Coca-Cola's vice president and chief scientific and regulatory officer, Rhona Applebaum (who also became president of ILSI in 2015), announced a major research effort to counter evidence linking sodas to poor diets and health. Applebaum did not mince words. Company-funded research, she said, was essential to rebut the "agenda-driven science" of advocates for soda taxes. Coca-Cola intended to train journalists and to engage scientists as partners to conduct both "defensive and offensive research." Otherwise, the industry would be at the mercy of "activists and crusading journalists."[2]

This effort was indeed major. A systematic search for research funded by Coca-Cola or performed by investigators with financial ties to Coca-Cola identified 389 articles published in 169 journals from 2008 to 2016. These studies typically concluded that physical activity is more effective than diet in weight control, sugars and soft drinks are harmless, evidence to the contrary is wrong, and industry-funded research is superior to that funded by other sources.[3]

The focus on physical activity is best illustrated by Coca-Cola's support of the Global Energy Balance Network (GEBN). The GEBN first came to public attention late in 2014 when Yoni Freedhoff, a Canadian physician specializing in obesity, was checking his Twitter feed and noticed a tweet from Applebaum. She mentioned that Steven Blair, a University of South Carolina exercise physiologist, would be using the GEBN to connect experts on energy intake and expenditure. Freedhoff had seen an earlier tweet from Blair about the GEBN, but, he said, "when Rhona gave her shout out, I knew something was up."[4] That "something" was Coca-Cola's sponsorship, unmentioned in the announcements.

Other founding members of the GEBN were James Hill of the University of Colorado and Gregory Hand from West Virginia University. Their primary message: lack of physical activity is responsible for obesity—not diet, and certainly not soft drinks. In a video posted on the GEBN website, Blair explained, "Most of the folks in the popular media and in the scientific press, you know, they're eating too much, eating too much, eating too much, blaming fast food, blaming sugary drinks and so on. And there's really virtually no compelling evidence that that in fact is the cause."[5] In the video,

Blair says that the GEBN had recently obtained funding but does not say from whom.

This omission was no mere oversight. Not only did Coca-Cola fund the GEBN, but reporters' emails suggest that the company was so actively involved in the group's development that there was some tension over its origins. Hill claims credit in a rather testy exchange with a Coca-Cola executive in May 2014: "I have been pushing the idea of a global energy balance network for 3 years. . . . I have invested my time, effort and resources into this idea. . . . I feel strong ownership of this idea and I was taken aback to find that you have moved forward on this idea without me."[6]

The emails reveal that a few months later, Applebaum distributed a draft proposal for the GEBN "tweaked from an earlier doc used to sell the concept into the Company." Her proposal positioned the GEBN as a weapon in the "growing war between the public health community and private industry over how to reduce obesity." As she put it, "Sides are being chosen and battle lines are being drawn. . . . The GEBN needs to quickly establish itself as the place the media goes to for a comment on any obesity issue." The GEBN, she said, needed to "devise, create, and implement a multi-year advocacy 'campaign'" to serve "as a counterforce to one-sided, regulation-driven proponents. Akin to a political campaign, we will develop, deploy and evolve a powerful and multi-faceted strategy to counter radical organizations and their proponents." Coca-Cola, she said, would kick-start the GEBN with a $20 million endowment yielding an annual budget of $1 million.[7]

After seeing the Applebaum tweet, Freedhoff wrote the GEBN and asked who was paying for it.[8] The reply: "GEBN has received support from private philanthropy, the University of Colorado, the University of South Carolina, the University of Copenhagen," and, almost as an afterthought, "including an unrestricted education gift from The Coca Cola Company."[9] Freedhoff passed this information along to Anahad O'Connor, a reporter for the *New York Times*, who observed that the GEBN's website was not alone in failing to mention the funding source. Press releases from the Universities of South Carolina and Colorado and an announcement by the GEBN organizers in the *British Journal of Sports Medicine* also neglected to mention Coca-Cola's sponsorship.[10]

This was enough to keep O'Connor busy for the next several months as he filed open-records requests and conducted interviews to learn more about the GEBN's relationship to Coca-Cola. He published his findings in August 2015 in an article that began on the front page and continued to an entire inside page. He reported that Coca-Cola had granted Blair more than $3.5 million and Hand nearly $1.5 million for energy-balance research since 2008 and had contributed $1 million to the University of Colorado's research foundation to start the GEBN. I was quoted in the article and soon heard from other reporters incredulous that researchers paid by Coca-Cola could argue that diet had nothing to do with obesity—an idea so self-serving and so far from scientific truth that it elicited immediate ridicule (see Figure 7.1).[11]

Members of Congress also were incredulous. Connecticut representative Rosa DeLauro issued a statement: "This research is reminiscent of the research conducted by the tobacco companies to mislead the public about the health risks of smoking. . . . This new group and their research are a sham. . . . People want to be healthy and they want their kids to be healthy and realize that drinks full of empty calories are not good for them."[12]

Coca-Cola's initial response to all of this came from its chief technical officer, Ed Hays: "Yes, we fund scientific research through GEBN and we are proud to support the work that scientists such as Dr. Jim Hill and Dr. Steve Blair do—because their type of research is critical to finding solutions to the global obesity crisis. At Coke, we believe that a balanced diet and regular exercise are two key ingredients for a healthy lifestyle."[13]

But a more considered response must have seemed necessary. This came a week later from the company's CEO, Muhtar Kent, in an op-ed piece for the *Wall Street Journal*: "Our company has been accused of shifting the debate to suggest that physical activity is the

FIGURE 7.1. A cartoonist's reaction to the uproar caused by revelation of Coca-Cola's funding of researchers associated with the Global Energy Balance Network. Steve Sack's cartoon appeared in the *Minneapolis Star Tribune*, August 14, 2015. ©Steve Sack, Cagle Cartoons, used with permission.

only solution to the obesity crisis. There also have been reports accusing us of deceiving the public about our support of scientific research. . . . I know our company can do a better job engaging both the public-health and scientific communities—and we will. . . . In the future we will act with even more transparency as we refocus our investments and our efforts on well-being."[14]

By "more transparency," Kent meant something quite extraordinary: Coca-Cola's website would post lists of its community and research partnerships for the past five years, and the lists would be updated regularly. On September 22, 2015, the company revealed the names of the hundreds of individual health professionals, scientific experts, and organizations it had funded in the United States since 2010, along with the amounts it had paid them. This funding totaled $21.8 million for research and $96.8 million for community partnerships over the five-year period from 2010 to 2015. Later, Coca-Cola launched similar transparency initiatives in Great Britain, Germany, Australia, and at least ten other countries.[15]

Transparency encourages analysis. Kyle Pfister of the advocacy group Ninjas for Health looked up the 115 individuals listed; 57 percent were dietitians, 20 percent academics, 7 percent medical professionals (mostly doctors), 6 percent fitness experts, and the rest authors, chefs, or food representatives.[16] The site revealed that from 2010 to 2015, Coca-Cola had contributed $700,000 to the Academy of Nutrition and Dietetics, $2.9 million to the American Academy of Pediatrics, and $3.5 million to the American Academy of Family Physicians, all groups that might otherwise be expected to advise avoidance of sugary drinks.

Analysis of transparency has consequences. Within a week, Coca-Cola had ended its embarrassing partnerships with these academies. By early November, the University of Colorado had returned Hill's $1 million grant to Coca-Cola. Its explanation? "While the network continues to advocate for good health through a balance of healthy eating habits and exercise, the funding source has distracted attention from its worthwhile goal."[17] On November 24, the Associated Press published emails exchanged between Applebaum and Hill. Later that day, Coca-Cola announced Applebaum's retirement. The GEBN disbanded a week later. By the end of the year, Applebaum had resigned from ILSI's board of trustees and ended her term as president. In further follow up, the *Denver Post* reported that Coca-Cola had paid Hill $550,000 for honoraria, travel, educational activities, and research from 2011 to 2015. In March 2016, Hill resigned from his position as executive director of the University of Colorado's Anschutz Health and Wellness Center.[18]

The GEBN leaders must not have expected such strong reactions. Soon after the August 2015 *Times* article, they issued a statement: "It is unfortunate the GEBN was characterized as a group that promotes physical activity at the expense of diet. Nothing could be further from the truth. . . . Coca Cola has no input into the activities of GEBN. GEBN is not about minimizing diet or even the role of sugar-sweetened beverages in development of obesity. That said, GEBN believes that both the food and the physical inactivity [*sic*] industries can play roles in helping reduce obesity."[19]

They accompanied this statement with responses to "questions raised by recent media attention." These responses repudiated Blair's video, defended the group's focus on energy balance, and suggested little understanding of the depth of public perception that the GEBN's interests were conflicted. To the question, "Does the Global Energy Balance Network believe that physical activity is more important than diet for obesity?" the answer began, "Absolutely not. . . . Dr. Blair's personal views as expressed in the video do not accurately reflect the position of GEBN and for that reason he asked us to remove the video from our website. . . . We believe that reducing consumption of sugar-sweetened beverages is one strategy that may help reduce obesity." To the question, "Was the GEBN website registered to Coca-Cola?" they responded, "Yes. This was a mistake on our part." As for "Do you still feel comfortable with funding from Coca-Cola?," the response was "Yes. We are enormously grateful to The Coca-Cola Company. . . . This funding was given as unrestricted funding. . . . This means that the company has no input into how the money is spent and there is no requirement to report anything to the company." Overall, the GEBN leadership noted, "We were clearly dismayed to see our organization portrayed as downplaying diet to benefit Coca-Cola, but we do accept responsibility for some mistakes we made, particularly with our website."[20]

The next day, my NYU colleague Lisa Young, a member of the Academy of Nutrition and Dietetics, received a letter, jointly signed by GEBN steering committee members James Hill, Steven Blair, Gregory Hand, and John Peters (a researcher working with Hill at the University of Colorado), that read, "The New York Times article alleged that The Coca-Cola Company is driving our strategy. This is not true. The Coca-Cola Company does not have any input into our organization. They provided unrestricted funds to set up GEBN, meaning they have no say in how these funds are spent. . . . Even now, we continue to believe that the world needs the GEBN. We need an organization to discuss (and yes, disagree) about the science of energy balance and how to use the knowledge we have to reduce obesity."[21]

I include these statements because they reveal the GEBN leaders' insistence that Coca-Cola had no input into the group's activities. The email record, however, tells a different story, suggesting that the company was actively involved in every aspect of the organization, from conception to recruitment of members to dissemination of research results. Because the GEBN leaders work for public universities in states with open-records laws, reporters and researchers requested the emails they exchanged with Coca-Cola. For example, Gary Ruskin at US Right to Know, a group best known for its advocacy for labeling of genetically modified foods, obtained emails containing internal company documents. These provide evidence that Coca-Cola executives worked closely with GEBN scientists to influence the direction of the research, hide its funding source, and promote the energy-balance strategy to professionals and the media.[22]

The AP's Candice Choi also requested emails. She used them to show that Applebaum had helped select the GEBN's membership, develop the group's mission and activities, suggest materials for its website, design its logo, develop its communications plan, offer media training to its leaders, and find a job for one investigator's child. Choi quoted an email from Hill to Applebaum: "It is not fair that Coca-Cola is signaled out as the #1 villain in the obesity world, but that is the situation and makes this your issue whether you like it or not. I want to help your company avoid the image of being a problem in peoples' lives and back to being a company that brings important and fun things to them."[23] *New York Magazine* classified that statement as "Despicable," with this explanation: "Desperate-to-please emails to their corporate masters surface from Coke-funded obesity 'researchers.'"[24]

The *BMJ* obtained emails related to Coca-Cola's attempts to influence journalists. From 2011 to 2013, Coca-Cola had worked with GEBN investigators to sponsor conferences for medical and science writers. The National Press Foundation, which often runs industry-

funded educational programs for journalists, assisted with these conferences. Speakers came from industry and academia but promoted
energy-balance approaches to obesity. In an email, Hill described the
2011 conference to Coca-Cola funders as a "home run," adding, "The
journalists told us this was an amazing event and they generated a lot
of stories." With respect to the one in 2013, Hill wrote, "The conference was a great success and even better than last year. These journalists came away with a much more realistic understanding of obesity.
Thanks again for your support." Although Coca-Cola contributed as
much as $45,000 to the University of Colorado Foundation to pay for
each conference, at least some of the participating journalists were
unaware of the company's sponsorship; they thought the conference
had been funded by the National Press Foundation and the University of Colorado.[25]

O'Connor of the *New York Times* obtained his own collection of
GEBN emails and sent them to me for review in January 2016. Along
with exchanges about speaking engagements and expense reimbursements, much of the correspondence is devoted to dinner plans and local basketball teams, suggesting close personal as well as professional
ties. The emails provide insight into the GEBN's attempts to recruit
members as well as Coca-Cola's attempts to influence research.

The GEBN's Recruitment Efforts

Emails in July 2014 refer to a survey sent to an unstated number of
candidates for GEBN membership, a list that eventually included
more than 140 individuals.[26] Responses came from 24 potential
GEBN members. One question asked whether there was anything
that might make candidates hesitant to join. Indeed, there was. Answers included examples like these: "The term Energy Balance will be
code to critics who will see this as an industry effort"; "The network
will whitewash this complex social problem which the food industry has helped to create"; "The single sponsorship"; and the GEBN
looks like "a marketing strategy and ploy for a potential sponsor (e.g.
Coke) to gain 'credibility' and avoid attention to products that could

be contributing to obesity." Although other responses were more favorable, these should have warned everyone concerned that Coca-Cola's sponsorship would appear to be conflicted. But the company viewed the survey responses as a go-ahead: "important information about features and benefits seen through the eyes of the potential members . . . Really great result from the survey, team!"[27]

Whether or not the GEBN organizers recognized the risk, they said as little as they could to potential members about Coca-Cola's sponsorship. The emails shed light on one recruitment effort aimed at Stephen Simpson, the director of the Charles Perkins Centre at the University of Sydney. In October 2014, Hill wrote that he planned to meet Simpson during a forthcoming trip to Australia: "I hope he might be someone we invite."[28] Later that month, the public affairs manager for Coca-Cola South Pacific sent Hill a briefing about his events in Australia, which noted that Simpson was "destined to be a key policy influencer in the obesity debate with the Centre focusing on a range of issues including fundamental biological research, food policy, food supply, population health and behavioral areas."[29]

In 2016, when I was a visiting fellow at the Charles Perkins Centre, I showed Simpson the emails related to Hill's visit. Simpson recalled that Hill had given an excellent and well-received presentation and had extended an invitation to join the GEBN. But even had he wanted to, Simpson could not accept. That Centre has a policy on relationships with industry that firmly precludes partnerships with single companies.

Coca-Cola's Research Funding: The ISCOLE Study, 2010–2015

The emails indicate that although Coca-Cola executives did not directly control the research they funded, they did review manuscripts in advance, craft press releases, and pay travel and dinner expenses as well as those for research. Indeed, executives' relationships to investigators were so close that they regarded the GEBN investigators as members of Coca-Cola's "team."[30]

In March 2016, Sandy Douglas, then president of Coca-Cola North America, updated estimates of the company's funding of research and partnerships since 2010 to $132.8 million. He further updated the figure to $135.4 million in October 2016 and to $138.3 million in March 2017; the company did a further update to $140 million in December 2017.[31] The more recent updates did not specify the proportion devoted to research as opposed to community partnerships, but the company has been generous to researchers. The email correspondence obtained by the *New York Times* between Coca-Cola executives and Peter Katzmarzyk at Louisiana State University bears on that point.

Katzmarzyk was the principle investigator on a five-year, logistically demanding study to identify the behavioral factors that most predispose schoolchildren to obesity. Called the International Study of Childhood Obesity, Lifestyle and the Environment (ISCOLE), it was funded from its start by Coca-Cola. The study began in 2010 and involved six thousand children, ages nine to eleven, in twelve countries. The investigators measured the children's physical activity with step counters, estimated how long they slept, and asked them to report how much time they spent watching television. They also asked the children to self-report their usual intake of twenty-three categories of foods for a week. The investigators divided the dietary responses into two broad categories, "healthy" and "unhealthy." Healthy diets contained vegetables, fruit, whole grains, and low-fat milk. Unhealthy diets were those with fast food, hamburgers, soft drinks, sweets, and fried food. The investigators did not look for a correlation between obesity and intake of sodas, soft drinks, or sugars, and they did not find one. Their results showed neither dietary pattern to be associated with overweight. Instead, they concluded that the most important correlates of obesity in children were low physical activity, short sleep duration, and frequent television viewing.[32]

Coca-Cola could not have asked for a better outcome. The subject line of Applebaum's email to the team said, "A great study is published!!" Her message began: "A very happy day!!" She attached the press release from Louisiana State: "Pennington Biomedical Research

Study shows lack of physical activity is a major predictor of childhood obesity." Her message continued, "Indeed, a glorious day!! I raise my glass to the researchers and the ISCOLE staff for being the First!![33]

The disclosure statement in publications from this study says, "ISCOLE is funded by The Coca-Cola Company. The study sponsor has no role in study design, data collection, analysis, conclusions or publications. The only sponsor requirement was that the study be global in nature." As an analysis of the emails makes clear, this statement does not fully describe the extent of Coca-Cola's actual involvement, not least because the researchers consulted with Coca-Cola in making strategic decisions about study design.[34] The emails also illustrate other points: the difficulties of recruiting international sites to a study funded by industry, the size of Coca-Cola's investment in this study, and concerns about the way Coca-Cola's sponsorship might affect public and professional perception of the credibility of this research.

In April 2012, for example, Katzmarzyk wrote that he was unable to induce the National Institute for Public Health in Mexico to agree to participate: "Just a footnote on Mexico. We definitely approached INSP [Instituto Nacional de Salud Pública] about being a site, but they did not want to play ball because of who was sponsoring the study. It looks like we still have some uphill work ahead of us on changing the landscape!"[35] To this, Applebaum replied, "Got to love it. An analogy—they're drowning, we throw them a line and they refuse to take it. . . . So if good scientists take $$$ from Coke— what?—they're corrupted? Despite the fact they're advancing public good? As you can see my opinion of such folks is pretty low because of how selfish it is. . . . you hit a nerve."[36]

The emails include the ISCOLE contracts, which show that Coca-Cola invested more than $6 million in the study (the international sites were particularly costly to manage). The correspondence provides no evidence of company involvement in the conduct of the study but does demonstrate that Coca-Cola officials kept close tabs on its progress. The company's payments to the investigators depended on successful completion of "milestones" such as recruitment targets, protocols, sampling frames, identification of sites, presentations, and publications.

The team was concerned about how Coca-Cola's sponsorship might appear to the public. Applebaum wrote Katzmarzyk that she just wanted "to clarify the understanding and agreement we have had regarding ISCOLE meetings held at The Coca-Cola Company. . . . Due to the potential for this very important study to be intentionally distorted by those who have concerns re our support, it has been agreed that Coca-Cola associates will not be in attendance. . . . The last thing we need is for ISCOLE and/or any of the scientists associated with same to be challenged and have the study's and/or the scientists' integrity/credibility compromised."[37] Katzmarzyk replied, "We need to maintain the separation between the sponsor and the investigators that we have worked hard to maintain since the beginning of the study. I think we have done a good job of this to date, and we have a bullet-proof relationship that should be the model for these types of industry-scientist partnerships in the future."[38] But whether accomplished consciously or unconsciously, this study, like so many others funded by food companies, produced precisely the result its sponsor wanted.

Applebaum's message to Katzmarzyk also referred to Coca-Cola's "Conflict of Interest Principles," which she had participated in developing as part of an ILSI project. These principles state that funders should make payments regardless of outcome and that funded investigators should adhere to accepted scientific standards, control how they design and conduct their studies, and disclose funding sources.[39] Applebaum said that research funded by Coca-Cola "is only valuable if it is conducted without conflict of interest and with absolute integrity."[40] But the emails suggest that neither Coca-Cola nor its funded investigators kept the boundaries sufficiently firm.

In his *Wall Street Journal* op-ed piece, Kent promised that Coca-Cola could and would do better. Doing better would not be easy. A later analysis of the transparency initiative identified more than nine hundred researchers who disclosed Coca-Cola funding in their published papers, but the company's website named only forty-two of them. An editorial on that study pointed out that "the incompleteness of its transparency lists ends up giving us a limited view of the extent to which [Coca-Cola] influences the published, peer-reviewed literature."[41] Even so, I do not believe that Coca-Cola officials were deliberately trying to hide this information; my guess is that they did not have readily accessible records of everyone they funded.

Although Kent was replaced as CEO a year later, the company appears to be following through on his transparency promises. Its updates show that Coca-Cola now reports funding fewer individuals and groups. In February 2016, the company reevaluated its funding program and established new guidelines for sponsoring "well-being scientific research." These indicated that Coca-Cola would no longer pay for studies in their entirety, either directly or through a third party (presumably ILSI or the ABA). The company said it would fund health research only if a non-Coca-Cola entity bears at least 50 percent of the cost. It would not pay third parties any compensation, incentives, or travel costs. It would no longer be the sole funder of programs involving the health community. And it closed down its Beverage Institute for Health and Wellness and its global Active Healthy Living programs.[42]

These actions suggest that Coca-Cola executives learned useful lessons from the GEBN experience. We can hope that the company will no longer be paying dietitians to do its public relations or overtly funding research aimed at producing desired results. Whether 50 percent funding will exert less influence on investigators remains to be seen, but the company deserves credit for recognizing that its former practices damaged its own reputation as well as the reputations of its funded investigators—and for at least trying to reduce conflicts of interest in its funded research.

The *Lancet* editors summarized their thoughts on the greater meaning of the GEBN experience on the journal's US cover for October 3, 2015: "Ultimately the goals of Coca-Cola and those of medical organisations and health researchers that wish to improve public health are very different. Moreover, medical health profes-sionals must guard against any possible conflict or perceived conflict when working towards the overarching goal of improving public health and preventing non-communicable diseases such as obesity and type 2 diabetes."[43]

Possible and perceived conflicts pose a dilemma for nutrition professionals as well, not only as researchers but also as members of advisory committees, the matter to which we now turn.

Conflicted Advisory Committees:
Then and Now

S HOULD EXPERTS BE PERMITTED TO SERVE ON DIETARY ADVI-
sory committees when they have financial ties to companies that
might profit from the committee's advice? Of course not, but they
often do. The UK Health Forum provided evidence for this contention in its collection of examples of inappropriate food-industry
influence over the deliberations of government and professional
advisory committees in such countries as Mexico, Chile, Guate-
mala, and Fiji, among others.[1]

Concerns about undue industry influence on committees are
anything but new. In the 1970s, conflicts of interest among nutrition committee members came to the attention of no less than a
US senator, Wisconsin Democrat William Proxmire. In 1974, Proxmire complained that the National Academy of Sciences' Food and
Nutrition Board, the group responsible for setting Recommended
Dietary Allowances (RDAs) for daily nutrient intake, was in the
pocket of the food industry. Proxmire was infamous for his annual

Golden Fleece Awards ridiculing taxpayer-funded research he viewed as frivolous (much of it was not). He also held scientifically questionable beliefs about vitamins: if some were good, more were better. In his view, the RDAs were too low, "arbitrary, unscientific, and tainted" and amounted to "one of the most scandalous conflicts of interest in the Federal Government." As he saw it, the board was "both the creature of the food industry and heavily financed by the food industry." Furthermore, he said it was in "the narrow economic interest of the industry to establish low official RDAs because the lower the RDAs the more nutritional their food products appear."[2]

In reality, the board was trying to stop the supplement industry from promoting large amounts of nutrients as beneficial when the science showed that excess intake was useless or harmful, but Proxmire was not especially interested in evidence. When the FDA proposed to set an upper limit of 150 percent of the RDA for over-the-counter nutritional supplements, he induced Congress to pass his Proxmire Amendment, which blocked the FDA from classifying "any natural or synthetic vitamin or mineral (or combination thereof) as a drug solely because it exceeds the level of potency which the Secretary determines is nutritionally rational or useful."[3]

Proxmire may have misjudged the science, but he knew his politics. As he wrote at the time, "Let's face it. The orthodox nutritional community is off base in supporting the FDA's attempt to regulate vitamins as drugs. It's foolish, wrong, and bad policy. It's so typical of the FDA—go after the little guy, the harmless vitamins . . . but overlook aspartame, DES [diethylstilbestrol], and thalidomide."[4] In this, he was mostly in error. The FDA had issued a warning about DES, and to this day its refusal to approve thalidomide is considered the agency's finest hour.

But Proxmire was right about the board's ties to industry. Those were revealed in 1980 during a dispute over the first edition of the US dietary guidelines, which advised reductions in intake of fat, saturated fat, and cholesterol (meaning, in effect, meat, dairy, and eggs) to reduce the risk of heart disease. The board opposed the guidelines so vehemently that it issued a counter-report, *Toward Healthful Diets*, arguing that fat restrictions were unnecessary for healthy people. This infuriated health advocates, who charged that at least six board members had financial ties to industries most affected by the guidelines. Sheldon Margen, a professor of public health at the University of California, Berkeley, for example, objected that "the board's range of expertise is too narrow, its ties with industry too close to avoid the suspicions of bias, its mandate is too ill-defined, and its mode of operation is too secret." Others criticized the board's support by an industry liaison committee whose members represented eighty food companies. The furor over the report so embarrassed the academy that it eliminated the industry panel, removed board members with strong ties to food companies, and appointed new members with fewer industry ties.[5]

That was not the only instance of early concerns about conflicted committees. I asked Ken Fisher, who in the 1970s had directed the nongovernmental Life Sciences Research Office (LSRO), about his experience appointing committees to review the safety of food additives. In 1958, Congress had defined two categories of food additives: new chemicals that needed to be proven safe before they could go into the food supply and substances with a history of common use—sugar, salt, flavorings, and the like—that could be considered generally recognized as safe (GRAS). In the early 1970s, questions about the safety of GRAS additives led President Richard Nixon to direct the FDA to evaluate them, and the FDA commissioned the LSRO to conduct the reviews. The LSRO appointed committees to do this work and was immediately confronted with the problem of what to do about candidates with ties to companies making or using the additive under consideration.

The review committees eventually issued 151 evaluations of more than four hundred GRAS additives. In a report on this work, Fisher said that the LSRO's policies on conflicts of interest were more rigorous than those of the government. The LSRO required candidates to report grants, contracts, and consultancies, as well as investments and holdings. It did not permit members with such ties to participate in discussions or vote on final decisions. Fisher told me that all members "were made aware of these conditions and all agreed—after some back and forth." He recalled "one conflicted member, who of his own volition, absented himself from the vote on the decision." He also recalled that committees "rejected several of the monographs on substances because they were incomplete and clearly biased in coverage of published positive or negative studies on certain substances."[6]

Fisher's comments suggested that conflicts of interest only rarely caused problems with GRAS reviews. But in *The Case Against Sugar* (2016), the journalist Gary Taubes presented the GRAS review of sugar (sucrose) as highly conflicted. His book notes that the chair of the overall GRAS review process was George W. Irving Jr., a former head of the scientific advisory board of the International Sugar Research Foundation, and that the GRAS committee relied heavily on materials provided by the Sugar Association. The 1976 GRAS review concluded that "other than the contribution made to dental caries, there is no clear evidence in the available information on sucrose that demonstrates a hazard to the public when used at the levels that are now current and in the manner now practiced."[7] According to Taubes, the Sugar Association took that to mean that "there is no substantiated scientific evidence indicating that sugar causes diabetes, heart disease, or any other malady." He has harsh words for critics of the idea that sugars are harmful. "If you get a chance," he advises, "ask about the GRAS Review Report. Odds are you won't get an answer. Nothing stings a nutritional liar like scientific facts."

The FDA's GRAS reviews still elicit concerns about conflicted interests. A 2013 analysis of the GRAS review process concludes that the industry ties of committee members not only threaten the integrity of GRAS reviews but also the integrity of the FDA's entire scientific enterprise. In a commentary on that analysis, I pointed out that without independent review of GRAS additives, it is difficult to be confident that the ones in use are safe.[8]

My questions to Fisher about GRAS review committees had induced him to search through notes packed away for decades.

Among them, he found memos indicating that Mike Jacobson had asked to have consumer representatives appointed to GRAS review committees, but, he said, "We opted not to do so as it would imply the other members of the [committees] were not consumers." Fisher was referring to Michael Jacobson, director of the Center for Science in the Public Interest (CSPI), whose concerns about conflicted advisory committee members also date back to the 1970s. Jacobson was arguing that if federal agencies insisted on permitting members with industry ties to serve on advisory committees, they should balance viewpoints with an equivalent number of consumer representatives.

Jacobson holds a doctorate in microbiology. He began his career working for Ralph Nader, cofounded CSPI in 1971, and retired as its director in 2017. CSPI's purpose is to improve the American diet, and it continues to be the largest nonprofit organization engaged in advocacy for a broad range of nutrition issues, among them conflicts of interest caused by food industry sponsorship. I served on the CSPI board for about five years in the early 1990s, remain a member, and subscribe to its monthly *Nutrition Action Healthletter*.

In 1976, Jacobson asked a member of Congress with a strong record of consumer advocacy, New York Democrat Benjamin Rosenthal, to help him survey the heads of university nutrition departments about their faculty's ties to food corporations. Jacobson told me why he had done this: "It was so obvious to me that professors were touting their academic affiliations while shilling for food manufacturers and trade associations. I thought it would be interesting and possibly useful to collect information about the matter."[9] Rosenthal introduced their report of the survey results, titled "Feeding at the Company Trough," into the *Congressional Record*, with this blunt statement:

> Nutrition and food science professors at Harvard, at the Universities of Wisconsin, Iowa, and Massachusetts, and at many other prominent universities work closely and often secretly with food and chemical companies. Professors sit on the boards of directors,

act as consultants, testify on behalf of industry at congressional hearings, and receive industry research grants. Many professors with corporate links also serve as "university" representatives on Federal advisory committees. . . . One can only come to the conclusion that industry grants, consulting fees and directorships are muzzling, if not prostituting nutrition and food science professors.[10]

The report named names: it characterized Fred Stare, the head of Harvard's Department of Nutrition, as a "food-industry apologist," but it also listed the industry ties of sixteen other eminent scientists, nearly all members of prestigious national committees issuing advice about nutrition and health. It proposed three strategies for countering conflicted interests: balance, disclosure, and new funding mechanisms. All merit comment from today's perspective.

To achieve *balance*, they wanted consumer representatives to be appointed to nutrition advisory committees. This seems entirely rational, but in my experience federal agencies view experts who avoid industry ties on principle as too biased to appoint, especially if they state those principles publicly. I was a member of the Dietary Guidelines Advisory Committee in 1995, but only because I had previously worked with the assistant secretary for health, Philip R. Lee, who insisted on my appointment. I served as a consumer representative on two FDA advisory committees in the 1990s, Food Advisory and Science Advisory, but have not been asked to join another federal committee since the publication of *Food Politics* in 2002. The FDA's current practice is to appoint one consumer representative to its committees, hardly enough to have much influence on decisions.

With respect to *disclosure*, the report comments on the failure of the named professors to state the full extent of their industry ties: "As long as collaboration with industry continues to be viewed by the academic community as ethical and respectable, it is important that the public know about potential sources of bias. . . . In such matters, respect for individual privacy must yield to society's right to know."

To help accomplish the third strategy, *funding*, the report raised the idea of a nonprofit, public interest group to "launder" industry contributions before they reach universities. But I doubt that such a group could maintain its objectivity if it depended on ongoing donations. I also doubt that companies would be willing to provide ongoing support for research that might risk producing unfavorable results.

CSPI has continued to view researchers' ties to industry as a threat to science. In 2003, it initiated its Integrity in Science project to demonstrate how investigators' financial ties to the chemical, pharmaceutical, and cigarette industries (not necessarily those making foods and beverages) affect research results and interpretation and to advocate for balance on advisory committees, full disclosure, and journalists' attention to conflicted scientific interests.[11] As part of this project, CSPI constructed a conflict-of-interest database listing about four thousand researchers identified through journal disclosure statements and other public sources as having accepted funding from industry. Conservative critics complained that the database unfairly implied that industry funding is necessarily corrupting and that CSPI's Integrity in Science project was "in reality, a platform for bashing science it doesn't like."[12]

To discuss such issues, CSPI hosted four conferences (see Figure 8.1). I spoke at the 2003 conference on food-industry influence, but food issues were never the primary focus of this project and seemed peripheral to it, perhaps because the effects of sponsorship were— and continue to be—better documented for other industries. Nevertheless, many investigators on CSPI's database were engaged in nutrition research, but they are not easy to locate without knowing what to look for. When I searched for "vitamin" as a research topic, up popped the names of 171 scientists, many of whose studies were funded by supplement companies.

CSPI ended this project in 2009, ironically for lack of funding, but continues to advocate for advisory committees free of industry influence. This group has been especially concerned about committees advising on treatment for high blood cholesterol, a risk factor for coronary heart disease. Such committees typically recommend the widespread use of statin drugs. But dietary approaches—reduced

Figure 8-1. As part of its Integrity in Science project, the Center for Science in the Public Interest (CSPI) held four conferences from 2003 to 2008 on conflicts of interest in research. The 2003 conference focused on corporate and political influences on research-based policy initiatives. Used with permission, courtesy of Michael Jacobson and CSPI.

intake of foods highest in saturated fat, trans fat, sodium, and added sugars—also work, cost less, and have fewer side effects.[13] Questions about who needs to take statins remain hotly debated, not least because when advisory committees are packed with members with financial ties to statin companies, they are more likely to recommend statins over dietary approaches and to advise these drugs for increasingly wide swaths of the population.[14]

In 2004, CSPI organized several dozen physicians and scientists (including me) to sign a letter calling for the appointment of independent panels to reevaluate the evidence for statin drugs versus dietary approaches. This concern remains highly relevant. In 2017, the editors of JAMA *Internal Medicine*, noting that clinical trials sponsored by statin companies report greater benefits and fewer adverse effects than non-industry-sponsored trials of the same drugs, urged physicians to "refocus efforts on promoting a heart-healthy diet, regular physical activity, and not smoking."[15]

Conflicts of interest are a constant concern about drug advisory committees, but what about committees issuing the dietary guidelines? This too has a history. The guidelines have been issued jointly by the USDA and the Department of Health and Human Services (HHS) every five years since 1980. They constitute the official statement of federal nutrition policy. Because they influence the rules governing nutrition education, school meals, food assistance, and food labels, every word of them is the target of intense food industry lobbying.[16]

To understand how conflicts of interest might affect the guidelines, it helps to understand how they are created. The process begins with appointment of a Dietary Guidelines Advisory Committee (DGAC). When I was on the DGAC in 1995, the agencies instructed us to review the research published since the previous edition and provide the best advice we could on that basis. We wrote a report summarizing that research and then wrote dietary guidelines based on our interpretation of what it meant. In 2005, the industry-friendly administration of President George W. Bush changed that process. The DGAC would continue to review and summarize the science, but the agencies would now write the actual guidelines. This took the guidelines out of the hands of scientists and put them into the hands of agency political appointees.

Conflicted interests among DGAC members can also make that process subject to industry influence. As special government employees, members must disclose conflicts of interest to the agencies. The agencies, however, are not required to make the disclosures public and usually do not. Candidates for committee membership who consult, do research, or work for food companies are not necessarily disqualified from serving. They are eligible for waivers, which the agencies often grant on the grounds—debatable, in my opinion—that qualified members who have no ties to industry are too difficult to identify.

These days, the White House itself grants waivers related to dietary guidelines. In 2017, White House Counsel Donald McGahn issued a waiver for Kailee Tkacz, a former lobbyist for the Snack Food Association and for the Corn Refiners Association, for which she was also director of food policy. The Corn Refiners Association, you will recall, represents producers of high-fructose corn syrup. McGahn explained that this waiver would allow Tkacz to advise the USDA about the dietary guidelines process. He said he had "determined that it is in the public interest to grant this limited waiver because of Ms. Tkacz's expertise in the process by which the Dietary Guidelines for Americans are issued every five years."[17]

Citizens who want to know about DGAC members' arrangements with food companies must file Freedom of Information Act (FOIA) requests or look up members' disclosure statements in published papers. Doing so reveals that in 1995, when I was on the DGAC, only three of the eleven members had ties to food companies, but the balance soon shifted: to seven of eleven members in 2000, eleven of thirteen in 2005, and nine of thirteen in 2010. Members of the 2000 DGAC, for example, reported financial ties "to two meat associations, four dairy associations and five dairy companies; one egg association; one sugar association; one grain association; five other food companies; six other industry-sponsored associations; two pharmaceutical associations; and 28 pharmaceutical companies."[18] Zara Abrams, a journalism student at the University of Southern California, looked up disclosure statements in published papers by members of the 2015 DGAC. By her tally, ten of the fourteen had consulting arrangements or research grants with companies producing meat, dairy, or processed foods.[19] Did such conflicts affect this DGAC's interpretation of the science? Several critics argue that they most definitely did.

Nina Teicholz's Critique: The DGAC's Nonrigorous Science

In 2015, the *BMJ* published what it called an "investigation"—what later appeared to be a commissioned editorial—by the journalist Nina Teicholz, sharply critical of the DGAC for weaknesses in its scientific review. Teicholz is the author of *The Big Fat Surprise* (2014), a book promoting the health benefits of fats and foods derived from animals. Her article objected to the DGAC's recommendation to reduce intake of saturated fats and, therefore, meat, arguing that it was largely based on reviews by heart and cardiology associations that receive substantial funding from food companies. "This reliance on industry backed groups," she wrote, "clearly undermines the credibility of the government report." She added, "It is surprising that unlike authors in most major medical journals, guideline committee members are not required to list their potential conflicts of interest. A cursory investigation shows several such possible conflicts: one member has received research funding from the California Walnut Commission and the Tree Nut Council, as well as vegetable oil giants Bunge and Unilever."[20]

As I noted earlier, the agencies do collect information about conflicted interests; they just do not release it publicly. CSPI identified eleven more errors of fact or interpretation in Teicholz's article and organized a letter signed by 180 scientists demanding its retraction (I did not sign it; although I viewed her analysis as scientifically flawed, I thought she was entitled to her opinion).[21] To deal with CSPI's letter, the *BMJ* asked two academics for independent reviews: Mark Helfand at the Oregon Health & Science University and Lisa Bero, with whom I had worked at the University of Sydney earlier that year. Both concluded that the Teicholz article had numerous factual errors but agreed with her contention that the DGAC process was insufficiently rigorous.

In Bero's view, "Teicholz's criticisms of the methods used by DGAC are within the realm of scientific debate." Helfand noted that the Arnold Foundation (which promotes evidence-based policy) had paid both Teicholz and the *BMJ* to publish this article; Teicholz had disclosed this funding, and the foundation's website lists a payment of $4,000 to the *BMJ* for "a report that analyzes the scientific research used to inform the Dietary Guidelines Advisory Committee recommendations." Helfand stated that "compared with other *BMJ* investigations and most investigative journalism, this article is poorly researched and poorly documented." He said the *BMJ*'s decision to publish the article was "regrettable" and "[The] article is better described as an opinion piece, editorial, or even an example of lobbying literature than an independent investigation." Nevertheless, he advised against retraction, in part because "it is clear that further investigation of the composition of the committee, as well as its conflict of interest policies and work group structure, are warranted." The *BMJ* chose not to retract but instead published a statement of Teicholz's conflicted interests as well as extensive corrections and clarifications that largely supported the points detailed in CSPI's complaint.[22]

Beyond the *BMJ* article, the Arnold Foundation also funded a group organized by Teicholz, the Nutrition Coalition.[23] This group lobbied Congress and succeeded in getting it to agree that the "entire process used to formulate and establish the guidelines needs to be reviewed before future guidelines are issued. . . . At a minimum, the process should include: full transparency, a lack of bias, and the inclusion and consideration of all of the latest available research and scientific evidence, even that which challenges current dietary recommendations."[24] On that basis, Congress granted a million dollars to the National Academy of Medicine to evaluate the guidelines process.

The academy dealt with this challenge by appointing a review committee, which released a report on the DGAC selection process early in 2017. The committee suggested that DGAC members be nominated by third parties, nominations be open to public comment, and members fully disclose conflicted interests. The committee's second report later that year recommended ways to strengthen scientific credibility and make the DGAC's decisions more transparent.[25]

Whether or how the agencies might use these recommendations to develop the 2020 guidelines was not public at the time this book went to press.

Neal Barnard's Critique: The DGAC's Cholesterol Advice

Breaking with precedent, the 2015 DGAC omitted advice to limit cholesterol to three hundred milligrams per day as a means of reducing heart-disease risk: "The 2015 DGAC will not bring forward this recommendation because available evidence shows no appreciable relationship between consumption of dietary cholesterol and serum cholesterol. . . . Cholesterol is not a nutrient of concern for overconsumption."[26] Eggs are the largest source of dietary cholesterol (one egg contains about two hundred milligrams). This change meant that Americans no longer needed to worry about the cholesterol in eggs.

As evidence, the DGAC report cited two review articles, both funded by independent sources. One found insufficient evidence to decide whether lowering dietary cholesterol reduces blood cholesterol. The second, a meta-analysis, found no association of eggs with heart disease risk or mortality but did find an association of eggs with an increased risk of type 2 diabetes and of heart disease in patients with diabetes.[27] "Insufficient evidence" is not surprising. Studies on eggs and cholesterol are particularly difficult to interpret because saturated fat raises blood cholesterol levels more than does dietary cholesterol, blood cholesterol levels in the general population are already so high that adding an egg or two makes little difference, and so many people take statins that the effects of dietary cholesterol are blunted. Nevertheless, the dropping of the cholesterol guideline seemed so gratuitous that Neal Barnard, president of the Physicians Committee for Responsible Medicine (PCRM), wondered whether DGAC members' ties to the egg industry might have influenced this decision.

PCRM advocates for plant-based diets and animal welfare. It and other such groups filed a lawsuit arguing that elimination of the cholesterol guideline violated the Federal Advisory Committee Act, which prohibits special interests from influencing committee members. They charged that the egg industry, through its Egg Nutrition Center (the education and research arm of the USDA-sponsored American Egg Board) deliberately organized research to cast doubt on a linkage between eggs and high blood cholesterol levels: "The Egg Nutrition Center's funding establishes financial relationships with key researchers at major universities and supports studies designed to portray eggs in a favorable light. These research funds . . . are used to fund studies designed in pursuit of the American Egg Board's mission 'to increase demand for eggs and egg products.'"[28]

The lawsuit noted that studies funded by the egg industry dominate research on dietary cholesterol. It pointed to a 2013 review concluding that the effect of dietary cholesterol on blood cholesterol "is modest and appears to be limited to population subgroups."[29] Of the studies reviewed in that paper, 92 percent were supported by the egg industry. Because one of the review's authors, Alice Lichtenstein, was vice-chair of the 2015 DGAC, the lawsuit suggested that Lichtenstein was in a position of particular influence over the cholesterol issue. She denies such influence: "The committee reviews the evidence, assesses current dietary intakes, and draws conclusions. This was not smoke and mirrors."[30]

The lawsuit also charged that four other members of the DGAC had direct ties to the Egg Nutrition Center, were nominated by it, or held positions at a Tufts University research center that actively sought egg-industry funding to evaluate support for the new cholesterol nonrecommendation. It quoted press comments to demonstrate the effect of the DGAC's decision: "Think of all those eggs you missed," and "Eggs are back."[31]

The legal brief may have been sparked by commitments to vegan diets and animal rights, but it is well worth reading for its lucid explanation of how easily egg studies can be manipulated to produce desired results. For example, if your study compares the effects of eating eggs to eating foods high in saturated fat or cholesterol, you won't see a difference. If your dietary intervention adds eggs but cuts

FIGURE 8.2. In October 2015, the Physicians Committee for Responsible Medicine (PCRM), a group committed to the benefits of vegan dietary practices, placed billboards in Texas, the home state of Republican representative K. Michael Conaway, to urge him to push for reinstating the cholesterol guideline in the forthcoming dietary guidelines. Used with permission, courtesy of Neal Barnard and PCRM.

calories or saturated fat, the effects will cancel each other. If you divide study participants into groups based on how strongly they react to dietary cholesterol, only hyper-responders will appear to be at risk. If you use a small study sample so results are not statistically significant, you can interpret them as showing no effect. And if you mainly include industry-funded studies in your meta-analysis, you will have a better chance of showing that eggs have no effect on blood cholesterol levels.

I can think of one more: do the obvious. A study funded by the Egg Nutrition Center demonstrates that eating eggs along with raw vegetables increases absorption of vitamin E. Of course it does; vitamin E is fat-soluble and requires fat for absorption. This study is especially relevant because its senior author was a member of the 2015 DGAC.[32] Shortly before release of the 2015 dietary guidelines, Barnard ran a billboard campaign pressing for reinstatement of the eat-less-cholesterol recommendation (Figure 8.2).

I was a reviewer on an early draft of the 2015 dietary guidelines, but that experience did not prepare me for what the guidelines said about cholesterol when they appeared early in 2016. To quote: "The

Key Recommendation from the 2010 Dietary Guidelines to limit consumption of dietary cholesterol to 300 mg per day is not included in the 2015 edition, but . . . individuals should eat as little dietary cholesterol as possible while consuming a healthy eating pattern. . . . Eating patterns that include lower intake of dietary cholesterol are associated with reduced risk of CVD [cardiovascular disease]."[33] This is head-spinning advice. If I am reading the guidelines correctly, they are saying that you don't need to limit cholesterol but should eat as little as possible. No wonder dietary advice seems confusing.

To return to the PCRM lawsuit: the judge threw it out of court in October 2016. On what grounds? "Undue influence," it seems, has no legal definition. The court ruled that it could find "no meaningful standard for deciding whether certain scientists exercised, or whether the USDA and HHS sufficiently guarded against, inappropriate influence in the DGAC."[34] In writing about this decision, *Business Insider* quoted Nina Teicholz, Neal Barnard, and me, the three of us in rare agreement about the absurdity of the ruling.[35]

Industry's Critique: Sugar Guidelines Are Not Science-Based

In 2015, WHO advised consuming no more than 10 percent of calories from added sugars.[36] So did the 2015 US guidelines. The guidelines have always advised eating less sugar, from the straightforward "avoid too much sugar" in 1980 and 1985, to the more complicated and obfuscating "choose beverages and foods to moderate your intake of sugars" in 2000 and "reduce the intake of calories from solid fats and added sugars" in 2010. Ten percent of calories translates to about fifty grams of added sugars a day, or twelve teaspoons, which is not exactly abstemious, but it takes only one sixteen-ounce soft drink to reach that limit. The Sugar Association immediately invoked the playbook to cast doubt on the science. It accused WHO of basing its advice on poor-quality evidence, and it called the US guideline "agenda based, not science based."[37]

Taking up this theme, ILSI sponsored a study concluding that "guidelines on dietary sugar do not meet criteria for trustworthy recommendations and are based on low-quality evidence."[38] Of the study's five authors, two disclosed grants from ILSI; one of the two was on the scientific advisory board of Tate & Lyle, a British supplier of sugar and sweeteners. Why the *Annals of Internal Medicine* chose to publish this ILSI-funded review is beyond me, but it hedged its bets by commissioning an editorial from two prominent advocates for sugar reduction, Dean Schillinger and Cristin Kearns of the University of California, San Francisco (UCSF). Their editorial demolished the review's arguments point by point, and chastised the journal: "When it comes to added sugars, there are clear conflicts between public health interests and the interests of the food and beverage (F&B) industry. . . . High quality journals could refrain from publishing studies on health effects of added sugars funded by entities with commercial interests in the outcome."[39]

This dispute was covered by the *New York Times* (which quoted me) as well as other publications. The AP's Candice Choi interviewed ILSI's executive director, who admitted that his group had initiated this study. Choi obtained emails revealing that ILSI had requested revisions of the review and that one author had failed to disclose grants from Coca-Cola and other companies with interests in making sugar appear harmless. The *Annals* had to correct the authors' disclosure statements and publish a clarification that ILSI had, in fact, reviewed and approved the review. All of this convinced Mars, Incorporated, a member of ILSI, to tell Choi that this study "undermines the work of public health officials and makes all industry-funded research look bad."[40] Soon after, as noted in Chapter 4, Mars withdrew from ILSI.

The authors' disclosure statement warned readers, "Given our funding source, our study team has a financial conflict of interest and readers should consider our results carefully." Yes, readers should. Unless ILSI and its commissioned authors believe that dietary guidelines ought to encourage eating *more* sugar, their review is pointless.

ILSI-sponsored guidelines for selection of advisory committee members argue that financial biases are immaterial unless candidates for membership derive a direct benefit from the committee's work. In ILSI's view, keeping members with conflicted interests off advisory committees bars "the most experienced and knowledgeable nutrition and food scientists from contributing their expertise on the panels informing public policy."[41] I think this is a hypothesis that has yet to be tested. ILSI's efforts, along with the others reviewed here, should make it clear that debates about the dietary guidelines are far more about politics than they are about science.

Co-opted? The American Society for Nutrition

NUTRITION PROFESSIONALS ALL OVER THE WORLD BELONG TO societies focused on research, education, and practice, many of which accept sponsorship by food, beverage, and supplement companies. In the United States, nutrition scientists and medical nutrition researchers generally belong to the American Society for Nutrition (ASN), nutrition educators to the Society for Nutrition Education and Behavior (SNEB), and dietetics practitioners to the Academy of Nutrition and Dietetics (AND). Other national nutrition organizations tend to represent more specialized interests. The Obesity Society, for example, represents medical and health professionals who treat that condition; its website promotes its "longstanding history of mutually beneficial partnerships with industry." Two much smaller nutrition societies deserve special mention for their unusual refusal to accept industry funding: the 1,400-member American College of Nutrition, which focuses on the application of research to clinical practice, and the World Public Health Nutrition Association, which has about 500 members.

Food companies support nutrition societies by helping pay for conference activities, publications, prizes, and scholarships. In return, they gain goodwill and what CSPI calls "innocence by association."[1] In their capture of nutrition organizations, food, beverage, and supplement companies participate in the increasing influence of corporations over American society.

Such effects are evident from two studies published in 2016. The first pointed out that at the same time that soft-drink companies were sponsoring the health-promoting activities of ninety-five health organizations, they were also lobbying against public health measures such as soda taxes. The second found evidence for substantial influence by corporate sponsors over the scientific program of a nutrition conference in Brazil; speakers who discussed promotion of healthful diets, for example, did not recommend avoiding unhealthful food products but instead called for motivating individuals to make better food choices. For such reasons, some experts view food-industry sponsorship of nutrition societies as "preposterous" and as creating "unfathomable" risks. Nutrition societies, they insist, must be transparent and accountable for how they get and use funds from food, drink, and other industries and for how those industries might affect their work.[2]

ASN is a good example of how food industry sponsorship produces troubling effects. It is the principal US association for doctoral-level academics and physicians who conduct nutrition research. It has about six thousand members (including me). Its very mission includes industry: to bring together "the world's top researchers, clinical nutritionists and industry to advance our knowledge and application of nutrition for the sake of humans and animals."[3] The society holds conferences, gives awards, and publishes four research journals, and it actively seeks food-industry donations for such activities.

ASN has a complicated history. It was formed in 2005 through the merger of three older societies: the American Institute of Nutrition (AIN—established in 1928), the American Society for Clinical

Nutrition (established in 1961), and the Society for International Nutrition (established in 1996). The oldest, the AIN, was founded in the 1920s to represent some of the first researchers engaged in identifying and characterizing the newly discovered vitamins and minerals. Their experiments, which often involved feeding diets of defined composition to rats, dogs, or chickens, appeared to constitute an entirely new field of study, one that called for its own professional society and journal. These scientists formed the AIN expressly to publish a journal to share research results—then and now the *Journal of Nutrition*. A history of the AIN published in 1978 mentions industry sponsorship in only one context, annual awards beginning in 1939 from Mead Johnson and in 1944 from Borden Dairy.[4]

In the early 1950s, medical researchers with interests in human—as opposed to animal—nutrition began publishing their own, clinically focused journal (now the *American Journal of Clinical Nutrition*) to compensate for the lack of nutrition education in medical schools.[5] In 1961, they formed a separate organization, the American Society for Clinical Nutrition, as a division of the AIN. Five years later, this society established its own industry-funded award, a gift from the Dairy Council to honor Elmer McCollum, the scientist who in 1912 had codiscovered vitamin A in milk. McCollum gets credit as the force behind the formation in 1915 of the National Dairy Council, that industry's principal trade association. The Dairy Council paid for publication of the AIN's 1978 history.

In 1968, the *Journal of Nutrition* began to list the AIN's corporate sponsors in every issue. The first sponsors included twenty-six companies, among them Coca-Cola, Hoffman–La Roche, Monsanto, Nestlé, Procter & Gamble, and Ralston Purina. The American Society for Clinical Nutrition began to list sponsors in 1979, when there were thirteen, mostly drawn from the same of companies sponsoring the AIN. Since the 2005 merger, ASN has represented researchers of all types: basic, clinical, and applied. Table 9.1 lists ASN's corporate sponsors in 2018. The society's journals list them with this introduction: "Industry organizations with the highest level of commitment to the nutrition profession are recognized as ASN Sustaining

TABLE 9.1. The American Society for Nutrition's Sustaining Partners, 2018

Abbott Nutrition	Kyowa Hakko USA
Almond Board of California	Mars
Bayer HealthCare	McCormick Science Institute
Biofortis Clinical Research	Mondelēz International Technical
California Walnut Commission	Center
Cargill	Monsanto Company
Corn Refiners Association	National Cattlemen's Beef Association
Council for Responsible Nutrition	Nestlé Nutrition, Medical Affairs
Dairy Research Institute	PepsiCo
DSM Nutritional Products	Pfizer
DuPont Nutrition & Health	Pharmavite
Egg Nutrition Center	Tate & Lyle
General Mills Bell Institute of	The a2 Milk Company™
Health and Nutrition	The Coca-Cola Company
Herbalife/Herbalife Nutrition	The Dannon Company
Institute	The Sugar Association
International Bottled Water	Unilever
Foundation	

Partners. ASN is proud to partner with these companies to advance excellence in nutrition research and practice."

In April 2016, I spoke to ASN's newly formed "blue ribbon" Advisory Committee on Ensuring Trust in Nutrition Science (the Trust Committee) about the risk of bias associated with industry funding. The need for this committee had become increasingly apparent. The previous year, Michele Simon, the supporter of plant-based diets who wrote the report about the USDA's sponsorship of dairy foods discussed in Chapter 5, published the results of an investigation of ASN's collaboration with the food industry. The title of her 2015 report aimed straight at the reputational risk: "Nutrition Scientists on the Take from Big Food: Has the American Society for Nutrition Lost All Credibility?" Its sponsor was the Alliance for Natural Health, a group in favor of approaches to health that incorporate functional foods (those formulated for health purposes), dietary supplements, and lifestyle changes.

Simon's report listed ASN's industry donors, described their influence at annual meetings and on policy statements, and exposed conflicts of interest resulting from members' financial ties. In response to these and other concerns about its sponsorship policies, ASN asked the Trust Committee to "establish recognized best practices that allow collaboration across industry, government, academia, and nonprofit, nongovernmental organizations . . . leading to the best science and policy possible, attained with the highest level of rigor, transparency and confidence."[6]

Pulling this off would be challenging given ASN's history of industry ties, but I thought appointment of the Trust Committee was an impressive step, especially because its members were distinguished experts in nutrition science, public perception, and conflicts of interest. If any group could rise to the challenge—create a policy that allowed industry funding but protected integrity—this one could.

I hoped the committee would deal with the question of whether industry sponsorship of ASN was even necessary. As a member in 2017, I paid annual dues of $190 (which included online journal subscriptions) and a registration fee of $420 for the annual meeting (which did not cover travel, hotel, or meals, and increased to $500 for the 2018 meeting). I asked the society's executive director, John Courtney, how much of its work is supported by the Sustaining Partners. He told me that they cover less than 4 percent of ASN's annual budget and that industry contributions are earmarked specifically for professional development, student prizes, and the like. ASN, he said in an email, "is a small player when it comes to receiving industry funding compared to others in the nutrition space."[7] Then why take the reputational risk?

ASN, he explained, "is a welcoming 'big tent' where all stakeholders in the nutrition research enterprise can participate, share latest research information, dialogue and debate, and develop relationships to advance the field and members' careers. . . . Many of our academic members value the opportunity to meet with industry counterparts as a growing number of graduates are being employed in the private sector and a growing portion of the total nutrition research funding comes from this sector." The ASN leadership believes that it should "welcome and convene all of the stakeholders and voices in the nutrition field to meet, discuss, share perspectives, and learn from each other in our quest for advancing global public health through the best nutrition science and practice."

Welcoming sounds good, but the society's "big-tent" approach makes it look like an arm of the food industry rather than an independent voice in debates about nutrition issues. ASN has a long history of allowing food companies to sponsor its conferences and symposia and of appearing to promote food-industry interests over those of public health. In *Food Politics*, I wrote about an ASN meeting in 1999 at which I went to a particularly memorable Kellogg-sponsored breakfast meeting for heads of university nutrition departments. It featured samples from the company's proposed line of foods with psyllium fiber, then undergoing test-marketing (they failed and soon disappeared). The Dairy Council and the National Cattlemen's Beef Association also sponsored sessions at that conference. This tradition continues. Kellogg still sponsors breakfasts; the one in 2017, which I did not attend, was listed as featuring a discussion of trust in nutrition science among other topics. Industry-sponsored sessions were interspersed throughout the scientific program; the ones that offered lunch were especially well attended.

I was interested to see that two of the society's most prestigious awards in 2017 went to leaders of the recently disbanded Global Energy Balance Network (GEBN); another went to a Coca-Cola executive involved with the GEBN.[8] ASN committees—not the ASN leadership—choose award recipients. The members of these particular committees may never have heard of the GEBN events, or perhaps they did not view them as germane to decisions about who deserved honors. But such awards make ASN appear to be untroubled by conflicted relationships with food companies.

It is not that ASN ignores the issue. As a speaker at a session on the US dietary guidelines, I was sent a prototype slide for disclosing conflicts of interest and instructed to display that information at the beginning of my presentation. I did so, but I could see from attending other sessions that compliance with this directive was haphazard or perfunctory. Speakers frequently omitted the disclosure slide or displayed it so quickly that it could not be read.[9] Judging from questions and comments after my and other sessions, conflicts of interest are a touchy issue for ASN members. Speakers and audience members commented that financial ties to food companies are either irrelevant or necessary and desirable.

Does sponsorship influence the content of conference sessions? If nothing else, sponsored sessions exclude speakers who might hold opinions contrary to the donor's interests. ASN permits corporate sponsors to organize and run "satellite" sessions for fees that in 2018 ranged from $15,000 to $50,000 each, depending on length and time of day. The 2017 program book identified these sessions as industry-sponsored, although not always prominently, and they were fully integrated into the overall scientific program. This makes them appear to be endorsed by the society, even though ASN specifically denies endorsing the content of satellite events.

ASN hosted ten satellite sessions during the 2017 annual meeting. Sponsors included the Almond Board of California, Cattlemen's Beef Board, National Dairy Council, Herbalife Nutrition Institute, Pfizer, Tate & Lyle, and the Egg Nutrition Center, among others. The Global Stevia Institute, for example, sponsored a session on the science, benefits, and future potential of this low-calorie sweetener. While eating a free lunch, participants could achieve the session's stated objectives: explore the latest scientific evidence for stevia's benefits and understand the science behind stevia's "naturality." Although satellite sessions look educational, they serve marketing purposes. Speakers at this particular session reviewed evidence for stevia's benefits. Some contrary evidence exists, but participants at that session were unlikely to learn about it.[10]

In 2018, in what I view as a partial improvement, ASN moved most industry-sponsored sessions to the weekend before the start of the annual meeting and labeled them "Preconference/Satellite" to distinguish them from the scientific sessions. But the sponsors still included groups such as the Hass Avocado Board, the Egg Nutrition Center, PepsiCo, and Herbalife, among others.[11]

More troubling are ASN's consistently industry-friendly positions on public health issues. The society's purpose is to promote research and communication among members, not to speak for them about policies about which members might hold diverse opinions. ASN's "big-tent" approach often appears to favor industry over public health, as several incidents demonstrate. Let's take them in chronological order.

Sponsoring Smart Choices, 2009

In May 2009 I received an email from ASN's program coordinator informing me that I had been nominated to join the board of directors of a new program, Smart Choices. This was a food-industry initiative in collaboration with leading nutritionists to put a stamp of approval on the front of packaged foods that met defined nutritional criteria. ASN was administering the program. My immediate reaction: Do not do this. Whatever this program did, it would make ASN appear to be endorsing products carrying the Smart Choices logo—a risky proposition. I wrote an open letter in the society's newsletter saying so and declined the invitation.[12]

Although Smart Choices seemed to be aimed at helping the public identify healthier food options, it seemed clear that its underlying purpose was to induce nutritionists to endorse highly processed "junk" foods as healthy. The program also appeared to be an industry-designed effort to head off a plan, then under consideration by the FDA, to regulate front-of-package food labels. In his response to my open letter, Courtney explained that ASN had competed for oversight of the program and would be responsible for the program's scientific integrity.[13] I was not reassured.

A few months later, William Neuman, a *New York Times* reporter newly assigned to cover the food business, asked to meet with me to discuss current issues in the nutrition world. When I mentioned

FIGURE 9.1. The Smart Choices check-mark logo appears near the upper-right-hand corner of this package of Froot Loops, indicating that the product meets the program's nutritional standards. The Smart Choices board set the upper limit for added sugars at 25 percent of calories but made an exception for breakfast cereals. Added sugars in Froot Loops come to 44 percent of its calories.

Smart Choices, he suggested we head for the nearest grocery store. Because breakfast-cereal packages are redesigned frequently, we went straight to that aisle. There on the shelf was the first product labeled with the Smart Choices logo: Froot Loops—a kids' cereal providing 44 percent of its calories from added sugars (Figure 9.1).

Neuman's article about this discovery appeared on the newspaper's front page in September with the title "For your health, Froot Loops." It reported that Michael Jacobson, CSPI's executive director, had resigned from the Smart Choices panel in disgust: "It was paid for by industry and when industry put down its foot and said this is what we're doing, that was it, end of story. . . . You could start out with sawdust, add calcium or vitamin A, and meet the criteria." Neuman also quoted Eileen Kennedy, president of the Smart Choices board and dean of the nutrition school at Tufts University: "You have a choice between a doughnut and a cereal. . . . So Froot Loops is a better choice."[14] This quickly got translated to Froot Loops being "better than a doughnut," or as the *Economist* put it, "It's practically spinach."[15]

The FDA and USDA jointly wrote to the Smart Choices program questioning whether its logo might encourage the public to select highly processed foods and refined grains instead of fruits, vegetables, and whole grains. Change.org filed a petition to end the program, distressed that nutrition experts were "happy to mislead the public about what constitutes a healthy/smart choice." Connecticut representative Rosa DeLauro asked the FDA to investigate, and that state's then attorney general, Richard Blumenthal, said he intended to investigate this "overly simplistic, inaccurate and ultimately misleading" program.[16]

By October, Smart Choices was history. The program announced postponement of all further activities pending the FDA's decisions on front-of-package labeling.[17] As *Forbes* explained, "[The] uproar over the program has conveyed a definitive message to industry: Don't try to disguise a nutritional sin with a stamp of approval."[18] The ASN board sent a short letter to members explaining that the society fully supported the decision to postpone the program until the FDA made some decisions about front-of-package labels. The letter quotes ASN's president at the time, James Hill (one of the founders, later, of the GEBN). He said that the society would "continue to provide nutrition science expertise within the dialogue on front-of-pack labeling in order to best serve the interests of the health of Americans."[19] I thought ASN should never have been involved in this enterprise in the first place and was lucky to have gotten out of it so easily. ASN's leaders should have realized the reputational risk of involvement with a food-marketing initiative but apparently did not.

Promoting Processed Foods, 2012

In a collaborative effort with the Academy of Nutrition and Dietetics, the Institute of Food Technologists (a professional society for food scientists), and the International Food Information Council (a food-industry group), ASN participated in writing a report promoting the importance of processed foods to nutritional health.[20] Food scientists and food trade associations have a vested interest in promoting processed food products; nutrition organizations do not, but their collaboration lends credibility to the report's conclusions.

Most foods are processed in one way or another, ranging from the minimal (washing, chopping) to the extensive (converting whole wheat to white flour). Processing often removes vitamins, minerals, and fiber while adding salt, sugar, and trans fats, making foods junkier. Independent nutrition groups generally recommend diets containing foods that are minimally processed.[21] But ASN's cosponsored report concluded "the processing level was a minor determinant of individual foods' nutrient contribution to the diet and, therefore, should not be a primary factor when selecting a balanced diet."

This report appeared in a supplement to ASN's *Journal of Nutrition* with a statement that its first author and the supplement itself were supported by the sponsoring industry groups. That statement also explained, "Publication costs for this supplement were defrayed in part by the payment of page charges. This publication must therefore be hereby marked 'advertisement' ... solely to indicate this fact." ASN's participation in the report made it appear to support industry marketing objectives rather than those of public health nutrition.

Opposing "Added Sugars" on Food Labels, 2014

In 2014, the FDA proposed including information about "added sugars" on its revised Nutrition Facts labels. As is customary, the FDA asked for comments on this proposal.[22] Consumer and public health groups supported putting "added sugars" on food labels, but the food industry opposed the FDA's proposal. So did ASN. In supporting the food industry's opposition, ASN explained that it had "concerns with FDA's rationale for the inclusion of 'added sugars' on the food label. . . . Conclusions regarding added sugars remain elusive based on insufficient evidence regarding the effects of added sugars (beyond contribution of excess calories) on health outcomes. . . . ASN recommends careful consideration of the totality of the scientific evidence, as well as consideration of compliance and other technical issues."[23]

ASN's insistence that sugar policy be strictly "science-based" positioned the group as opposing a widely supported public health initiative. Eventually, the FDA not only ruled in favor of putting "added sugars" on the Nutrition Facts panel but also set a daily value of 10 percent of calories as an upper limit.[24] ASN's position on the science may have been technically correct, but it ignored the public health implications. In contrast to naturally occurring sugars in foods, added sugars are unnecessary. Nobody in or out of ASN thinks people should be eating *more* sugar. Encouraging people to eat less sugar is a reasonable public health objective, and ASN should have supported this measure.

Defending "Natural," 2015

In response to petitions from consumer groups, the FDA requested public comment on the meaning of "natural" on food labels. Marketers of processed foods love the word because it is so frequently, but incorrectly, interpreted as meaning organic and healthy.[25] The FDA's current policy leaves much room for ambiguity: "From a food science perspective, it is difficult to define a food product that is 'natural' because the food has probably been processed and is no longer the product of the earth. . . . The agency has not objected to the use of the term if the food does not contain added color, artificial flavors, or synthetic substances."[26]

Consumer groups want the FDA to clarify that this definition also excludes seemingly unnatural substances such as high-fructose corn syrup, foods that are genetically modified, or, perhaps, stevia's "naturality." They petitioned the FDA to come up with a more restrictive definition. But ASN argued for a more expansive definition that would allow the addition of synthetic vitamins. ASN correctly stated that many Americans interpret "natural" on processed foods to mean no pesticides, no artificial chemicals, and no GMOs, and that even more believe that it *should* mean these things. But the society argued for permitting the addition of synthetic vitamins because the diets of many Americans lack "important nutrients of public health concern"—a debatable contention, given the lack of evidence for widespread signs of nutrient deficiency in the general population. Marketing vitamin-fortified foods as "natural" opens the door to other "healthy" synthetic additives. Once again, ASN was supporting industry marketing interests against what some members of the society might prefer "natural" to mean.

Promoting Food Industry Sponsorship, 2016

In 2016, I accepted an invitation from ASN to serve as an adviser for its Early Career Nutrition Interest Group, which provides networking and mentoring for postdoctoral fellows and early-career faculty at annual meetings and also sponsors an award competition. ASN requires all groups running social and professional-development sessions at annual meetings to raise their own funding for hotel-room space, audiovisual support, and food. In the past, the Early Career group's events had been sponsored by PepsiCo, Abbott Nutrition, and DuPont, for a total cost below $5,000. I thought ASN could easily cover these costs from annual and meeting dues, and said so, but was overruled.

One last example, this time from ASN's use of social media. In September 2016, the online news magazine *Slate* published an article that asked, "So what if the sugar industry funds research? Science is science," arguing that funding sources are irrelevant to the conduct or outcome of research.[27] Whoever does social media for ASN supported this "science-based" position. ASN linked to the article on its Twitter feed with this comment: "Evaluating science on factors beyond data and methods impairs efforts to understand and advance nutrition science."[28] Industry funding is indeed a factor "beyond data and methods," but it skews the science. While many members might agree with ASN's position, others might not, and the organization has no mechanism for polling members on such questions.

ASN is a relatively small society, but it represents research faculty at universities and medical centers throughout the world. Although its actions establish ethical norms for the field, it places high value on the inclusiveness of its connections to food companies without regard to their ethical or reputational implications. ASN's apparent support of food-industry objectives makes it seem to be favoring commercial interests over those of science or public health. It appointed the Trust Committee to address this problem. In August 2018 as this book went to press, the committee had submitted its findings and recommendations for publication but could not release them until completion of peer review. Whether the ASN board would approve the recommendations was as yet uncertain.

International Implications

ASN is an American society, but the issues that beset it are typical of nutrition societies throughout the world—US nutritionists just do not hear much about them. Critics have long objected to the ubiquitous presence of Big Food marketers at congresses of the International Union of Nutritional Sciences, but these take place only at four-year intervals.[29] The last two were in Granada (2013) and Buenos Aires (2017) and did not get much press coverage in the United States.

But in 2017, the *New York Times* began to publish a series of investigative reports collectively titled "Planet Fat." These articles describe in riveting detail the marketing methods used by international food companies to promote sales of highly processed food products in developing countries—Brazil, Ghana, Senegal, Colombia, Mexico, Malaysia, India, Chile—and, inadvertently, to promote the rapid rise in obesity and its health consequences in such countries.

The article about Malaysia is especially relevant to our discussion because it deals with the influence of food companies on the research and opinions of the country's leading nutritionist, Tee E-Siong. Tee heads the Nutrition Society of Malaysia, a group funded by Nestlé and other food companies. He also is scientific director of ILSI in that region.[30] The *Times* headline got right to the point: "In Asia's fattest country, nutritionists take money from food giants."[31] In particular, Tee was senior author on a study sponsored by Nestlé and Cereal Partners Worldwide (a joint venture between Nestlé and General Mills). The study examined how Nestlé's Milo (a sugar-sweetened, chocolate-flavored, vitamin-enriched malted milk drink) affected children who consumed it at breakfast. Unsurprisingly, the study found that children who drank Milo consumed more of the nutrients it contains. It also noted that Milo-consuming children were more active and had healthier weights than children who did not consume the drink—just the kinds of results Nestlé and Cereal Partners must have hoped for.[32]

Of the study's twelve authors, four were employed by its sponsors. The paper's disclosure statement noted that the funders "had no influence over the design or analysis of the research" but also noted that the authors who worked for the funders "critically revised the manuscript for intellectual content." If so, how could there be no influence? A spokesperson for Nestlé told the *Times* that the company's review of the manuscript was routine and aimed only "to ensure that the methodology was scientifically correct."

In response to this article, an anonymous Malaysian scientist objected to suggestions that industry funding might influence the quality of Tee's science. Instead, he wrote, Tee's Milo investigation "is a valid and important scientific study that added an important contribution to the ongoing research about food intake and obesity." Such comments induced David Ludwig, a Harvard specialist in childhood obesity, to post a detailed critique of the study's design and methods—low participation rate, unmatched comparison groups, unvalidated methods, and statistical problems—concluding that the results were weak and susceptible to confounding.[33]

The *Times* further quoted Tee: "There are some people who say that we should not accept money for projects, for research studies. . . . I have two choices: Either I don't do anything or I work with companies." But other choices exist and are worth considering. The *Times* writers must have thought so, too. This research, they said, "exemplified a practice that began in the West and has moved, along with rising obesity rates, to developing countries: deep financial partnerships between the world's largest food companies and nutrition scientists, policymakers and academic societies." If professional nutrition societies are embedded in partnerships with food companies, they are, or can appear to be, front groups for the food industry, not independent sources of scientific advice about diet and health.

Nutrition Education and Dietetics Societies: Industry Influence

NUTRITIONISTS WHO ADVISE THE PUBLIC OR INDIVIDUALS about diet and health are highly diverse in training and outlook, as are the groups they belong to. Professionals who call themselves nutritionists range from people who are self-taught or have completed rather casual online programs to those who have been awarded advanced doctoral and postdoctoral credentials. Some nutritionists are certified or licensed, but many are not. I hold a New York State license in nutrition and dietetics, number 000007 (I was a charter member of the committee that developed it), but I also have a master's degree in public health nutrition obtained eighteen years after my doctorate in molecular biology, both from the University of California, Berkeley. Nutrition is a field in which credentials vary widely.

The best-regulated credential is that of Registered Dietitian Nutritionist, authorized by the largest of the nutrition societies, the 100,000-member Academy of Nutrition and Dietetics (henceforth, the Academy). I am not a member of the Academy; although I completed its internship requirements while working on my public health nutrition master's degree, I lacked some of its undergraduate course requirements. I do belong to the Society for Nutrition Education and Behavior (SNEB), which has only about 1,100 members. Both groups are mainstream in that they represent practitioners with traditional academic training in nutrition. Both have long histories of receiving food-industry sponsorship, but the internal struggles over whether to accept funding from food companies occurred much earlier for SNEB—indeed, right at its start.

Early Struggles: The Society for Nutrition Education

In the early 1960s, university faculty and nutrition practitioners involved with nutrition education did not think the existing nutrition societies were doing nearly enough to address public confusion about diet and health. They founded SNEB in 1968 as the Society for Nutrition Education (SNE) and began publishing the *Journal of Nutrition Education* in 1969. This new society would need funding, but its founders could see that food-industry sponsorship might entail reputational risk. Some thought the risk worth taking; others did not.

George Briggs, for example, a professor in the University of California Berkeley's then newly established Department of Nutritional Sciences, was on the board of the industry-funded Nutrition Foundation (which we will meet in Chapter 13). He feared that if the new journal was "sponsored directly and solely by The Nutrition Foundation, the strong food faddist group in California would continue to complain loudly and clearly that the 'powerful food industry' is behind the undertaking and it has little or no concern for the eventual consumer."[1] The foundation did make a contribution, but only a small one (it was more interested in research than education). As recalled by Joan Gussow, a former president of the society, nutrition scientists tended to view SNE members as a "radical fringe" whose dietary advice was insufficiently based on evidence.[2]

FIGURE 10.1. The goal of nutrition education is to help the public choose foods and meals that promote health, but the goal of food (and restaurant) companies is to sell as much of the most profitable items as possible. Because these aims are often contradictory, they make nutrition education inherently incompatible with the goals of food companies. Sidney Harris ©1979 The New Yorker / Condé Nast, used with permission.

The SNE board sought industry donations, but food companies had little interest in investing in a group likely to advise the public to avoid processed foods, salty snacks, and sugary drinks. As Gussow wrote in 1979, food companies did not want nutrition educators to recommend eating less of their products. Instead, they wanted educators to provide information about nutrients so consumers could add up the numbers and figure out for themselves how to meet their requirements: "There is, of course, not the remotest possibility that the average consumer—a category that includes children, illiterates, those unable to do quadratic equations and so on—can or will do this."[3]

In Gussow's view, the goals of food companies and those of nutrition educators are *inherently* incompatible: "Any company or any industry's ultimate goal is to sell products. . . . Much of what the educator *ought* probably to be teaching in affluent countries is restraint, and nonconsumption of the very overprocessed food products from which many food producers make their greatest profit."[4] Figure 10.1 illustrates this problem.

By the late 1970s, SNE had about five thousand members, many working for food companies. Differing opinions about food company sponsorship led to contentious arguments in committee and annual meetings and threatened to split the society. When McDonald's produced a video and wanted SNE to cosponsor it, some members of the board voted yes; while others were aghast. In 1978, the SNE board accepted a supposedly no-strings-attached grant from the potato industry for a campaign to promote consumption of potato chips and the inclusion of potato chips in school vending machines and lunch programs.[5] These kinds of incidents led to what Gussow recalls as open warfare at position-statement meetings, with nutritionists who favored ties to food companies viewing any criticism of the industry as anticapitalistic and unacceptable. When I first attended SNE meetings in the 1980s, such debates were commonplace.

Today's Society for Nutrition Education and Behavior ("and Behavior" was added in 2012) has one-fifth the membership of its peak in 1979, and it lists only four food-industry sponsors: the American Frozen Food Institute, Canned Food Alliance, Dairy Council of California, and Egg Nutrition Center/American Egg Board (the egg checkoff). In 2014, evidently to resolve still-ongoing arguments about food-company donations, SNEB developed a policy for accepting external funding for the society itself and for events at its annual meeting. This policy requires that donations come from diverse sources, be aligned with the society's mission, and serve the interests of both the donor and the society. Donors must agree that acceptance of funds does not imply endorsement of the donor or its mission, products, or services.[6]

In effect, this policy divides food companies into two categories: those that produce acceptable "good" foods versus those that do not. The policy does not define the criteria for acceptability or give examples, but I am told that SNEB has a long list of companies from which it is actively seeking donations. Canned foods and dairy foods evidently fall into the good-food category, but the overall standards remain unclear. Food companies sponsoring the 2017 annual meeting included Wegmans (a grocery chain), Sorghum (a checkoff program), Chobani (a yogurt maker), and Nestlé, which hosted a lunch of Lean Cuisine (packaged frozen meals) and Nescafé. The program guide marked the sponsored sessions with corporate logos.[7]

SNEB's present compromise—to accept funding from some companies but not others—cannot help but imply endorsement of the full range of products of the sponsoring companies. In the case of Nestlé, that means chocolate bars, ice cream, and aggressively promoted (and largely unnecessary) drinks for children. As for dairy and canned foods, some SNEB members—vegans or those concerned about saturated fat or animal welfare—might prefer that dairy foods not be consumed at all; others might be uncomfortable with the added salt or potential leakage of chemical contaminants in canned foods. Dividing foods into good and bad is a slippery slope. Endorsements, even those for "healthy" foods, have no real meaning for health; their purpose is marketing.

Current Struggles: The Academy of Nutrition and Dietetics

Until 2012, the Academy of Nutrition and Dietetics was known as the American Dietetic Association. It was founded in 1917 and launched its journal in 1925; both are still going strong. Many Academy members work for food companies or support food-industry goals, but in recent years they and their organization have been criticized for such ties and for their apparent willingness to promote products of questionable health benefit.

In the wake of the collapse of the GEBN, for example, dietitians were found to comprise the majority of experts paid by Coca-Cola, some of them to promote small cans of Coke as a healthy snack. In 2015, Coca-Cola ended its partnership with the Academy; as publicly reported, neither Coke nor the Academy "pursued an opportunity for sponsorship renewal."[8] After many years of exhibiting at the Academy's annual conference, Coca-Cola and McDonald's ended their participation in 2016. In the wake of AP reporter Candice Choi's exposure of its recruiting dietitians to use social media to oppose soda tax initiatives, the American Beverage Association also said it would stop such payments.[9]

But a month later, Choi reported that Kellogg was paying dietitians an average of $13,000 a year to join a Breakfast Council of "independent experts" to use social media to promote Kellogg cereals. Choi explained that this council "deftly blurred the lines between cereal promotion and impartial nutrition guidance. The company used the council to teach a continuing education class for dietitians, publish an academic paper on the benefits of eating breakfast cereals, and try to influence the government's dietary guidelines."[10]

The Academy's stated mission is to improve the nation's health and advance the profession of dietetics through research, education, and advocacy. It explicitly engages with policy: "As a leader in food and nutrition issues, the Academy provides expert testimony at hearings, lobbies Congress and other governmental bodies, comments on proposed federal and state regulations, and develops position statements on critical food and nutrition issues."[11] In 2002, I wrote in *Food Politics* about how this group's positions on food issues often appeared to be more favorable to the interests of its food-company sponsors than to the health of the American public. They still sometimes appear that way.

The Academy began seeking corporate sponsorship in the early 1980s.[12] By the mid-1990s, reporters observed that dietitians' reliance on such funding meant that "they never criticize the food industry."[13] With such a large membership of nutrition professionals who advise the public about diet and health, it is understandable why food companies would want to capture the Academy. But its 2018 list of corporate sponsors is surprisingly short (Table 10.1) and is getting shorter as a result of public criticism and pressures by Academy members to clean up the group's sponsorship policies.

TABLE 10.1. Corporate Sponsors of the Academy of Nutrition and Dietetics, 2018

Academy national sponsor

National Dairy Council

2017 conference exhibitor supporters

American Pistachio Growers

Campbell Soup Company

Ingredion

Lentils.org

Premier Protein

SPLENDA® Sweeteners

Sunsweet Growers

The a2 Milk Company™

NOTE: *Contribution levels per category are not disclosed.*

The Academy recognizes reputational risks: "In its relations with corporate organizations, the Academy is mindful of the need to avoid a perception of conflict of interest and to act at all times in ways that will only enhance the credibility and professional recognition of the Academy and its members. . . . The Academy will authorize no commercial use of the name and logo that would diminish that value or damage that reputation."[14] But because the organization does not always adhere to its stated policies, it gets into trouble with the press as well as with some of its members.

The Academy's apparent endorsement of Kraft Singles is a good example. Although the Smart Choices fiasco should have taught nutrition societies that stamps of approval on processed food products inevitably look like endorsements, the Academy got involved in another such scheme. In 2015, its foundation developed a labeling program to put the Academy's Kids Eat Right seal on products meeting certain nutrition standards. The first product to qualify? Kraft Singles.

Kraft Singles are "cheese" slices, in quotation marks because they are not cheese. They are a "pasteurized prepared cheese product" with a list of ingredients so long that one reporter said "it read like a novel."[15] The foundation defended Singles as a way for kids to get more vitamin D and calcium. An exposé of this partnership in the *New York Times* gave the last word to Andy Bellatti, a dietitian we will hear from again in this chapter: "You would think an organization that has come under fire for so many years for its relations with food companies might pick something other than a highly processed cheese product for its first endorsement."[16]

Endorsement? The *Times* account noted that although "the academy emphatically denied that the label was an endorsement . . . Kraft itself told the *Times* it was the first time the academy was endorsing a product." But the Academy insisted that "contrary to recent published reports . . . The Academy Foundation does not endorse any products, brands or services. The Kids Eat Right logo on KRAFT Singles packaging identifies the brand as a proud supporter of Kids Eat Right."[17] ABC News quoted the Academy as stating, "The academy has never once endorsed any product, brand or service, and we never will."[18]

But to anyone outside the Academy, the Kids Eat Right logo *was* an endorsement. The comedian Jon Stewart certainly thought so. Kraft, he pointed out, is not legally allowed to call this product cheese: "Turns out the Academy of Nutrition and Dietetics is an Academy the same way this [Kraft Singles] is cheese."[19]

Embarrassed members of the Academy protested the Singles endorsement. Two weeks later, Kraft dropped the logo, putting an end to this "textbook case of corporate PR gone horribly wrong."[20] Did the Academy learn anything from this incident? Not enough, apparently. This organization continues to get bad press for its financial ties to food companies, especially the ones permitted to exhibit at its annual Food and Nutrition Conference & Expo (FNCE).

It has been years since I attended the Academy's annual FNCE (pronounced "fencie"), but I certainly remember the vast expanse of food-company exhibits surrounded by participants eagerly collecting free samples. I took my share and left with two shopping bags full of what I like to call "dietetic junk foods," highly processed food products marketed as nutritious or healthy. Not much has changed. In

2016, my NYU colleague Lisa Sasson sent an email from the event to announce her personal annual "FNCE award for most outrageous product and claim." Her winning product: SweeTARTS Mini Gummy Bites, candies with twenty-four grams of sugar per twenty tiny pieces—but no artificial colors or flavors. These are made by Nestlé and display a label helpfully pointing out that "enjoying confections in moderation can be part of a balanced diet and an active lifestyle." Indeed they can, but candy is candy whether or not its colors and flavors are natural.

Reporters loved the 2016 exhibits, as who would not? Sheila Kaplan of *Stat News* led off her account with the Sugar Association's declaration, "We make food with lots of vitamins and minerals taste good!" and "Because it's all-natural, you can consume it [sugar] with confidence."[21] Choi tweeted a photo of a page from a pamphlet: "Sugar Association's tips for pleasing picky eaters—sprinkle a little sugar on vegetables before cooking."[22] Her account titled "Do candy and soda makers belong at a dietitians' conference?" quoted Lucille Beseler, the Academy's president, defending Sugar Association participation: "Academy members know the difference between marketing and science, and use their professional judgment to evaluate exhibitors' products and programs."[23]

About the free items distributed throughout the exhibit halls, Beseler said, "I'm not so weak-minded that I would make a decision based on receiving a pen." To this, Academy member Bellatti commented, "We truly wish the topic of corporate influence was approached by [the Academy] with greater awareness, curiosity, and understanding as to how we, as a profession, can recognize it and improve our actions to elevate the registered dietitian credential. This is not about 'weak-mindedness'; it is about larger systemic forces. Pretending they don't exist will not make them go away."[24]

The Academy's alphabetical list of FNCE exhibitors in 2017 was so long that I gave up counting when I reached one hundred but was still only in the Cs. I checked for Coca-Cola and McDonald's; both were missing, but the Sugar Association was back and so was PepsiCo. Even so, FNCE's food-company sponsorships seemed somewhat less overwhelming than in the past, undoubtedly because of turmoil within the organization about those linkages.[25]

I date the turmoil to 2013 when Michele Simon published an investigation of the Academy's relationships with food companies subtitled "Are America's Nutrition Professionals in the Pocket of Big Food?"[26] Her report detailed the group's financial ties to purveyors of foods of questionable health benefit and correlated those ties to the Academy's policy statements on nutrition and health. She also listed fees paid by food companies to exhibit at annual meetings ($15,000 to $50,000), their sponsorship of educational activities for which dietitians get continuing education credits ("the best nutrition education money can buy"), the frequent lack of disclosure of industry ties by conference speakers—and the increasingly vocal concerns of members about such issues.

Simon's report on the Academy, unlike her later one on the American Society for Nutrition, elicited widespread press attention, as well as a dismissive comment from the Academy's president at the time, Ethan Bergman: "There is one indisputable fact in the report about the Academy's sponsorship program: We have one. . . . As members of a science-based organization, I encourage you to not take all information you see at face value, always consider the source (in this case, an advocate who has previously shown her predisposition to find fault with the Academy) and seek out the facts."[27] Simon is not an Academy member, and neither am I. But other dissenters, Andy Bellatti among them, are fully credentialed members.

Bellatti and colleagues established an organization of their own—Dietitians for Professional Integrity (DFPI)—expressly to induce the Academy to end inappropriate corporate sponsorships. Bellatti earned his master's degree in clinical nutrition from my NYU department and is a practicing dietitian. In an email, he explained that he and others founded DFPI in 2013 in response to Simon's report and the embarrassing press coverage of the Academy's industry ties: "As a vocal critic of these ties, I saw an important opportunity to mobilize like-minded dietitians and create an organized movement calling for sponsorship reform."[28]

DFPI has made great progress in building this movement. The DFPI website explains that all successful social movements "began with a group of people who expressed their dissatisfaction with the status quo in hopes of mobilizing others. . . . We believe Big Food has a starkly different mission from that of a health organization." The site provides resources for advocates and guides for preventing conflicts of interest in the Academy's continuing-education and sponsorship programs. In 2013, DFPI produced a report on the Academy's conflicts of interest at its annual meetings, beginning with the FNCE tote bag printed with the names of the sponsors and continuing on to the industry handouts and other "educational" materials, the exhibit statements, and a newly instituted ban on taking photographs at exhibits, presumably to eliminate evidence that might embarrass the organization.[29] DFPI also confronts the potential loss of income incurred by rejecting food company sponsorship. Because the Academy is so large, DFPI calculates that eliminating food industry funding would cost members an additional $8 a year. As I will soon explain, the Academy's official estimates are higher.

I asked Bellatti if he could assess DFPI's impact on the Academy's activities. He replied that DFPI considers its main purpose to be raising awareness. Many Academy members, he says, "are unfamiliar with the various repercussions and consequences of corporate sponsorship—and certainly unaware of research about this topic in the field of bioethics." From the early 1990s on, the Academy consistently denied that sponsorship even required discussion, but DFPI and other members have convinced the leadership that they must open the sponsorship issue to debate, not least because DFPI members have succeeded in getting their local city, county, and state dietetic associations to develop guidelines for responsible sponsorship. DFPI keeps the issue of the Academy's corporate relationships in the news, making it more difficult for the academy's leadership to ignore the problem. DFPI also has normalized dissent within the Academy. Bellatti is pleased that non-DFPI dietitians were responsible for the petition to "Repeal the Seal" on Kraft Singles: "We were thrilled. . . . [The Academy] could no longer say sponsorship concerns were 'fringe.'"[30] In July 2018, having achieved much of what it set out to do, DFPI went inactive, turning "the baton" over to its colleagues in the Academy.[31]

As I see it, DFPI has forced the Academy to at least go through the motions of dealing with the effects of its sponsorship history and the current problems caused by its food-industry ties. The Academy may still be stumbling in these dealings, but it has come a long way from its previous insistence on a "total diet approach" to advising clients and the public. That approach famously stated that "all foods can fit" and "there is no such thing as a good or a bad food," meaning that dietitians could never advise eating less of any food product or category.[32] The Academy's current policies repudiate those messages, but mainly on paper. Its actual practices leave plenty of work for DFPI still to do.

For years, the Academy's code of ethics addressed food-industry sponsorship obliquely: "The dietetics practitioner," the code stated, "is alert to situations that might cause a conflict of interest or have the appearance of a conflict . . . provides full disclosure . . . promotes or endorses products in a manner that is neither false nor misleading."[33] In 2002, the Academy's president promised to confront the issue of "industry's real or perceived influence on the content of the organization's messages . . . head-on."[34] But in 2006, its ethics committee maintained that the existing policies, "if scrupulously practiced and enforced . . . should allay any public concerns about potential conflicts of interest impairing the integrity of dietetics research and practice."[35]

In 2014, perhaps in response to Simon's report and internal pressures from DFPI and other members, the Academy appointed a Sponsorship Advisory Task Force (SATF). Academy leadership considered corporate sponsorship a "mega issue" for discussion in 2015 and organized a sponsorship summit meeting at which delegates debated such matters as transparency, confidentiality, legalities, vetting processes, and endorsements. A task force report on its work explained that the Academy's dealings with the sponsorship issue had been "propelled into the forefront of member interest due to a specific sponsorship decision," a reference to the Kraft Singles episode.[36] Reading between the lines, the report revealed serious struggles within the organization about the implications of food-industry sponsorship.

The task force itself was divided; some members wanted no industry sponsorship at all, whereas others thought restrictions of any kind were unnecessary and counterproductive. They compromised by recommending acceptance of sponsorship from companies making products aligned with the Academy's vision, mission, and scientific-integrity principles (which mainly involve accuracy and disclosure). The compromise also stipulated that the Academy should not put its logo on food products.[37] The Academy's board approved these recommendations early in 2016—as a pilot project—with a one-word change: it added "broadly" as a modifier of "aligned." Sponsors' products now needed only to "broadly align" with the Academy's mission and principles, leaving considerable wiggle room for acceptance.[38] The Academy's website explains the policy and its rationale: "The Academy is transparent about our sponsorship program and does not tailor messages or programs in any way due to corporate sponsors. . . . Corporate sponsorship enables the Academy—as it does for non-profit organizations and associations nationwide—to build awareness of the Academy and our members. . . . The Academy builds and maintains our reputation by scrupulous attention to facts, science and honesty."

This statement suggests that the Academy's leadership wants food-industry sponsorship to continue and hopes—despite experience—that "scrupulous attention to facts, science, and honesty" will protect its reputation. The Academy president's letter to members announcing the sponsorship policy came with several attached documents, among them task-force guidelines for estimating the risks and benefits of sponsorship by particular companies and a score sheet for rating companies on their now-broad alignment with the Academy's mission. The attachments also included a set of nutrient standards for marketing foods to children and for general health promotion. One such standard: "The Sponsoring Entity enhances nutrition or health status of the general population or specified targeted markets." The task-force guidelines would seem to preclude sponsorship by the makers of food products with salt or sugar added above some cutoff point, yet the Sugar Association had booths at annual meetings in 2016 and 2017. For reasons not publicly explained, the Academy must have made an exception in this case. Having a policy is one thing; implementing it is another.

The president's letter included additional documents from staff of the Academy and its foundation estimating the financial impact of the task-force recommendations. These documents included complicated analyses of what would be needed to replace the current $1.3 million in sponsorship revenue—an average of $17.17 per member, twice DFPI's estimate. This, the staff report said, would have dire effects: "The last time the Academy raised rates beyond inflation . . . 7% of Academy members dropped their memberships." Academy staff predicted reductions in members' purchases of books, in registrations for continuing professional-education programs, and in registration fees for FNCE attendance, as well as in overall advertising and FNCE revenues: "In conclusion, the issue of replacing sponsorship revenue with increased membership dues is complex . . . and requires a balanced approach to achieve an acceptable outcome for the long-term viability of the Academy and the profession." The analysis produced by the foundation implied that without corporate funding, it would have to stop giving scholarships.

The temporarily approved policy—to accept sponsorship by the makers of good foods but reject funding by makers of the bad—may look reasonable, but the devil is in the details. As long as the Academy continues to accept funding from the makers of highly processed food products, questions will continue to be raised about the professional integrity of the Academy and its members.

Neither the Academy nor its members like having to deal with these issues. I know this because whenever I say anything about Academy sponsorship in talks or in writing, I am deluged with objections to the idea that sponsors might influence professional opinion or action. Members tell me that it is unfair to single out the Academy when other nutrition societies do the same or worse, and they say I am insufficiently sympathetic to their having to belong to the Academy whether they agree with its policies or not.

All of us who belong to nutrition societies for professional reasons are faced with the problem of sometimes disagreeing with their policies. Nutrition professionals are human, and humans believe themselves—ourselves—to be immune from the influence of sponsorship. Whether or not they intend to, nutrition societies appear to endorse their sponsors' products. When the Academy allows the Sugar Association to exhibit at its annual FNCE, it may be constrained from advising the public to cut down on sugar intake—a situation that looks like a conflict of interest and leads to a loss of trust and, sometimes, to ridicule.

Food-company sponsorships of professional societies create difficult dilemmas for members, and each of us must find our own way to deal with them. We would have an easier time negotiating these dilemmas if our professional associations set higher ethical standards for relationships with food companies, established stronger policies, and followed the spirit of those policies as well as the letter. What professional societies do matters, not only in the United States but also internationally.

Justifications, Rationales, Excuses: Isn't Everyone Conflicted?

U NTIL NOW, I HAVE BEEN TALKING ABOUT THE PURPOSE and consequences of food-industry sponsorship—the hazards. It is now time to fulfill my promise to respond to objections that industry funding is essential, raises no special concerns, and requires no particular management. Medical ethicists observe that responses to questions about industry funding generally fall into two categories: some professionals (like me) see financial conflicts of interest as too problematic to ignore, whereas others view any intervention as unnecessary and a cause of more harm than good. These diverse viewpoints, they find, track closely with overall ideas about how societies should be managed—whether market forces need to be curtailed or encouraged, for example.[1] With that observation in mind, let us take a look at the principal reasons typically given to justify acceptance of food-industry funding. Some of these reasons are well-grounded in reality, and some contain grains of truth. Others, however, represent wishful thinking that contradicts the large body of empirical evidence for how gifts affect human behavior.

I want to begin with the reality of today's research environment: it is harshly competitive for university scientists. Their appointment, promotion, tenure, and career advancement absolutely depend on their winning grants, publishing in prestigious journals, and achieving national and international recognition for their research. Universities expect faculty to obtain grants to pay for research supplies, equipment, and the salaries of technicians, graduate students, and postdoctoral fellows. Increasingly, faculty are also expected to raise part or all of their own salaries. As a nutrition professor at a large state university explained to me, her institution typically pays only 10 to 40 percent of salaries and expects faculty to generate the rest from grants. She insists that faculty members would not ask food companies for funding if they did not have to: "It's a high-pressure system and it's not getting any better with the current administration's cuts to science funding and increasing power to industry."[2]

The current administration is not the first to cut research funding; previous administrations also did so. Until recently, government granting agencies—mainly NIH and the USDA—funded about half of all food, nutrition, and agriculture research. But by 2013, industry and foundations accounted for 70 percent of food-related research. This shift occurred as a result of two simultaneous trends: a decline in federal funding and a sharp increase in private funding that began early in the twenty-first century.[3]

Universities actively encourage industry partnerships. My university's medical school, for example, has an Office of Industrial Liaison to facilitate "the commercial development of . . . products to benefit the public, while providing resources to the University to support its research, education, and patient care missions."[4] The University of Colorado, Boulder, former home of the GEBN, says it "has a long history of partnering with industry and is putting new attention to expanding those partnerships."[5] In 2016, when I was a visiting fellow at the University of Sydney, its vice-chancellor announced a forthcoming strategic plan: "We must more fully engage with the community, industry and business in order to ensure that our work is relevant and impactful."[6] Coca-Cola's gift to the GEBN—and its aftermath—are understandable in the context of the double messages universities send to their faculty: take the money, but maintain high ethical standards.

The transition to industry's funding a greater portion of research might not matter if government and industry paid for the same kinds of research. But they do not. Industry funding—as we have seen—most often goes for projects aimed at product development, product defense, or other marketing advantages, leaving support of basic research to the government and foundations. By one estimate, 80 percent of industry research funding goes for product development, whereas only 20 percent supports basic and applied research. Of federal support for everything except defense research, the opposite is true; 80 percent goes for basic research.[7]

Government nutrition priorities understandably favor studies of obesity and its consequences that are likely to have the greatest impact on public health, but this means there is less money for studies of dietary intake, food composition, or other areas of basic nutrition science. The 2014 farm bill established the Foundation for Food and Agriculture Research (FFAR) to help pay for studies in key areas, nutrition and health among them. Congress granted $200 million to FFAR on the condition that it raise equivalent matching funds. That funding, presumably, would have to come from industry, which explains why FFAR's board and advisory committee include representatives from Kellogg, PepsiCo, and Cargill, among other food corporations.[8]

Even within the USDA, partnerships with industry are encouraged. The USDA's cash-strapped Agricultural Research Service (ARS) explains: "ARS encourages its scientists to seek external funding. . . . External funding is appropriate to further scientific goals . . . and could also strengthen partnerships with stakeholders."[9] ARS engages in research partnerships through cooperative agreements with universities, food companies, and trade associations. These agreements require the cooperating entity to contribute at least 20 percent—but no more than 50 percent—of the total funding for a project in the form of salaries, material resources, or financial support.[10]

The USDA posts lists of its many cosponsored ARS projects, but the listings do not identify the cooperating group. To find out who they are, I went to the agency's annual reports, which cite a few publications resulting from the USDA's research partnerships. Most partners are university faculty, but a few are food companies.[11] Those few demonstrate that having the USDA as a cofunder does not change the typical outcome of industry-funded studies: most favor the interests of the cooperating sponsor. Table 11.1 gives some examples. For food companies, the partnerships make sense. The USDA picks up half or more of the costs, and the favorable research results appear more credible when they come from a government agency. The lead author of the avocado, pear, and rice studies summarized in the table was Victor Fulgoni, whose consulting firm, as I mentioned in Chapter 1, helps food companies obtain "aggressive, science-based claims" for their products.[12]

The USDA seems unconcerned that such partnerships may give the appearance of serving the interests of industry rather than public health. Members of the USDA's research staff tell me that industry funding often drives their research agenda; they would not otherwise be doing the kinds of studies industry partnerships require. As for trust: children may believe that sponsorship has no influence on professional action or opinion, but at least some adults know better; recognizing that a food company sponsored a study is all it takes to decrease confidence in the results—whether or not that study was cosponsored by a government agency, nonprofit group, or both.[13]

To be fair, the USDA's cooperative studies with food companies occasionally produce results unfavorable to the sponsor's interests. The no-benefit study of honey versus sugar reviewed in Chapter 4 was cosponsored by the USDA and the National Honey Board. A respectable journal published that study; another published what must have been the equally unwelcome results of a project cofunded by Dairy Management, Inc., a clinical trial finding that diets high

TABLE 11.1. Examples of Studies with Favorable Results Funded through Cooperative Agreements with the USDA's Agricultural Research Service, 2014–2018

FOOD OR INGREDIENT	RESULT	FOOD-COMPANY COSPONSOR
Avocados	Improved dietary intake and weight[1]	Hass Avocado Board
Blueberries	Improved cognition in older adults[2]	US Highbush Blueberry Council
Eggs	Effects on heart disease inconclusive[3]	American Egg Board, Egg Nutrition Center
Pears	Improved dietary quality, reduced obesity[4]	Pears Bureau Northwest
Rice	Improved nutrient intake[5]	USA Rice Federation
Salmon, farmed	Reduced cardiovascular risk[6]	Cooke Aquaculture, Canada
Walnuts	Calories overestimated[7]	California Walnut Commission

NOTE: Source notes are located in the "Notes to Tables" on pages 287–290.

in saturated fat (from dairy and other foods) raised blood levels of heart-disease risk factors.[14]

One explanation for the favorable results of industry-funded studies is that professional journals do not like to publish studies with negative results. If a hypothesis does not make sense in the first place, failing to prove it is no great accomplishment; such studies should be and are rejected by peer reviewers and editors. But even when a hypothesis does make sense, journals tend to publish studies with positive results at higher rates.[15] Of this "publication bias," David Katz, director of the Yale-Griffin Prevention Research Center, explained in an email that it has nothing to do with who pays for the studies: "We ran the first ever placebo-controlled trial of an intravenous nutrient mix widely used to treat fibromyalgia, funded by NIH. The methods were state-of-the-art. The results, however, were negative. . . . We found it nearly impossible to publish the paper, settling for a rather low-impact journal. . . . It is VERY difficult to publish negative results, regardless of funding source."[16]

Publication bias can drive the direction of research if scientists believe they need positive results to publish in high-impact journals.[17] But at least one investigation of this effect concludes that study design is a more important factor. When negative studies are designed well—meaning that they ask important questions, test them rigorously, and interpret their results fairly—journals publish them at the same rate as those with positive results. Unconscious influence is a better explanation for the positive results predicted by industry funding. The various rationales offered for its value ignore the large body of evidence for the power of funding effects.

The Rationales: Conflict of Interest (COI) Bingo

These justifications are stated so frequently that Daniel Goldberg, professor of public health ethics at the University of Colorado, Denver, considers them ripe for satire. Typical rationales, he says, "suggest no familiarity whatsoever with the substantial evidence base regarding motivated bias and its impact on human behavior. . . . Any reasonable attempt to justify deep relationships with commercial industries must begin by acknowledging the evidence rather than trotting out tired justifications that have mostly been contradicted by the evidence."[18]

Goldberg must have been especially inspired by the exposé of the Global Energy Balance Network in the *New York Times*, because the next day he tweeted this message: "I'm so tired of insipid rationalizations given for deep conflicts of interest, I made this handy #COIBingo chart." He later explained that the chart, reproduced in Figure 11.1, grew out of his exasperation with having to listen repeatedly to the same tired excuses for financial ties to industry.[19]

Although I have mentioned some of these reasons in previous chapters, a few deserve further emphasis or more critical examination. We have already seen how "Money doesn't influence me," and

COI BINGO

Sponsorship is required to bring in top experts	Don't throw the baby out with the bathwater	It's just a pen	Scientists control the work	Sponsor has no influence
It's an educational gift	My patients/ the data always takes precedence	Science speaks for itself	We're in charge	It's easier to work with than oppose industry
It's more complex than that	Studies are expensive	**CREAM*** FREE SPACE	This is not corrupt	Do you want to impede progress?
We're fully transparent	Money doesn't influence me	That is just an oversight	This is just a consulting relationship	Innovation
Management is sufficient	Disclosure is sufficient	No evidence of causation	How dare you	Scientific integrity means everything to me

COIbingocards

*(cash rules everything around me)

FIGURE 11.1. Professor Daniel Goldberg's satirical Conflict of Interest (COI) Bingo card lists the rationales commonly used to justify financial ties to industry. These justifications ignore the large body of research demonstrating the profound influence of industry funding on the design, interpretation, and outcome of research. The word "CREAM" in the center Free Space stands for "Cash Rules Everything Around Me," a reference to a 1993 rap song by the Wu-Tang Clan. Reproduced from Goldberg DS, "COI bingo," *BMJ* 2015, 351:h6577, ©2015, with permission from BMJ Publishing Group Ltd.

"Sponsor has no influence" are countered by substantial evidence to the contrary. Funding effects are real but typically occur at an unconscious level.[20] Goldberg despairs at the lack of recognition of these effects. The evidence exists; scientists ought to know about it.

But they often do not. Let us look at the one rationale that I myself invoke: "It's more complex than that." This rationale gives me a chance to say once again that industry funding does not inevitably bias research or opinion. While I was working on this book, I met Susan Jebb, a highly respected nutrition scientist at Oxford University who sometimes does research funded by food companies. When the UK government appointed her to lead its "responsibility deal," a partnership with industry to improve public health, the British press harshly criticized her industry connections. The *BMJ* reported that she had conducted at least ten industry-funded projects between 2004 and 2015 with a total value of £1.37 million; some of her funders were industry partners in the responsibility deal. The *BMJ* particularly noted that she was one of several investigators on a clinical trial funded by Coca-Cola to discover whether a diet drink containing green-tea extract, fiber, and caffeine would promote weight loss. The trial found that it did not, a rare example of an industry-funded study with unfavorable results.[21] But why do a study like this in the first place? Jebb explained to the *BMJ*,

> Personally, I am pleased that this was tested by independent scientists and not the company themselves and that the results of this research are now in the public domain. . . . Everything I do, whether in my research or as chair of the responsibility deal, is to try to improve public health. I do think that requires discussions with the food industry, and I think it is appropriate that we should be encouraging them to invest in research conducted by independent scientists.[22]

In an op-ed piece in the *Guardian*, Jebb argued for making a distinction between industry funding of research conducted by independent investigators and personal payments to individuals for consulting or advising.[23] Does this distinction hold? Jebb may be an example of a scientist who is not influenced by funding source. But regardless of her personal integrity, her acceptance of industry funding *appeared* to be a conflict of interest. Unfair? Perhaps. Complicated? Definitely. With complexities in mind, let us move on to some of the other rationales.

"Don't throw the baby out with the bathwater" refers to the contention we just heard from Jebb that industry funding, at least with appropriate safeguards, is a public good—needed, useful, and with no undesirable effects. GEBN founder James Hill says industry and academia *should* collaborate: "Whereas academia specializes in the front end of the continuum, the research end, specifically the ideation and testing of research hypotheses to improve peoples' lives, industry specializes in the back end of the continuum, or the implementation end, evaluating, marketing, and selling the results of research to profit from improving peoples' lives. By working together on that continuum, academia and industry can help better achieve each other's mission."[24]

Others agree and suggest that the pejorative term "conflict of interest" should be replaced by the less confrontational "*confluence of interest*."[25] Because the purpose of research is to benefit individuals and society, this rationale views researchers, universities, and industry as stakeholders with common interests in the same research system. Katz, who writes frequently about such matters, suggests some caveats. To ensure confluence rather than conflict, the "rules of research engagement must apply. The researchers must be authorized to publish results be they favorable or unfavorable to the company's interests. The researchers must be autonomous; methods must defend against bias; and there can be no *quid pro quo*."[26]

In debates on industry funding of research, defenders point to areas of basic research in which food-company interests align with public health interests, such as efforts to reduce salt, sugar, and fat in foods and to identify the benefits of vitamins and minerals. Perhaps, but the inherently divergent goals of public health and industry make alignment difficult. Corporations, devoted as they must be to maximizing shareholder value, tend to push the research agenda in the direction of studies likely to contribute to profits. They have much less interest in funding investigator-initiated basic research.[27]

"How dare you" expresses the outrage I often hear from defenders of industry funding who react to any discussion of these issues as a personal, ad hominem attack. This too has a history. In 1993, when many medical and scientific journals had begun to require disclosures of conflicts of interest, the Harvard epidemiologist Kenneth Rothman accused their editors of McCarthyism, of negating "the principle that a work should be judged solely on its merits. By emphasizing credentials, these policies foster an ad hominem approach to evaluating science . . . abridging the right of honest scientists to an impartial hearing of their work."[28]

I have a more recent, personal example. In response to one of my blog posts about industry-funded studies, a reader, identified only as "Ombudsman," posted this sarcastic comment: "We all owe a debt of gratitude to Dr. Marion Nestle, professor at New York University, for selflessly delivering a massive trove of conflict of interest charges impugning more than 400 of her colleagues in the field of nutrition research. In so doing whistleblower Nestle bravely exposes inexcusable failures by unnamed peer reviewers of some 70 separate papers to properly vouchsafe professional ethics and scientific integrity."[29] The anonymous writer followed this by listing the names of 409 individuals whose integrity I allegedly impugned but whose connection to the five posted abstracts I still cannot figure out.

"Ombudsman" undoubtedly would agree with obesity researcher David Allison, who discloses considerable funding by food companies but views it as scientifically irrelevant: "We should reject ad hominem reasoning when we judge the quality of evidence, including judging research by its funding source. In science, three things are relevant: the data, the methods that generated the data . . . and the logic that connects the data to the conclusions. We should do everything we can to strengthen the rigor and transparency of those three things, and any focus on ad hominem attacks is not only uncivil, but also unscientific."[30]

Are concerns about the well-documented effects of industry funding uncivil, ad hominem, and unscientific? I think not. They do, however, raise questions about a system in which food companies deliberately engage university faculty in their marketing objectives and in which biased research, loss of trust, misleading advice and the appearance of undue influence occur as a result. Occasionally, the outrage seems hypocritical. Consider, for example, a 2017 editorial signed by ten researchers who plead with fellow scientists to speak out against ad hominem attacks, arguing that "there is a common—indeed, near universal—view that those who are linked with for-profit companies are heavily conflicted whereas those employed in public or academic institutions, generally speaking are not." They insist that "the critics themselves should also be required to disclose financial and non-financial sources of potential bias." These authors did not disclose their own.[31]

The corollary of concerns about ad hominem attacks is that the funding source is irrelevant to the science: "Science speaks for itself" and "Scientific integrity means everything to me." Jeffrey Drazen, editor of the *New England Journal of Medicine*, presented the "Only science counts" argument in a debate in the *New York Times*: "It is not who pays for the research, it is the trial design, execution and open reporting that lead to research integrity. We should focus on these factors, not on the sources of research support."[32] A writer in the *Guardian* says, "What's especially annoying is that the 'who funded it?' question—often by people with axes to grind—overrides the inquiries that the public rightly ask. 'What do we actually know?' 'Do scientists agree on this?' 'Is this a proper study and how can I tell?'"[33] These are indeed important questions, but the conduct of the science is rarely an issue in industry-funded studies. On balance, the "Science is science" argument confirms the point of the COI Bingo card. It fails to acknowledge evidence demonstrating that industry funding biases research and opinion.

"Do you want to impede progress?" suggests that attempts to manage conflicts of interest will stifle innovation. If I may quote Katz again from his confluence discussion: "A blithe, dismissive, and undifferentiating contempt for industry funded research is contempt for virtually all advancement in modern pharmacotherapy, immunization, and medical technology—all of which are applied daily to the relief of miseries, and the extension of countless lives." Maybe so, but unmanaged industry funding creates risks that can well outweigh benefits.[34]

Nonfinancial Bias: A Non–Conflict of Interest

I wish that Goldberg had included an additional statement in his COI Bingo card, the one I hear most frequently in connection with funding from the food industry: "Nonfinancial interests are just as biasing." The most forceful exposition of this rationale appears in a commentary by M. B. Cope and David Allison. Both disclose multiple financial connections to food companies but argue that intellectual and ideological beliefs and the desire for career advancement are even more biasing than funding source. Personal beliefs, they say, "fueled by feelings of righteous zeal, indignation toward certain aspects of industry or other factors" constitute what they call "white hat bias," a term they define as "the distortion of information in the service of righteous ends."[35]

Sandro Galea, dean of the school of public health at Boston University, describes a typology of nonfinancial conflicts that includes career goals and ideological beliefs but also "network-based" biases resulting from commitments to particular methods of investigation. He cites nutritional epidemiology as an example. Scientists in this field, he says, "can advance their career through publishing articles that promote the interests of nutritional epidemiology . . . with researchers having an incentive to design, conduct, and publish work that reinforces what is network normative and being less likely to publish work that does not do so."[36]

The Stanford statistician John Ioannidis charges that nonfinancial interests raise concerns about scientific integrity and that scientists' beliefs in particular theories or in their own research results—and their need for grants or career advancement—bias their research agendas.[37] With respect to nutrition research, Ioannidis goes even further. Observational research in nutrition, he says, is so subject to ideological biases that nutrition scientists who write about such matters ought to be disclosing their beliefs in the benefits of "a vegan diet, the Atkins diet, a gluten-free diet, a high animal protein diet, specific brands of supplements, and so forth."[38] In other words, Ioannidis wants *dietary* disclosures in addition to financial disclosures. Here is mine. As anyone who knows me can tell you, I love food, am an omnivore, and practice what I preach: a largely but not exclusively plant-based diet that occasionally includes junk foods and often includes sweets—in moderation, of course.

Perhaps in response to such pressures, *Nature* journals announced that beginning in February 2018, they would expect authors to disclose nonfinancial as well as financial competing interests. These, it said, could include "a range of personal and/or professional relationships with organizations and individuals, including membership of governmental, non-governmental, advocacy or lobbying organizations, or serving as an expert witness." Their rationale for this requirement? "Transparent disclosures that allow readers to form their own conclusions about the published work are the best way to maintain public trust."[39] I occasionally do peer reviews for *Public Health Nutrition*. This journal now asks its peer reviewers to disclose nonfinancial as well as financial interests, which it specifies as personal relationships, academic competition, political, ideological, religious, or scientific preconceptions, and organizational or institutional affiliations.

These kinds of nonfinancial disclosures make no sense to me. Career goals, intellectual interests, political views, and dietary ideology can indeed bias research, but I see clear distinctions between personal and professional biases and financial biases. Invocation of white-hat bias and requirements for nonfinancial disclosures strike me as defenses of industry funding and as ways to cast doubt on the far-better-documented effects of financial conflicts. In my experience, *all* researchers—at least the good ones—are passionate about their science. All good scientists want to get grants, produce exciting results, publish in prestigious journals, advance in their careers, win national and international recognition, and take satisfaction in knowing that their work makes a valuable contribution to knowledge or society.

When I was a graduate student in molecular biology at Berkeley, resisting pressures to produce desired results was such an integral and insistent part of our training that we had a joke about it, the ironic "Never repeat an experiment that works on the first try." As students, we were supposed to try to catch each other in having missed controlling for some alternative explanation for our results. My doctoral adviser insisted that I endlessly repeat experiments before he would sign off on them. I now see that this system was designed expressly to overcome our human tendencies to favor the findings we wanted and to ignore those that were inconvenient. Most scientists are well aware of pressure-to-succeed biases, do everything they can to account for them, and address the limitations of their studies in their publications. Institutions manage these human tendencies with institutional review boards, audits, education, and ethical standards.[40]

I can think of three reasons why financial interests merit separate consideration from nonfinancial interests. First, nonfinancial interests are *intrinsic* to the research enterprise. All scientists want to demonstrate that their hypotheses are correct. All want to advance professionally. It is impossible to eliminate personal, intellectual, and ideological beliefs and goals and still do science. In contrast, avoiding financial conflicts merely requires not taking the money.

Second, nonfinancial biases are deeply inconsistent; they depend on individual beliefs, desires, and hypotheses that vary enormously from one investigator to another. Science benefits from these differences, and they do not constitute conflicts. But financial ties consistently bias research outcomes to favor the sponsor. As the editors of *PLoS Medicine* summarize these distinctions, financial ties to industry are optional, a matter of personal choice, unnecessary to scientific progress, and well established to influence the design, execution, interpretation, and conclusions of research.[41]

Third, ideological and intellectual biases can usually be deduced from a study's hypothesis—what it is trying to prove. But financial biases are only obvious when they are disclosed. For these reasons, legal scholar Marc Rodwin views the focus on nonfinancial interests as compromising the law's definitions of conflicts of interest, journalist Tim Schwab points out that this focus greatly benefits industry, and Lisa Bero sees the idea of white-hat bias as a "red herring" aimed at deflecting attention from the need to reduce, manage, and disclose financial conflicts.[42]

Bero's comment about disclosure takes us to two more statements in the COI Bingo card: "We're fully transparent" and "Disclosure is sufficient." In response to one of my published commentaries on conflicts of interest, a reader wrote, "I would argue that research supported by industry groups and trade associations can be on par with that funded by other sources, provided that the proposals undergo rigorous scientific peer review . . . the study design, methods and goals are clearly stated upfront, funding sources are clearly stated, and the results submitted for review and publication in recognized scientific journals."[43] That may well be, but evidence to date provides little reassurance that these measures are sufficient to counter the unconscious and unrecognized effects of industry funding. Few institutions have measures in place to deal adequately with financial influences, not least because the conflicts cannot be observed, let alone dealt with, unless they are disclosed.[44] If anything, the COI Bingo card's "It's more complex than that" also describes the situation with disclosure, a topic so complicated that it merits a chapter on its own.

12

Disclosure—and Its Discontents

WHEN I ACCEPT SPEAKING INVITATIONS, I EXPECT THE HOST to pay travel expenses and an honorarium. If I am invited by a food company, I donate the honorarium to my NYU department or the university's library. But I do not enjoy talking about any of this. Talking about personal finances is always uncomfortable in our society, but with respect to ties to food companies, disclosure can also have unpleasant consequences: public exposure, ridicule, loss of trust and opportunities, and the like. I can well understand why scientists resist disclosure requirements, especially when they have extensive financial ties to disclose.

I learned about disclosure and its discomforts the hard way. In the mid-1990s, I edited a collection of papers on Mediterranean diets for the *American Journal of Clinical Nutrition*. The papers appeared as a separate supplement paid for by the International Olive Oil Council (IOOC) through a grant to Oldways Preservation & Exchange Trust, a group devoted to promoting the taste and health benefits of traditional diets and their principal foods and ingredients—olive oil conveniently among them.[1] The IOOC was Oldways' principal sponsor at the time.

Oldways conferences, typically held in olive-growing countries, brought together food writers, chefs, restaurateurs, and academics to learn about the benefits of Mediterranean diets and, of course, the benefits of olive oil. The food professionals I met at these conferences wanted to know more about the history and role of food in society as well as the science behind diet and health. I remain grateful to Oldways for introducing me to the greater food community, not least because these conversations directly inspired the development of food studies programs at New York University.

With Walter Willett of the Harvard School of Public Health, I cochaired Oldways's first international conference on diets of the Mediterranean in 1993. Many speakers raised provocative questions about the definition of these diets, their relevance for people living outside the region, the health effects of olive oil and other components, and the effects of following Mediterranean diet patterns on food production systems. I thought the conference talks were exceptionally interesting and deserved publication, and I volunteered to take on editing responsibilities. At the time, it did not occur to me that sponsorship by the IOOC and Oldways would influence the publication's credibility, or mine. The authors were not paid and neither was I. But the journal's editor, Norman Kretchmer, set me straight. The IOOC had an economic interest in promoting sales of olive oil. Oldways was a partner in that goal. This supplement had commercial implications.

Journal supplements generate revenue for their publishers (the one I worked on cost about $20,000). Because sponsors pay for them, they can be considered advertising, which is why supplement page numbers are identified by the letter s. In part to protect me, Kretchmer insisted on a rigorous external peer review, refused to publish one paper he thought lacking in academic quality, and demanded full disclosure on the title page: "Sponsor: Oldways Preservation & Exchange Trust through a grant from The International Olive Oil Council, Administrator of the United Nations Olive and Olive Oil

Agreement." Authors did not disclose competing interests; this journal did not require such statements until 2002.

As published, the papers presented academically rigorous arguments for the benefits of Mediterranean diets, but they also raised critical questions—evidently too critical. That 1995 journal supplement ended my relationship with Oldways; I was not invited to another of its conferences for the next twenty years. Ironically, on the basis of subsequent, universally favorable research, the United Nations Educational, Scientific and Cultural Organization (UNESCO) placed the Mediterranean diet on its "Representative List of the Intangible Cultural Heritage of Humanity" in 2013, and the 2015 US dietary guidelines promote this diet as one of three exemplary eating patterns. But lesson learned: when work is funded by industry or an industry-funded group, it needs to promote industry interests unambiguously if the relationship is to continue.

Disclosure Policies

Journals have responded to the all-too-human reluctance to expose financial ties by making disclosure requirements increasingly explicit. Today, most scientific and health-professions journals, including nutrition journals, require authors to say who paid for their research and to declare any financial relationships they might have with relevant funders. Table 12.1 summarizes the ways food companies contribute to both categories. They can pay for all or part of the research expenses or can merely donate products to be tested in a study (vitamin supplements, for example). Financial ties to investigators include a longer list of possibilities. Full funding is likely to be more influential than partial funding, but even small contributions can exert influence, as we have seen.

By now, most professional journals follow the disclosure guidelines of the International Committee of Medical Journal Editors (ICMJE). This group provides a model disclosure form, which asks authors to say whether they or their institutions received payment or services from a third party at any time for any aspect of the submitted work,

TABLE 12.1. Funding by Food, Beverage, or Supplement Companies: A Taxonomy

Research support
Complete support
Partial support
Donation of products or materials
Participation in some or all of the research process

Researchers' financial ties
Salary
Stock ownership
Patent ownership
Consulting
Service on advisory committee or board
Service as expert witness or advocate
Honoraria for speaking, writing, or participation
Travel funds, lodging, meals

specified as "including but not limited to grants, data monitoring board, study design, manuscript preparation, statistical analysis, etc." With respect to competing interests, the ICMJE questions cover the preceding three years and ask about patents or other "relationships or activities that readers could perceive to have influenced, or that give the appearance of potentially influencing," what appears in the submitted work.[2]

Journals have considerable leeway in applying these guidelines. I have written occasional commentaries for *JAMA Internal Medicine*, which, like other journals in the *JAMA* network, demands especially diligent adherence to disclosure policies.[3] In 2016, an editor asked that I verify the accuracy of my disclosure; its policy requires authors to list all "potential conflicts of interest, including relevant financial interests, activities, relationships, and affiliations" as well as "all financial and material support for the research and the work." The *JAMA* policy is specific about potential conflicts: "employment, affiliation, grants or funding, consultancies, honoraria or payment, speakers' bureaus, stock ownership or options, expert testimony, royalties, donation of medical equipment, or patents planned, pending, or issued with any organization or entity with a financial interest in or financial conflict with the subject matter or materials discussed in the manuscript."[4]

The American Society for Nutrition (ASN) has uniform disclosure policies for authors and editors of all its publications. Its guidelines apply not only to authors but also to their close relatives—spouses, children, siblings, in-laws—and are also highly specific about the ways in which potential conflicts might occur:

- Serving as an officer, director, member, owner, trustee, or employee of an organization . . . or as an expert witness, advisor, consultant, or public advocate (with or without compensation) on behalf of an organization with a financial interest in the outcome;
- Receiving support, including grants, contracts or subcontracts, fellowships, consulting agreements, or gifts (e.g., chemicals, experimental diets, trips) . . . during the time the research was conducted, or over the past 3 years;
- Being employed; having rights to patent applications, patents, sales, licensing, or royalty agreements; serving on an advisory board or speakers' panel; or owning shares in a company or organization that may gain or lose financially.[5]

Even though ASN has strict disclosure guidelines, its journals publish many studies sponsored by food companies. How is this possible? The guidelines make it clear that editors do not see it as their job to prevent or manage authors' conflicts of interest: "The disclosure of a potential conflict of interest does not necessarily exclude an article from consideration for publication; the goal of disclosure is transparency." Transparency is good. Management—taking action to minimize the hazards of the disclosed financial ties—would be better but would require editors (some with financial ties of their own) to deal with awkward personal and professional issues.

ASN applies its guidelines to peer reviewers as well as editors. Its requirements for supplement guest editors are even more stringent: "Supplement coordinators must disclose all compensation from the sponsor for editorial services on manuscripts published in the supplement publication and/or for attending, speaking at, or organizing a meeting or symposium, including reimbursements for travel expenses." Had these guidelines been in place when I edited the supplement on the Mediterranean diet, I and all the other authors would have had to disclose our participation in the Oldways conferences and our paid travel and meals. Our nonfinancial level of commitment to Mediterranean diet practices should have been evident from our articles.

Avoiding embarrassing disclosures is one reason for not getting involved in financial relationships with food companies in the first place.[6] My current conflict-of-interest declaration says, "Professor Nestle's income from New York University's retirement plan and a small stipend support her research, manuscript preparation, and website at FoodPolitics.com. She also earns royalties from books and honoraria from lectures to university and non-profit groups about matters relevant to this publication."

I had to go into much greater detail on the federal disclosure form I filled out as an external reviewer of an early draft of the 2015 dietary guidelines. Completing this form was a tortuous exercise involving hours of looking up federal tax returns and reviewing my annual NYU faculty activities reports to try to recall all my consultant fees, lecture honoraria, payments for articles, book royalties, and travel and hotel reimbursements during the required three-year period. The form also demanded a statement of intellectual interests. For this, I explained that dietary guidelines are one of my major research and professional interests, that I had been a member of the 1995 Dietary Guidelines Advisory Committee, and that I wrote about the history, development, and politics of dietary guidelines in the 1988 *Surgeon General's Report on Nutrition and Health*, in articles published in the 1990s, and in my books *Food Politics* and *What to Eat*. I also disclosed that I had been writing about the 2015 dietary guidelines process on my blog and was frequently interviewed and quoted by reporters about that process. My views were no secret. I was appointed anyway, presumably because the agencies wanted my input.

Disclosure Discontents

With respect to disclosure demands, I try to do the best I can with what feels even to me as intrusively personal. I am guessing that most other nutrition professionals also try to do the best they can. But much evidence exists that some investigators are so uncomfortable or offended by disclosure requirements that they forget to comply or do so reluctantly, with overkill, or with sarcasm.

Not everyone discloses, and many disclosures are incomplete. The Integrity in Science project run by CSPI documented frequent nondisclosure in leading medical and scientific journals. More recently, Lisa Bero and her colleagues reported that one-third or more of authors in the studies they examined had undisclosed conflicts and that a similar percentage of published reviews omit statements of funding sources. An analysis of Coca-Cola's transparency initiative found a smaller, but still significant percentage; 17 percent of its funded researchers did not disclose the funding.[7]

To pick just one example: researchers later involved with Coca-Cola's GEBN coauthored a study questioning the validity of the National Health and Nutrition Examination Survey (NHANES), a major source of data linking sugary drink consumption to weight gain and its consequences. Their conclusion and its implication: NHANES data are physiologically implausible and should be ignored. The authors provided no funding or conflict-of-interest statements, but word must have gotten out. Two days after publication, the journal ran a correction listing the authors' financial ties to food companies and this statement: "Funding for the study was provided by an unrestricted research grant from The Coca-Cola Company."[8]

In my year of collecting industry-funded studies, I posted one with the longest disclosure statement I had ever seen—nearly two full pages of printed text. Nine of the study's sixteen authors reported not only a breathtaking array of financial ties to food companies but also payments that looked irrelevant: honoraria from the USDA, travel support from professional societies, spouses' employment, and a sister's grant for a cookbook.[9] This seemed like overkill. I wondered if the authors were mocking disclosure requirements, and I wrote the editor of the journal to ask whether its policies required such extensive revelations. He replied, "We give our authors considerable freedom and leeway regarding disclosures. This is easier for an online journal as page length is not a limitation. For the manuscript in question, the authors provided this level of disclosure of their own accord and we accepted it."[10]

I wrote about the statement on my blog.[11] I also sent it to Yoni Freedhoff, who followed up with a consultation with Chris MacDonald, an ethicist colleague. MacDonald said, "To a non-scientist, it reads like a bit of a joke. Maybe the authors are tweaking the noses of the editors, and of those who think disclosure of financial ties is an important thing. . . . Simply dumping information on people is a poor way to satisfy the relevant obligations."[12] Our posts led two of the authors, John Sievenpiper and David Jenkins, to initiate a conference call with us. They explained that this is what the ICMJE requires and that they did not want to be accused of holding back. I suppose scientists with extensive industry ties lack clarity about where to draw the line, but I thought such ties could have been summarized in a sentence or two.

A year later, Sievenpiper participated in a debate published in the *Canadian Journal of Diabetes*, taking the position that sugar does not cause chronic disease. His disclosure statement described support from Canadian foundations and professional associations but did not mention his financial ties to the sugar, corn sweetener, and soda companies itemized in that earlier disclosure. The journal published a correction beginning with "The publisher regrets . . ."[13] Not following guidelines for disclosure sometimes leads to more serious consequences. My failure to insist on a coauthor's full disclosure of potential conflicts of interest was the offense most responsible for our having to retract our article, an experience I would rather have avoided.[14]

The late David Sackett, considered the "father of evidence-based medicine," suggested another way to take care of requirements he must have found objectionable. In a post on the *BMJ*'s website, he wrote, "David Sackett has been wined, dined, supported, transported, and paid to speak by countless pharmaceutical firms for over 40 years, beginning with two research fellowships and interest-free loans that allowed him to stay to finish medical school."[15]

The purpose of disclosure is to alert reviewers or readers to the need to consider potential biases. If authors do not disclose industry affiliations and those affiliations are revealed later, it can look as if the authors are hiding something. The appeal of disclosure requirements is that they recognize conflicts of interest as a problem and suggest a mechanism for dealing with them—avoidance. But like much else about conflicted interests, disclosure issues are complicated. Disclosure can have unintended consequences. Among physicians, it sometimes produces perverse effects. Disclosure has been shown to encourage physicians to provide even more biased advice, to reinforce their feelings of immunity from industry influence, and to justify being influenced on the grounds that people have been warned. Patients sometimes have more—not less—trust in advice that discloses industry funding.[16]

But the most serious pitfall of disclosure is that it gives the impression of taking care of the bias problem and eliminating the need to do anything about it. Most American colleges and universities require faculty to file annual conflict-of-interest statements disclosing financial ties to corporate entities (mine certainly does), and some institutions take this requirement seriously. Cornell University's policy, for example, is noteworthy for its explicit penalties for noncompliance. Researchers who do not submit disclosure forms by a specific date may no longer act as principal investigators, accept grants, receive salary from grants, get salary raises, or, if untenured, continue as a faculty member.[17]

One reason why academic institutions, professional journals, and government agencies have adopted disclosure requirements is that they are relatively easy to implement, are only minimally disruptive, and make individuals—not their institutions—responsible for preventing, managing, or eliminating conflicted work. This leads some writers to argue that there is only one effective method for dealing with industry-induced conflicts: ban the funding. Banning, however, ignores the financial benefits of partnerships and the realities of the current research-funding environment. Attractive as the idea might be in theory, it is unlikely to happen in practice. The best that can be done to deal with conflicted interests is to disclose them but also to manage their potential pitfalls. Disclosure is helpful, says Bero, but it is not a panacea.[18]

At the moment, disclosure requirements are widespread, but compliance, enforcement, and management are highly inconsistent. Plenty of scientists still view disclosure demands as akin to McCarthyism. Plenty are distressed by efforts to make disclosure even more transparent through new PubMed policies or FOIA requests. PubMed.gov is a searchable database run by the US National Library of Medicine and NIH. Since 1997 the site has provided free access to the abstracts and, sometimes, the full texts of nearly 27 million scientific papers. In 2016, CSPI organized a letter signed by sixty-two interested scientists (including me) to those agencies asking them to list information about funding and competing interests along with the published abstracts. Five US senators also urged such disclosure. A year later, PubMed quietly announced that it would henceforth add this information when publishers provided it, although it would not add the disclosures to abstracts already released.[19]

I wished this decision had come sooner. The *Journal of Nutrition* has included funding information with abstracts for years, but most nutrition journals do not. To find disclosure statements for most of the articles mentioned in this book, I had to log on to NYU's online library, search for the journal, and find the article I wanted to see—a tedious and sometimes futile process. If NYU did not subscribe to the journal or if the journal's listings were incomplete, I had to order the articles through interlibrary loan. PubMed's decision should make this process much easier—if publishers start providing the information with their abstracts (I saw little sign of their doing so by mid-2018). Nevertheless, this was an important decision; it indicated that NIH considers disclosure fundamental to the scientific enterprise. CSPI and the senators issued congratulatory statements.[20]

FOIA Discontents

Disclosure remains a contentious topic, but FOIA requests for emails from academic researchers are even more contentious. Many states have their own public-records laws, which are variations of the federal FOIA. These allow any citizen to request copies of documents— including emails—produced by government agencies and employees. Researchers who work for state universities are subject to these laws.[21]

Although Congress passed FOIA to promote transparency as a means of countering government corruption, its success in achieving that goal is hotly debated. Critics complain about the frustrations of the FOIA process: government agencies take years to release documents and redact them excessively.[22] Are FOIA or open-records requests a way to shine light on otherwise-hidden food-industry influence? Or are they instead methods for harassing scientists whose work or opinions the requester dislikes? As I see it, the answer depends entirely on one's point of view about how the requests are framed, their purpose, and whose emails are targeted. I have no personal stake here. I retired from a private university exempt from such requests.

But I am impressed by how much we now know about food-industry methods from emails obtained through open-records requests to public universities. Coca-Cola's strategies for engaging researchers are only one example. On the other hand, if you are a researcher subject to a FOIA request, you might have quite a different view. You might consider FOIA an attack on science. You might think FOIA legitimate in theory but view it as enabling witch hunts, especially when FOIA requests are used as fishing expeditions into private correspondence.[23] That, contrary to expectation, is the view of the Union of Concerned Scientists (UCS), a group that has long advocated for transparency in science. UCS characterizes FOIA as "freedom to bully." It complains that "well-heeled special interests across the political spectrum . . . companies, organizations, and activists [who] may disagree with researchers' findings" are using these requests to harass scientists by going after "all materials on a topic in a university's possession, including researchers' draft papers, emails, and even handwritten notes." Strategies like these, UCS says, "can curb the ability of researchers to pursue their work, chill their speech, and discourage them from tackling contentious topics."[24]

UCS's principal concern is harassment of researchers by industry. It notes that two-thirds of open-records requests come from corporations, and it particularly objects to the chemical and fossil fuel industries' use of FOIA to harass environmental and health researchers who report harm from their products. UCS has produced a guide to help scientists respond to FOIA attacks.[25] Andrew Rosenberg, who directs the Center for Science and Democracy at UCS, insists that the group is not entirely opposed to FOIA requests. His group views inquiries aimed at specific targets as justifiable—those related to Coca-Cola and the GEBN, for example. Rosenberg says UCS objects only to fishing expeditions aimed at harassment, and he argues that FOIA should not be used as the primary means of exposing scientists' financial ties. Although UCS calls for clear and consistent policies regarding transparency in science, it makes no suggestions for what those might be.

Arguments about use of FOIA create a dilemma. Policies that block corporations from obtaining scientists' emails also block requests from public health advocates. Paul Thacker, a journalist who advocates for transparency in corporate research funding, views the UCS report as part of a backlash against transparency initiatives. He sees the benefits of transparency as greatly exceeding its costs. Thacker and NYU journalism professor Charles Seife wrote an article critical of UCS's position: "So long as scientists receive government money, they are subject to government oversight; so long as their work affects the public, journalists and other watchdogs are simply doing their jobs when they seek out possible misconduct and questionable practices that could threaten the public interest."[26] Their article appeared on the *PLoS Biologue* blog but was so forcefully challenged that *PLoS* deleted it on the grounds that the criticisms were "not consistent with at least the spirit and intent of our community guidelines."[27]

That article and others provide compelling examples of the value of open-records requests for exposing corporations' engagement with scientists, and scientists' cooperation with corporate interests. Thacker points out that it is only through emails obtained via FOIA that we know how pharmaceutical companies edit journal articles and prepare testimony for authors, how the National Football League manipulates research on concussions, how Monsanto secretly recruits scientists to advocate for genetically modified foods, and how Coca-Cola attempts to influence high-ranking government officials to minimize concerns about sugars and the role of diet in obesity.[28]

Such exposure works both ways, of course. I am a strong supporter of organic production practices (they use fewer toxic pesticides and do better at regenerating soil), but emails obtained by the *New York Times* show that companies producing organic foods have engaged academic researchers to produce favorable studies, publications, and testimony. Thacker concludes that scientists at public universities have no more right to try to hide their emails than any other public officials, and he points out the hypocrisy of researchers saying they love transparency in science—until it affects them personally.[29]

How you view use of FOIA is most likely to depend on how you feel about its targets. Greenpeace, for example, filed an open-records request to the University of Washington to obtain funding records for a scientist considered to be "a denier of overfishing." Although the scientist had obtained millions of dollars in research funding from many seafood-industry groups over the years, he did not always disclose this in publications. His supporters viewed the request as undeserved, and the scientist used a defense straight out of COI Bingo: "Greenpeace can't attack the science because they don't do science. Instead they attack the messenger."[30]

We have seen that FOIA helps expose industry influence that would not otherwise be known. One last example: a directive in a House appropriations bill to exempt checkoff programs from FOIA requests. The bill says the commodity research and promotion boards overseen by the USDA are not federal agencies and are paid for by producers and industry stakeholders, not taxpayers. On this basis, the appropriations committee wanted the USDA to recognize that checkoff boards are not subject to FOIA.[31]

We can only speculate about which lobbying group might have achieved insertion of that directive, but in 2015, the Associated Press used FOIA to obtain emails from one checkoff, the American Egg Board (AEB). These showed that the AEB was engaged in a coordinated, well-funded campaign to undermine the growth of Hampton Creek, a company making an egg-free mayonnaise substitute called Just Mayo. The AEB thought Just Mayo's threat to egg sales had reached the point of crisis. It attempted to stop Whole Foods Market from selling Just Mayo, pushed Unilever to oppose Hampton Creek, induced the FDA to go after the product's labeling, threatened the company's CEO, paid bloggers to discredit the company, and recruited a crisis-management firm to campaign against the company.[32]

The AEB publicly stated that it had nothing to do with these actions, but the emails contradicted its denials. Eventually, the AEB was unable to stop Hampton Creek. The USDA investigated, chided the AEB for exceeding its mandate, and required ethics training for its members. The AEB's actions did cause some debate over whether checkoffs are government or industry programs. As the Congressional Research Service explained in an analysis of the appropriations-bill provision, the USDA currently considers checkoff boards to be subject to FOIA, but checkoff groups say that FOIA requests divert time and funds away from research and promotion. I told a reporter that the House bill was yet another congressional attempt to protect corporate food interests, no matter how undemocratic the results. FOIA was designed to hold government accountable. Commodity groups are happy to have their checkoff programs run by the USDA when convenient, but they want the programs to be considered nongovernmental and exempt from FOIA. They cannot have it both ways.[33]

Like much else discussed in this book, disclosure issues are complicated. They create personal and professional discomfort and raise questions that are not easily answered. The most difficult questions have to do with how to prevent conflicts of interest or to manage them once they are disclosed. The remaining chapters address those questions, beginning with the history of early management attempts.

Managing Conflicts: Early Attempts

I BEGAN THE RESEARCH FOR THIS BOOK WITH A GREAT DEAL OF curiosity about when nutrition professionals first recognized the need to manage conflicted relationships and when and why the editors of nutrition journals first insisted that authors disclose funding sources and competing interests. I had the impression that concerns about conflicted interests were relatively recent. It never occurred to me that attempts to insulate researchers from undue industry influence began decades ago. Some of the history was readily available, but I had not known about it. Other aspects were only just coming to light through analysis of recently discovered historical documents. Because this history bears directly on today's attempts to manage industry-induced conflicts of interest, it is worth recounting. For our purposes, it begins in the 1940s with The Nutrition Foundation, an organization created for the express purpose of pooling donations from food companies into a common research fund.

The Nutrition Foundation, 1942–1985

In the days before NIH funded basic research, money available for this purpose was limited. Scientists realized that research grants from food companies could compromise their independence and sought ways to accept industry funding while maintaining their integrity and reputations. The solution? The Nutrition Foundation. In 1942, Karl Compton, president of the Massachusetts Institute of Technology, agreed to head the board of trustees of this foundation, which had just been established through donations from fifteen leading food manufacturers, among them Campbell's Soup, General Foods, Quaker Oats, and United Fruit. As he explained, the foundation would create a "strong" and "independent" program to support two kinds of research: basic nutrition research aimed at improving the food, diet, and health of the American public, and applied food-science research to help food companies with technical problems and product development.[1]

I put "strong" and "independent" in quotation marks because they have specific meanings in this context. In the foundation's view, "strong" meant adequately funded. Its funding model was to persuade as many food companies as possible to donate $10,000 a year for five years. Later, it encouraged smaller companies to contribute as little as $500 a year. By 1947, fifty-four food, beverage, and supplement companies had committed to such contributions.

By "independent," the foundation meant firmly separating the funding from the science. To achieve this, it created a scientific advisory committee to take full responsibility for reviewing applications and awarding grants—although decisions had to be approved by the foundation's board of trustees. Because the trustees included food-industry representatives, this requirement should have set off alarm bells. It put the board in a position to control the research agenda, even though its approval process appeared to be pro forma.

We know this from a history of the foundation published in 1976 by Charles Glen King, who ran the scientific advisory committee for years.[2] In his view, "the work of this committee and its rapport with the trustees were of such a quality that no grant recommendation to the board of trustees was denied or restricted in any way during my 21 years of experience as Director or President." This statement should also raise questions about the independence of the advisory committee. If members wanted to remain on it, and if the committee wanted companies to continue donating to the foundation, everyone would need to meet the trustees' and donors' spoken or unspoken expectations. Gifts, as we have seen, create obligations.

Researchers who obtained grants from the foundation could use the money to support graduate students, postdoctoral scholars, or staff and to buy equipment and supplies. The foundation awarded its first grants in 1942: thirty-six awards totaling $123,890. For example, William Rose at the University of Illinois received $3,600; Stanford University's George Beadle got $6,000; Cornell University's Vincent du Vigneaud was awarded $3,800. Small as these grants may seem, they contributed to some highly distinguished careers. Rose went on to win a National Medal of Science, and Beadle and du Vigneaud eventually won Nobel Prizes. The foundation soon increased the amounts; it gave out nearly $2 million to investigators at sixty-two institutions in 1943.[3]

Despite King's protestations of independence, some nutrition scientists must have had doubts. King quotes an unnamed member of a nutrition society as saying, "Of course you will have to scratch the back of your member companies occasionally and do little favors according to their interest!" But King insisted the foundation was not run that way. The foundation's charter specified that "no founder or sustaining member of The Nutrition Foundation, Inc., shall refer to his membership in this corporation in his advertisement of his products; or make any other commercial reference to said membership." King's history quotes a speech given to the foundation's trustees in 1972 by its then president, William Darby: "The Nutrition Foundation must provide leadership of integrity. It will not become a lobbying agency and must remain scientifically detached in debates affecting any particular segment of the food industry."

Nevertheless, some skepticism is in order. Yes, the grant recipients got essential funding, for which they thanked the foundation in their published papers. But surely the food-company donors expected some return on their investment? The foundation's leaders evidently thought so. They established an industry advisory committee that kept member companies apprised of the foundation's work, gave them early information about study results, and provided informal access to leading nutrition scientists. There were, of course, tax advantages. If I am dubious about the claims of independence, it is because the foundation's funding model required repeated commitments from participating companies and, therefore, created ongoing pressures to please.

Over the years, the foundation expanded its activities beyond giving out research grants. From the start, it published its own journal, *Nutrition Reviews* (which still exists), but it gradually took on additional missions. It helped establish similar foundations in other countries, gave awards, published books, funded conferences, and entered into partnerships with other nutrition organizations. Its financial needs grew accordingly.

Pressures to please may well explain why foundation executives sounded so much like representatives of the food industry whenever they made public statements about nutrition and health. Reporters came to view foundation officials as spokesmen for the food industry. In 1962, for example, King told a reporter that Rachel Carson's just-published book *Silent Spring* seemed to be "bordering on hysteria." The reporter identified King as the head of a "research-sponsoring organization largely supported by the food industry."[4] In 1967, Horace L. Sipple, who was then the foundation's executive director, suggested that mothers could fix their families "hot dogs and malted milks or even pizza for breakfast. 'It's better than nothing at all,' he said" (a statement reminiscent of the assertion, decades later, that Froot Loops is better than a doughnut).[5] In 1974, the foundation's president, William Darby, denounced academics concerned about the hazards of agricultural chemicals for their McCarthyite attack on the pesticide industry,[6] and in 1982 he said of the 1980 dietary guidelines, "I don't think we should look at food-stuffs as being dangerous things. . . . If we cut down on animal products such as lean red meats we remove one of our best sources of protein, B vitamins and iron" (a statement that may be scientifically correct but ignores the public health implications of processed meat consumption).[7]

By the time Darby made that statement, nutrition science was changing. Government research funding, which had increased rapidly after the end of World War II, had begun to focus on cancer, heart disease, and other chronic conditions rather than vitamins and minerals. Food companies were closing their basic-research units and shifting resources to marketing. When mergers and acquisitions consolidated the food industry, fewer companies were available to contribute to the foundation's work, and its financial situation deteriorated. In 1985, the foundation solved its financial problems by merging into ILSI, thereby confirming its status as a food-industry front group.[8] The moral: it takes more than pooling funds from food companies to maintain research independence. This moral is also evident from another example: Fred Stare's research fund at Harvard.

The Fred Stare Era at Harvard, 1942–1976

Stare founded the Harvard Department of Nutrition in 1942, chaired it until 1976, and remained involved with it until the 1990s (he died in 2002). In part because he so actively solicited contributions from the food industry and others, Stare also came to be viewed as a front man for the food industry rather than as an independent scientist.

His method for assuring "independence" was to require that all donations be entirely unrestricted. He pooled the contributions into a common Fund for Research and Teaching and, later, into endowment funds. In his autobiography, Stare explained, "It would have been easy to get generous support from the food industry if we would have conducted research on specific food products and hopefully improved them. But we were not a Department of Food Technology or Food Science. My major effort was to convince these leaders of the food industry that they should be willing to provide unrestricted funds for support of basic research . . . in addition to support of food technology which might result in improved products."[9]

He was persuasive—this was Harvard, after all—and the fund grew. By the mid-1950s Stare had already obtained more than forty grants from private sources. Eventually, his sponsors included drug companies, supermarkets, unions, meat companies, sugar companies, fast-food companies, and every imaginable food or beverage trade association, as well as major food, agriculture, and even tobacco companies. From 1942 to 1986, he collected nearly $21 million in unrestricted funds. By 1990, the endowment alone came to more than $9 million and produced an income of $800,000 a year. Stare boasted that these funds accounted for only a fraction of the department's outside support: "In our most productive years (1955–76), government funds averaged 80 percent of our total support and *unrestricted* private funds approximately 20 percent."[10] Stare personally contributed to that 20 percent: "Honoraria, book royalties, and fees from my syndicated columns have all gone to a fund that provides unrestricted support." He explained, "By giving personally to the financial support of the Department, it has been easier to get support from other private sources."

But Stare ran into precisely the same difficulty faced by the Nutrition Foundation: the need to please donors to get ongoing support. For this reason, or perhaps because his personal beliefs coincided with those of his donors, he was widely recognized as a nutrition scientist working on behalf of the food industry. His public statements consistently defended the American diet against suggestions that it might increase the risk of heart or other chronic disease. He, like officials of the Nutrition Foundation, could be counted on to state the industry position on matters of diet and health and to assure reporters and Congress that no scientific justification existed for advice to avoid food additives or eat less sugar.[11]

We now know much more about the depth of Stare's food-industry ties from documents that came to light in 2016 when Cristin Kearns and colleagues at the University of California, San Francisco published an analysis of internal documents of the Sugar

Research Foundation (SRF), the forerunner of today's Sugar Association. The documents included letters between the SRF and Mark Hegsted, a faculty member in Stare's Harvard department, about the SRF's sponsorship of a research review on the effects of dietary carbohydrates and fats on cardiovascular disease. The review, written by Stare, Hegsted, and another colleague, appeared in two parts in the *New England Journal of Medicine* in 1967. The letters show that the SRF not only commissioned and paid for the review but also pressured the Harvard authors to exonerate sugar as a factor in heart disease, then and now the leading cause of death among Americans. Other documents from the mid-1960s demonstrate that the SRF withheld funding from studies suggesting that sugar might be harmful.[12]

I wrote the editorial that accompanied the paper about the Harvard scientists' work; in it, I explained that studies at the time suggested that diets high either in sugar or saturated fat were associated with a higher risk of heart disease.[13] But the SRF wanted scientists to ignore sugar and focus on fats. The Harvard investigators had previously published research implicating *both* sugars and saturated fat as risk factors for heart disease, as their two-part review makes clear. Figure 13.1, which I adapted from their study, compares sugar and saturated fat "consumption" (in reality, amounts in the food supply—a proxy for consumption) to the risk of death in fourteen countries. In those countries, sugar and fat availability are indistinguishably correlated with mortality—an association that suggests but does not prove causation. To strengthen the case against saturated fat, the Harvard investigators appear to have cherry-picked the data by giving far greater credence in their conclusions to studies implicating saturated fat than they did to those implicating sugars.

These authors are all deceased and cannot be asked what they were thinking at the time. Hegsted's role is especially puzzling. He was well-known for developing the "Hegsted equation" for predicting the rise in blood cholesterol that occurs in response to consumption of specified amounts of saturated fat and dietary cholesterol.[14] But he was also revered in the public health community for promoting healthful diets in general, including diets reduced in sugar. As

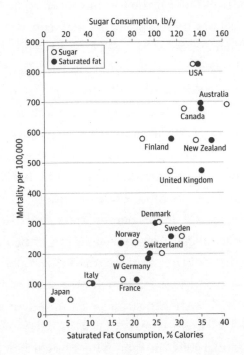

FIGURE 13.1. The close correlation between sugar and saturated fat "consumption" (availability in the food supply) and overall mortality in fourteen countries. Correlation does not necessarily imply causation; a high intake of either sugars or saturated fats also correlates with other dietary and lifestyle factors that can affect mortality. Reproduced with permission from *JAMA Intern Med.* 2016, 176(11):1685–1686, ©2016 American Medical Association. All rights reserved.

he testified in 1977, "The diet of the American people has become increasingly rich—rich in meat, other sources of saturated fat and cholesterol, and in sugar. . . . What are the risks associated with eating less meat, less fat, less saturated fat, less cholesterol, less sugar, less salt, and more fruits, vegetables, unsaturated fat and cereal products—especially whole grain cereals. There are none that can be identified and important benefits can be expected."[15]

Nevertheless, the 1967 reviews dismissed the need to reduce sugar consumption. How important were these papers? It is hard to say. They were not cited among the more than nine hundred references to a book-length report on sugars and health issued by the FDA in 1986 (which concluded that sugars caused tooth decay but not much else). A more recent analysis of the 1960s debates about sugar and fat, which refers to my editorial, ignores the cherry-picking and instead suggests that the focus on sugar-industry funding constitutes a "conspiratorial narrative" obscuring a more complicated history of uncertainty in nutrition science.[16]

Since 1980, US dietary guidelines have consistently called for eating less sugar, although mainly to reduce "empty" (nutrient-free) calories or to prevent tooth decay. Only in 2015 did the guidelines finally advise eating less sugar as part of an eating pattern to reduce risks for chronic disease, the same year that WHO deemed sugar a major risk factor for obesity, type 2 diabetes, and other chronic conditions. With respect to saturated fat and sugar, overall dietary advice remains much the same as it has been since 1980, but the reasons for the advice about sugar have expanded. This expansion may be why the balance of media concern about fat and sugars has shifted. *Time* magazine says scientists were wrong about fat and "butter is back," and journalists write books arguing that sugar causes chronic diseases ranging from obesity and type 2 diabetes to gout and dementia.[17]

Food companies have responded to these trends by trying to remove as much sugar as they can from their products, an example of "nutritionism" in action. This term was coined by the Australian sociologist Gyorgyi Scrinis and popularized by Michael Pollan to describe the reductive use of single nutrients or food components as proxies for dietary patterns that affect disease risk. Sugars and saturated fat are both markers of Western dietary patterns associated with overeating, overweight, obesity, and related chronic diseases. Food companies benefit when dietary advice focuses on single nutrients or foods—it makes marketing easier.[18]

The Nutrition Foundation and Harvard examples show that pooling industry funds is insufficient to avoid conflicts. But these examples illustrate one additional point: the need for disclosure. The 1967 reviews acknowledged support from several government and private sources, among them the Nutrition Foundation and the Harvard Fund, both known—at least to insiders—as funded by industry. But the authors did not mention funding by the SRF. At the time, this omission violated no rules; medical journals did not begin to require disclosures until the 1980s.

Nutrition Journals: Disclosure Policies

From the start, nutrition investigators voluntarily disclosed who paid for their studies. In its first two years of publication, 1928 and 1929, the *Journal of Nutrition* included forty-eight research reports and commentaries, most of them dealing with the effects of vitamins or minerals on rats. Of these, eleven articles acknowledged external funding, mostly from universities or the USDA, but four acknowledged funding from food or drug companies: Northwestern Yeast, Mead Johnson, Eli Lilly, the National Livestock and Meat Board, and General Foods.

For decades, disclosure of funding sources in journal articles remained voluntary. In 1960, a new editor of the *Journal of Nutrition*, Cornell nutrition professor Richard Barnes, added this note to its guidelines for authors: "Financial support should be listed as a footnote to the title. Credit for materials should be listed as a footnote to the text."[19] But "should" referred to where the information should be placed, not to the need to include it. In the late 1960s, when I published my dissertation research, acknowledging sources of funding was expected as a courtesy to the funder or was required by federal granting agencies as a condition for support. My papers included footnotes saying, "This work was supported in part by Research Grant CA 10641 from the National Cancer Institute, United States Public Health Service."[20]

Only in 1990 did the *Journal of Nutrition* introduce new instructions. Authors would henceforth need to provide "a statement of financial or other relationships that might cause conflict of interest."[21] The journal introduced this requirement without explanation. I tracked down several editors listed on the 1990 masthead to ask if they could recall what had prompted the new disclosure requirement.

Robert Cousins, now eminent scholar and director of the Center for Nutritional Sciences at the University of Florida, told me that he and Alfred Merrill had been invited to serve as associate editors by the journal's editor, Willard Visek: "Willard was an MD and attended meetings of medical journal editors. . . . The conflict requirement may have developed from that exposure also. He may also have seen that some authors had ties to industries that could be conflicts."[22] Cousins was referring to meetings of the Council of Biology Editors, now the Council of Science Editors, an organization of editors of about eight hundred science journals.[23] Among these journals was the *New England Journal of Medicine*, which in 1984 became the first to require authors to disclose their ties to drug companies.

The other associate editor, Alfred Merrill, now the Smithgall Institute Professor of Molecular Cell Biology at the Georgia Institute of Technology, recalled that the journal had seen many cases in which papers came from authors who had potential conflicts of interest because of either the funding source or their own affiliations. "Our policy," he said, "was to evaluate the science at face value, and if solid, publish the papers but ensure that issues that were of potential concern (e.g., funding source) were clearly stated. Statement of the funding source seemed important since there were a lot of studies funded by the National Dairy Council and other groups with industry connections." Visek, he added, "was very emphatic that the guiding principle for the journal should be the scientific rigor and not whether what was found would be out of vogue."[24] Merrill mentioned an example to illustrate that point: a study sponsored by the egg industry reporting that cholesterol from any source, not just eggs, raised blood cholesterol levels.

Although Merrill did not give me a specific reference for that study, I could see why he thought of an example like that. In 1993, he had written an editorial about another study sponsored by the egg industry. Egg sales had been declining for forty years by then, and the egg industry was actively sponsoring research to counter advice to reduce cholesterol intake. Merrill's editorial referred to a 1992 study by J. L. Garwin and colleagues of eggs modified to be lower in saturated fat. Garwin's group measured the effects of eating the modified eggs on the blood cholesterol levels of human volunteers. The study, sponsored by the developer of the modified eggs, concluded that people on cholesterol-lowering diets could consume a dozen of these eggs a week with no noticeable effect (not surprising, given that their overall diets counteracted any effect of eggs on blood cholesterol).[25]

Readers wrote letters to the editor objecting to the study's methods and conclusions. One pointed out, "The 'modified' eggs command a premium price in the marketplace that we think is unwarranted, and the fact that this article was published in THE JOURNAL OF NUTRITION could be taken to indicate that the nutrition community accepts the claims of the 'modified' egg producers."[26]

In his editorial, Merrill noted two separate concerns about the egg study: "The first regards the criteria for academic speculation about the possible explanations for experimental observations; the other deals with the possible commercial impact of such speculation. . . . Because various interpretations can be given to statements in any manuscript, it will remain important for authors to identify possible conflicts of interest." He noted that Garwin's article disclosed the funding source but added, "As these issues become more complex, it may be appropriate for THE JOURNAL OF NUTRITION to encourage authors (and reviewers) to identify all sources of possible conflict of interest."[27] But the journal had required precisely this information since 1990, suggesting some concern about whether authors were fully complying. I mention these details because Merrill's 1993 editorial is the *only* discussion of the need for disclosure I can find in any American nutrition journal prior to the 2000s. In contrast, writers in medical journals had been arguing about disclosure issues for many years.

Authors publishing in the *American Journal of Clinical Nutrition* also voluntarily disclosed funding beginning with its inaugural issue in 1952. That first issue contained three reports about the effects of vitamins that acknowledged sponsorship by one or more supplement companies—Merck, Wm. S. Merrill, Chas. Pfizer, Hoffman–La Roche, and Wyeth. Perhaps because of widespread voluntary compliance, this journal's instructions to authors did not mention disclosure until 1981, when it advised acknowledging "the sources of support in the form of grants, equipment, drugs, or all of these." Only in 2002 did the journal add, "Each author is required . . . to disclose any financial or personal relationships with the company or organization sponsoring the research," and it also specified that "such relationships may include employment, sharing in a patent, serving on an advisory board or speakers' panel, or owning shares in the company."[28] I asked D'Ann Finley at the University of California, Davis, a long-serving member of the journal's editorial staff, if she could tell me why the editors had added the statement. She too suggested that editors must have heard these issues discussed at meetings of the Council of Biology Editors and thought they should follow its guidelines.[29]

The *Journal of the American Dietetic Association* (since 2012, the *Journal of the Academy of Nutrition and Dietetics*) published its first issue in 1925 and introduced requirements for funding disclosure in 1992. Instructions that year said, "Authors should also disclose financial support or gifts of equipment or supplies in an acknowledgment" and should make sure that "any financial or other relationships that might cause a conflict of interest have been brought to the attention of the editor." It introduced an ethics statement the next year and, in 1995, a separate conflicts-of-interest section: "Authors must inform the Editor in writing of any financial arrangements, organizational affiliations, or other relationships that may constitute a conflict of interest." Beginning in 2001, the editors' calls for this information became increasingly strident: the instructions that year said, "Authors must inform . . ."; those in 2002 said "authors **must** inform . . . ."[30]

To summarize: two kinds of disclosure statements are at issue here—revealing funding (who paid for the study itself, in part or in total) and revealing competing interests (authors' financial ties to relevant companies). Historically, authors acknowledged funding sources voluntarily. Their failure to do so did not become an issue until food companies began to pay for studies more expressly designed to meet marketing objectives. The journals I have just mentioned began to require disclosure in 1990, 1992, and 2002, respectively. The *Journal of Nutrition Education and Behavior* required disclosure of study funders even earlier—in 1989—but to this day does not require authors to disclose their personal financial conflicts.

This history suggests that some journal editors viewed disclosure as essential; others not so much. But nutrition journals generally lagged behind medical journals in demanding disclosures by authors. This brings us to the present. Disclosure matters but is only the first step in management of conflicts of interest. It is now time to look at what is being done—and what ought to be done—to deal with the conflicts induced by food-industry funding.

Beyond Disclosure: What to Do?

H OW BEST TO PREVENT AND MANAGE THE CONSEQUENCES OF food-company sponsorship? In 2017, *JAMA* devoted an entire issue to conflicts of interest (COIs), those affecting nutrition as well as medical science. Figure 14.1 displays the cover of that issue. Its articles, editorials, commentaries, and patient-education page describe the problems caused by conflicted interests, but the included papers had little to say about how to manage them beyond recognizing that conflicts exist and disclosing them.[1]

We know why food, beverage, and supplement companies fund research partnerships. Nestlé, for example, explains sponsored research as helping its "ambition to become a major partner in solving key societal challenges . . . while simultaneously evolving our food and beverage portfolio."[2] Companies like Nestlé want research aimed at product development, but most such companies also want results that can help counter unfavorable information about their products or promote their benefits. Unfortunately, funding from food

FIGURE 14.1. The cover of the May 2, 2017, issue of JAMA demonstrates that financial conflicts of interest are a highly visible issue—in both medical science and nutrition. The COI (conflict of interest) certificate floating over the list of contents states, "A conflict of interest exists when professional judgment concerning a primary interest (such as patients' welfare or the validity of research) may be influenced by a secondary interest (such as financial gain). Perceptions of conflict of interest are as important as actual conflicts of interest." Used with permission, courtesy of Howard Bauchner, editor-in-chief JAMA and JAMA Network. ©2017 American Medical Association. All rights reserved.

companies can make nutrition scientists' work appear less trustworthy and, sometimes, can make the work less trustworthy.

The issue is not whether nutrition professionals should engage with food companies. Of course we should. The issue is about payment for our engagement. Payments create obligations, some recognized, but some not. Because industry funding is so strongly associated with unconscious biases, collusion with marketing objectives, and silence about public health initiatives, it is worth asking whether nutrition professionals should *ever* accept food-industry funding. And if we do, is there a way to establish guidelines that will help preserve trust and integrity? Are there policies that universities, journals, and professional societies could establish to protect themselves—and the individuals they serve—against risks of bias and threats to reputation?

In theory, preventing conflicts of interest is easy: just say no to the money. But when researchers are under intense pressure to bring in external funding, this approach may seem undesirable or impossible. What should they do? Dealing with the conflicts caused by food-industry funding is best viewed as a three-step process: recognize, disclose, and manage.

The first step is essential: recognize the influence. As we have seen, funding by food companies puts recipients at risk of producing biased research or opinions, appearing to have sold out, being criticized publicly, and losing opportunities to serve on prestigious committees. Recognizing conflicts of interest does not solve the problems they cause, but it establishes a starting point for the struggle to figure out how to avoid or manage them.

I use "struggle" advisedly. Recognition has to be more than superficial. For example, in 2016 I was asked for advice by an obesity-research group at Harvard University about how it should deal with support from food companies. Its invitation explained, "If we are to accept industry funding, we want to have a process in place that maximizes the probability that academics, policy makers, and the public will consider the research valid. We recognize that food-company sponsored research in the area of obesity research is inherently conflicted. Our goal is not to minimize the conflicts; rather it is to be relentlessly transparent."³

I gave high marks to this group for recognizing the problem it faces but a failing grade for assuming that transparency would solve the problem. The lack of commitment to managing the inherent conflicts gave me the impression that these researchers want some magical way to get away with taking industry money without consequences. If nutrition departments and organizations viewed acceptance of industry funding as a cause for serious concern and struggle, they might try harder to establish norms that promoted greater scientific and professional integrity. That kind of cultural shift could also encourage their members to follow such norms.⁴

In a thoughtful commentary in the JAMA COI issue, Dariush Mozaffarian, dean of the Friedman School of Nutrition Science and Policy at Tufts University, mentioned that food companies bias research results, promote harmful products, create misleading marketing campaigns, target children, lobby, co-opt organizations, and attack science and scientists (citing my book *Food Politics* as a reference). He justified acceptance of food-industry support on the basis of the diversity of food companies and the opportunity for nutrition professionals to influence what the companies do and make. He recommended deciding about industry funding case by case on the basis of the suitability of the industry partner, the alignment of goals, the balance of risks and benefits, and the assurance of academic independence and transparency. Ideally, he said, "the industry sponsor should have no role in project design, implementation, analysis, or interpretation." But he noted that in many cases, "the industry partner may wish to provide input to the study design, as well as additional project features; the acceptability of this input should be balanced against the principles summarized previously, with all roles documented in advance. Conversely, the decision to report and publish the findings must be fully retained by the academic partner, and the industry funding must be transparent and fully acknowledged—these principles must not be negotiable."⁵

I am not sure that balancing industry input with such principles can ever minimize unconscious bias; that hypothesis has yet to be tested. I agree that Mozaffarian's nonnegotiable principles for engagement with food companies—independence of the authors' decision to publish and full disclosure of industry ties—are excellent starting points. But I think our profession needs to do a better job of recognizing food-industry influence as a serious problem requiring serious attention to management strategies. We also need to do better about disclosure.

By now, the idea that research integrity requires full disclosure of financial ties ought to be a given. As one of the *JAMA* COI authors put it, "When authors are lax about reporting their relationships or other COIs to editors, and journals publish that authors have nothing to disclose, readers may feel betrayed, critics may be offended, and bloggers and other 'COI watchers' who scour the literature for failures to disclose become energized to expose the breach of trust."[6] Our profession needs to normalize disclosure and make it less uncomfortable and onerous.

Federal agencies try to normalize disclosure by requiring research institutions to maintain and enforce disclosure policies, but the degree of institutional commitment and faculty compliance varies greatly. How might institutions encourage faculty to report financial ties more freely? One suggestion has been to soften the language: replace "conflicts of interest" with "relevant relationships." Universities—some more than others—take disclosure enforcement seriously. As noted earlier, Cornell University informs faculty that "disciplinary measures and sanctions will be imposed when they fail to report as required or when they fail to comply with management plans."[7] But what actually happens when disclosure turns up something questionable? What do institutions actually mean when they talk about managing conflicts of interest?

In 2016, WHO established a management Framework of Engagement with Non-State Actors (FENSA). This grew out of the agency's recognition that conflicts of interest "could be the highest in situations where the interest of non-State actors, in particular economic, commercial or financial, are in conflict with WHO's public health policies, constitutional mandate and interests." The FENSA policy forbids any involvement whatsoever with the tobacco and firearms industries. It requires other industries to demonstrate clear benefits to public health; to support WHO's scientific and evidence-based approaches; to protect WHO's integrity, independence, credibility, and reputation; and to be fully transparent.[8]

This may seem like strong policy, but sixty nongovernmental organizations (NGOs) criticized an earlier draft of the FENSA policy for failing to distinguish between "public interest actors, who are guided by a public health mission, and private entities, guided by market profit-making logic."[9] These groups wanted WHO to ban *all* industry groups from lobbying the agency about anything. WHO, they said, must stop "developing FENSA under contradictory objectives: both as an instrument to attract voluntary financial resources for WHO and, at the same time, as a safeguard to protect its mandate. It can't be done."[10] In 2017, the NGOs called on WHO member states to choose the next WHO director general based on the candidates' commitment to promoting the agency's public health mission free of commercial influence.[11]

FENSA deals exclusively with WHO's official relationships with the food and other industries. It does not apply to industry relations within WHO's member states. But member countries have asked WHO for guidance about how to manage food-company sponsorship of their nutrition programs, particularly those for breast-feeding, product fortification, and childhood overweight. In response, WHO appointed a committee—a "consultation"—to propose guidelines for dealing with industry-induced conflicts in national nutrition policies and programs. The consultation's 2016 report produced these *nonbinding* conclusions and recommendations: Countries have a duty to ensure that food, beverage, and supplement companies do not exert undue influence over public health missions. Countries should assess the risks of engagement with food companies, do what they can to prevent conflicts of interest, and set clear rules for engagement. But advocates argue that these too are insufficient to protect against corporate interests.[12]

Advocates much prefer the clarity—the unambiguity—of WHO's 2016 guidance for managing the inappropriate marketing of foods for infants and young children. In this situation, WHO recommends that member states set policies that do not allow infant-formula companies to donate free samples to health facilities; provide gifts or coupons to health care staff, parents, or families; host events, contests, or campaigns in health care facilities; distribute educational materials to parents; or sponsor meetings of health or science professionals.[13] These management policies imply that workers at health care facilities should not accept gifts from infant-formula companies and that nutrition professionals should not attend meetings sponsored by such companies. This second implication explains why advocates were disappointed in my decision to speak at the Nestlé scientific symposium, an incident I discussed in Chapter 1.

But in the United States, ILSI, which never misses a chance to defend the interests of its member food companies, has taken the lead in setting management guidelines for conflicts of interest. In 2009, ILSI brought together a group of academics, former government officials, and representatives of Coca-Cola, PepsiCo, Mars, and other companies to develop a checklist for "achieving unbiased research results from industry-funded activities." The companies paid for this effort. ILSI published the report in its own journal, *Nutrition Reviews*, but several other nutrition journals considered the report so important that they reprinted it.[14] The ILSI checklist dealt with the integrity of research, its control by investigators, disclosure of financial ties, and the accessibility of data. Four years later, ILSI sponsored a second such effort involving many of the same players. This second group reviewed and analyzed previous frameworks for industry engagement, as well as the results of interviews with representatives of seventeen nutrition and health organizations. It came up with similar recommendations, although it made two new suggestions: using

TABLE 14.1. Consensus Principles Governing Public-Private Partnerships (PPP) for Food and Nutrition Research, 2015

Prerequisite principle

1. Have a clearly defined and achievable goal to benefit the public.

Governance principles

2. Articulate a governance structure including a clear statement of work, rules, and partner roles, responsibilities, and accountability, to build in trust, transparency, and mutual respect as core operating principles— acknowledging there may be "deal breakers" precluding the formation of an effective partnership in the first place.

3. Ensure that objectives will meet stakeholder partners' public and private needs, with a clearly defined baseline to monitor progress and measure success.

Operational principles

4. Considering the importance of balance, ensure that all members possess appropriate levels of bargaining power.

5. Minimize conflict of interest by recruiting a sufficient number of partners to mitigate influence by any single member and to broaden private-sector perspectives and expertise.

6. Engage partners who agree on specific and fundable (or supportable through obtainable resources) research questions to be addressed by the partnership.

7. Enlist partners who are committed to the long term as well as to the sharing of funding and research data.

8. Along with government and the private sector, include academics and other members of civil society (e.g., foundations, NGOs, consumers) as partners.

9. Select objective measurements capable of providing common ground for both public and private-sector research goals.

10. Adopt research questions and methodologies established by partners with transparency on all competitive interests, ideally in the precompetitive space.

11. Be flexible in implementing the PPP process.

12. Ensure ongoing transparent communications both among partners and between the PPP and the public.

SOURCE: Alexander N, Rowe S, Brackett RE, et al., "Achieving a transparent, actionable framework for public-private partnerships for food and nutrition research," *Am J Clin Nutr.* 2015, 101:1359–1363. Six of this statement's ten authors reported current or previous financial ties to food companies.

a third party to work out the details of engagement and blinding of funding sources (keeping them unknown to researchers). The group did not discuss the feasibility of such actions.[15]

In 2015, some of the same authors participated in yet a third set of recommendations, this one developed at a meeting sponsored by the American Society for Nutrition through a cooperative agreement with the USDA. Six of its ten authors had industry affiliations (although two of the six said they had no conflicts to report). Table 14.1 summarizes the consensus principles that emerged from that meeting. They are based on the idea that transparency, good governance, and robust communications "may significantly enhance public confidence."[16] The principles emphasize public benefit (number 1 on the list) and alignment of interests (number 3). They introduce the idea that multiple funders will mitigate conflicts of interest (number 5)—another hypothesis that has yet to be tested. What I do not see in these industry-influenced principles is a pledge that funders will keep their hands off everything having to do with the design, conduct, interpretation, and presentation of the research.

These principles may appear reasonable, but they leave much room for industry involvement, especially if the definition of "civil society" in number 8 includes food companies and if being "flexible" in the public-private partnership process (number 11) permits food companies to set the research agenda. In his article in the JAMA COI issue, Mozaffarian proposes his own set of management principles. His suggestions go further than those shown in the table: they emphasize the need to deal with the suitability of the industry partner, assess the balance of risks and benefits, and provide guarantees of full academic independence. Mozaffarian also urges advocacy for more federal funding for nutrition research, a vital policy objective often forgotten in these discussions.

The ideas presented here all deserve praise for recognizing that financial conflicts present problems that require more than disclosure to manage. But the apparent purpose of such frameworks is to allow researchers, institutions, and societies to take industry funding while maintaining public trust in what they do and say. Given current realities, I am not sure this outcome is realistic. Even if it is, some of the suggestions seem especially questionable.

These frameworks often include admonitions to assess the risks of loss of reputation, credibility, or trust and to balance them against benefits. The Charles Perkins Centre (CPC) at the University of Sydney, for example, established a committee to assess whether prospective corporate sponsors are aligned with the CPC's core mission; whether they will refrain from influencing the design, conduct, and publication of research; and whether an association with them will not embarrass the institution. The CPC's guidelines are explicit about the risks: furthering commercial interests of industry in ways contrary to the CPC mission; being perceived by others as being biased, "captured," or compromised (regardless of whether the perception has a basis in fact); diverting efforts away from high-quality research or education; discrediting the CPC as an "honest broker" of knowledge and skills; and biasing the results in the sponsor's interests.[17]

The CPC guidelines assume that industry engagement is appropriate and necessary but requires firm oversight. With the risks stated so starkly, however, it becomes difficult for the CPC to justify taking corporate funding. Because this framework blocks engagement in programs funded by a single company, it protected the CPC's director from getting caught up in Coca-Cola's GEBN. And as we have seen, aligning the goals of food companies with those of public health nutrition is also likely to pose difficulties.[18]

Lisa Bero views the task of assessing the suitability of corporate sponsors as a slippery slope. WHO, for example, may refuse to engage with tobacco and firearm companies, but it permits engagement with companies that make alcoholic beverages, soft drinks, and infant formulas—products with questionable health effects or marketing practices. It is not easy to distinguish among corporations, trade associations, and front groups working on behalf of products that conflict with public health or have complicated nutritional profiles (fast foods, for example, may be high in saturated fat and sugar but also contain valuable nutrients). Where are the boundaries to be drawn?

Funding from multinational food companies may be unacceptable, but what about funding from the makers of "healthy" food brands owned by those same multinational corporations?[19]

The slipperiness of this slope does not stop groups from trying to set criteria for suitability. Dietitians for Professional Integrity (DFPI), the dissident group within the Academy of Nutrition and Dietetics, set up a rating system for sponsorship acceptability. On health grounds, its system automatically disqualifies the makers of alcohol, soft drinks, confectionary, and processed meats. It awards points for nutritious ingredients, sustainable methods of food production, fair-trade practices, animal welfare, low environmental impact, and social responsibility. Companies achieving a certain point level are acceptable for sponsorship; those below that number are not.[20]

Another classification scheme, NOVA (not an acronym), groups foods into four categories according to their degree of processing: (1) natural, unprocessed, or minimally processed foods; (2) processed culinary ingredients such as oils, butter, sugar, and salt; (3) foods processed in basic ways, as in making bread or cheese, canning, freezing, or other such methods; and (4) ultraprocessed foods such as soft drinks or packaged snacks. The NOVA scheme automatically disqualifies makers of ultraprocessed foods as sponsors on the grounds that these foods are deliberately formulated to be habit forming, are heavily advertised, are falsely promoted as healthful, and cause "troublesome effects on global nutrition and health."[21]

Sugary beverages are an easy target for exclusion; they contain sugars and water but nothing else of redeeming nutritional value. Their alternative, bottled water, is better for health but not for the environment. Most candy goes in the same category as soft drinks, but once you go beyond sugar the nutritional assessment becomes more complicated; some candy is made with nuts or dried fruit. Even the most heavily processed foods have some nutritional value. If it were up to me, I would be hard-pressed to decide which food-industry sponsors are acceptable. All food companies want to sell more of what they make; this alone makes alignment with the goals of public health inherently questionable. Given the complexities, it may be that the best we can do is to agree that conflicts of interest exist and ask what can realistically be done to manage them.

By the early 1990s, universities in the United States were already having trouble managing the risks of industry partnerships. They still are having trouble—even though they now have policies in place. They had no choice about setting these policies. Federal granting agencies not only require the policies but also audit them to make sure they are implemented and enforced.[22] Agency rules leave the details of management to the discretion of each institution but suggest that institutions require researchers who report conflicted interests to disclose them both to the public and to coinvestigators, to modify their research plans or disqualify themselves from participating in research, to reduce or eliminate the conflict (selling equities, for example), or to sever their conflicted relationships. Federal rules also recommend that institutions appoint independent, third-party monitors to oversee conflicted investigators' research designs, conduct, and reporting.

Mitigation policies put research universities in a difficult position. Universities want faculty to do groundbreaking research, bring in grants (and the overhead dollars that come with them), and win acclaim. But universities do not worry only about the reputational risks of industry sponsorship; they also worry that working for industry might distract faculty from institutional commitments. Faculty members who devote time to industry partnerships may neglect obligations to students and the institution. My university, NYU, permits up to one day a week for consulting activities, but other institutions may permit less.

Pressures on universities to promote highly active research programs—but also more ethical practices—create tensions. NYU's policy on conflicts of interest and ethics takes up thirty-three pages of small print. It requires faculty to disclose industry affiliations; I am told that most do. Administrators determine whether conflicts exist; investigate, manage, or eliminate the conflicts; and impose sanctions if necessary.[23] NYU's central administration delegates conflict management to the deans of its various schools. In mine,

NYU's Steinhardt School, the dean of faculty affairs is responsible for reviewing the annual conflict forms, flagging any that need further attention, and referring potential problems to the university official in charge. In 2017, for the first time in the years I have been filling out these forms, I received an email acknowledgment of its review along with a statement that mine posed no problems. Administrators tell me they are working on a new policy that may require review of flagged COI forms by a faculty committee. These actions suggest increasing recognition that a problem exists and that the university is responsible for addressing it.

Some universities already manage conflicts through faculty committees, which help decide whether the outside financial activities of faculty conflict with federal or university policies and, if so, how to manage such conflicts. The University of California system has had such committees for years, although its campuses interpret the policies in different ways.[24] The Berkeley campus explains why it is so diligent about managing conflicts of interest: "It's the law. It's university policy. It's the right thing to do."[25]

What triggers committee concerns? Cornell University has a guidance matrix for this purpose. Beyond protecting the institution, the matrix aims to protect students and postdoctoral researchers from unwittingly getting caught in situations where funders interfere with the conduct or publication of their work. Staff of Cornell's Office of Research Integrity review faculty's disclosure statements and refer those that involve consulting agreements, equity holdings, or licenses for committee review. If the committee finds that a conflict exists, it can and does impose sanctions.[26]

Problems may be infrequent, but this is not just a theoretical exercise. Past and present members of such committees relate alarming stories of instances, fortunately rare, in which faculty spend most of their time working on private business or consulting arrangements, fail to inform students of commercial interests in their work, and appear more loyal to the funder than to their institutions. A member of one conflict-oversight committee told me that its members viewed their job as reducing incidents of flagrant stupidity that might exploit students or reflect badly on the researcher and university. This was the first time I had heard anything said about the potential harm to students of conflicted research—a point that also deserves far greater emphasis.

Medical societies, as we have seen, are also taking conflicts more seriously. Some require speakers at annual meetings to disclose financial ties when submitting abstracts; some have committees in place to review such relationships and audit disclosures at meeting sessions. As mentioned earlier, speakers at the American Society for Nutrition meeting I attended in 2017 often omitted disclosures or presented them too quickly to be understood, and I saw no evidence that this situation was being audited. Nutrition professionals still have a long way to go to create a culture that views conflicts of interest as a problem worth serious attention. Bero proposes that reforms similar to those used to manage pharmaceutical and tobacco-industry sponsorship be applied to nutrition research. The nutrition field, she says, badly needs enforced policies requiring journals and societies to deal with financial conflicts, improved methods for evaluating studies for bias, a research agenda independent of corporate interests, and independent funding sources for nutrition research, or, at a minimum, a pooling of industry funds administered by an independent party.[27]

I agree, and the sooner the better. While waiting for the culture of research to improve, what should stakeholders—everyone who participates in or is affected by industry funding of nutrition research and practice—do to bring improvement about? This question brings us to the last chapter and the conclusion of these discussions.

15

Stakeholders: Take Action

For our purposes, "stakeholders" is the policy-wonk term for groups or individuals who stand to gain or lose from food-industry partnerships with nutrition professionals. By this point we are thoroughly familiar with the risks of these partnerships: biased opinions, distorted research agendas, skewed study results, compromised dietary advice, loss of professional opportunities, and, not least, reduced public trust. It is now time to turn to what we and other stakeholders in this situation can—and should—do to prevent, interpret, and manage these risks.

When I first begin working on this book, I wanted to be able to answer some basic questions: Should the food, drink, and supplement industries fund public health research? Should nutrition scientists and their societies accept industry funding? What should universities and nutrition journals be doing to protect *their* scientific integrity? Most critical, I wondered how we, as private citizens, ought to deal with these matters in our own lives. I wanted to be able to explain how industry-induced conflicts affect all of us and to show

how we could hold corporations, nutrition professionals, universities, government agencies, and journalists who write about such matters accountable for maintaining higher ethical standards. Here is how I have ended up thinking about these questions.

Should Food Companies Fund Nutrition Research?

If we lived in an ideal world, food companies would sell products that are good for us and minimize the creation, manufacturing, and aggressive marketing of junk foods. Nobody forces food companies to make and sell junk foods. Even though many people have come to love them, these products are about profits, not health. I like the way the ethicist Jonathan Marks addresses this point: "If a food or beverage company wishes to have integrity, it cannot make claims that it is promoting health while aggressively marketing low-nutrient, high-calorie leading brands that exacerbate obesity and associated non-communicable diseases."[1] Even for products that are "healthy" or "healthier," there is no valid reason—other than profits—to engage university scientists or government in marketing research.

I fully understand that food companies are neither charities nor social service agencies and that they are required to meet stockholders' demands for higher and more immediate returns on investment.[2] I also understand that the food industry needs research to help create new products and desires research to support its marketing objectives. But when food companies ask me where they are supposed to get this research if they do not fund it themselves, I think they are asking a marketing—not a scientific—question.

For marketing research, food companies have choices. If they do not do in-house research, they can contract with firms whose business it is to do this kind of research. But once they start partnering with USDA laboratories or offering grants to university researchers, they are introducing an unnecessary bias into the research process. Research aimed at technical aspects of product development and marketing strategies has its place in universities, usually in food-science departments or business schools. But when companies want research in order to make health claims for their products, they are distorting the research agenda. There is a big difference between "Let's fund a study to prove our product is healthy" (marketing) and "Let's fund a study to learn about whether or how diets might affect health" (science).

Unilever, one of the few food companies still actively engaged in in-house research, has an explicit policy on research integrity: its science must be driven by hypothesis and be rigorous, objective, and transparent. Unilever applies these principles to its own researchers as well as to its university partners. Nestlé, also still actively engaged in research, insists that its partnerships adhere to principles of academic freedom, ethics, and integrity. Coca-Cola, after the public exposure of its too-cozy involvement with sponsored researchers, now limits its funding to 50 percent of a study's cost.[3] These companies deserve credit for recognizing the hazards of research partnerships and for attempting to protect against those hazards. Whether their methods will reduce researchers' unconscious biases is uncertain, but these companies seem to be trying to respond to the need for a more objective research environment. Other companies that care about research objectivity should also establish integrity policies and stick to them. The policies should make clear that once the money is granted, donors will stay out of the entire scientific process—design, conduct, interpretation, publication, and presentation. Even so, the donors will still have established or influenced the research agenda by the very nature of the research they agree to support.

In thinking about how best to create a firewall between donors and scientists, the idea that comes up most frequently is to pool contributions from multiple donors and have them administered by an independent third party. Previous attempts to do this by the Nutrition Foundation and Harvard, as I discussed in Chapter 13, did not sufficiently protect against charges of bias. Because so much industry-funded research is aimed at product development or sales, I doubt that food companies would willingly contribute to a fund they could not control, especially if their money happened to support studies that produced inconvenient results. Coca-Cola, for example, partnered with the US Centers for Disease Control and Prevention (CDC) on obesity campaigns focused on physical activity but refused to fund CDC programs in which it had no immediate commercial interest.[4]

One current model for pooled donations is the nonprofit Foundation for the National Institutes of Health (FNIH), authorized by Congress to collect funds from private donors to support research and education. The FNIH is highly successful; in 2016 it distributed more than $55 million, mostly for research partnerships. This money comes from hundreds of donors, ranging from grateful patients to huge corporations, who contribute amounts ranging from a few hundred dollars to millions. The top category includes twelve donors: five makers of alcoholic beverages, five drug companies (some of which make dietary supplements), the National Football League, and the Bill & Melinda Gates Foundation. Beyond alcohol companies, I can find only one other food or beverage company on the current donor lists—the National Dairy Council in the $25,000–$49,000 category.[5] Why are food and beverage companies so strikingly absent from contributing to the FNIH? I am guessing that it is because NIH typically focuses on basic rather than marketing research.

But here, too, the lines blur. The FNIH actively seeks donors for specific projects and permits them to specify areas for research (thereby letting them influence the research agenda). This earmarking was evident in a front-page story in the New York Times about a pledge from several companies selling alcoholic beverages to provide $67.7 million to the FNIH for a study to determine whether one drink a day prevents heart attacks. This project may sound like science, but the vested interest of the funders, the size of their donation, and the research question sent up warning flags. The director of NIH's alcohol institute assured the reporter that the trial would be "immune from industry influence."[6] I thought this statement came right off the COI Bingo card, as it implied ignorance of research on funding effects. Subsequent reports indicated even deeper ties between that director and the alcohol industry and led the NIH to suspend enrollment, conduct an investigation, and stop the trial.[7]

Given these difficulties, I can think of only one option that might actually work: an industry-wide program for research paid for by a mandatory tax or levy. Making contributions mandatory would eliminate the problem of having to please donors to ensure ongoing funding.[8] The idea would be to require *all* food, beverage, and supplement companies with sales over some set level to pay a fee in proportion to sales revenues. A government agency, private foundation, or some other independent group could collect the funds and administer them in much the same way as NIH currently distributes grants. Such systems have their own sources of bias, but the biases would not be commercial.

But in practice? I score the feasibility of this idea as zero, at least in the United States. Food companies do not like taxes and invariably oppose them (USDA checkoffs are an exception, but those funds are for marketing, not science). It is hard to imagine how the US tax code or Congress would allow something like this. But anything short of a mandatory levy is a compromise that permits industry funding to bias the research, induces conflicts of interest, and leads to undesirable consequences. Some other kind of compromise might also be worth trying if anyone can come up with a good one.

Should Nutrition Scientists and Their Professional Societies Accept Industry Funding?

Here I want to address my nutrition colleagues directly. The dilemma: if you take food-industry money (which you want and may need), you run risks (which you do not want). Engage with industry? Certainly. Take the money? Not if you can help it. In the absence of professional standards for managing conflicted interests, you are on your own to deal with problems that arise. This suggests that, to the extent you can, it is best to avoid the conflicts and avoid rationalizing them. If you find yourself in a conflicted situation, get help in dealing with it.[9]

The risks can no longer be ignored. As our institutions and professional associations increasingly recognize the hazards, which I believe they will, the "opportunity costs" of industry funding will rise. These costs already include the downgrading of industry-funded research in commissioned literature reviews, the rejection of such research by journals with high ethical standards, and the exclusion of conflicted experts from prestigious advisory and review committees—all with consequences for academic promotion and tenure. James Hill, one of the founders of the GEBN, should have been aware of these risks. He was an author on a commentary about public-private partnerships complaining that some of his colleagues view taking research money from food companies "as a last resort, something that could negatively affect tenure and promotion, and trainees are warned not to pursue it."[10] My guess—and hope—is that the number of colleagues viewing industry funding as a problem will increase.

Anything other than refusing the money involves compromises. Setting a policy should help you deal with compromises. Create a policy that can help you decide what kind of funding is acceptable and under what circumstances. Recognize that your biases will be unconscious; design your studies to control for unconscious biases; insist that your sponsor keep hands off the entire research process; and fully disclose the sponsorship. As lipid researcher Martijn Katan continually reminds me, all industry funding does not deserve blanket condemnation; Unilever-sponsored research led to his discovery of how trans fats increase the risk of heart disease.[11] True, but much industry-funded research is about marketing, not science. It helps to be crystal clear about the difference.

Developing a policy to protect your students and postdoctoral fellows is also a good idea. Of all the stakeholders in industry-funded research, they are the most vulnerable. Should they be permitted to accept industry-funded travel awards, scholarships, fellowships, or grants? Awards and honors are unlikely to cause problems for them, but if they are working on industry-sponsored projects, they need to be well informed about the risks. At the very least, they must be able to conduct their research and publish their results without interference from corporate sponsors. When trainees ask me how to handle awkward situations caused by industry sponsors (who appear to be attempting to control the research agenda, micromanage the research, set restrictions on publication, and the like), I suggest they talk to their supervisors and, failing that, ask for help by scheduling an appointment with a counselor in their university's research integrity office.

Our professional societies also need policies. As long as they continue to accept funding from food companies and ignore the reputational consequences, they are failing to set appropriate ethical standards for the profession. World Obesity, a coalition of about fifty international organizations, developed a system for categorizing potential donors by their degree of risk. This group does not accept donations from the makers of tobacco, firearms, or alcohol. It carefully scrutinizes the makers of soft drinks, snack foods, baby foods and infant formulas, breakfast cereals, cookies, cakes, and confectionary.[12] But regardless of what professional societies intend, acceptance of industry funding implies endorsement of the sponsoring company and its entire line of products. To categorize the makers of "healthy" foods as acceptable sponsors but those of "unhealthy" foods as unacceptable puts professional societies on a slippery slope, best avoided.

In creating policies for dealing with industry donations, nutrition societies are recognizing their roles in setting ethical standards for research, practice, and public advocacy. Ideally, they should aim for a complete phasing out of industry funding. While working toward that goal, their interim policies should at least call for donations to be unrestricted and for complete transparency about donors, amounts, and proportions of budgets. Policies could also deal with disclosures at annual meetings, restrictions on company logos on meeting bags or other gift items, and elimination of industry-funded satellite symposia. They could also address situations in which industry funding is solely about marketing, such as advertising in journals and exhibit-hall booths.[13] Whatever the policies turn out to be, professional societies should make them fully transparent to members and to the public.

What Should Universities and Nutrition Journals Do to Protect Their Scientific Integrity?

Because the culture of the workplace sets ethical standards, any institution employing researchers or practitioners should promote the integrity of work performed under its auspices. Institutions should train investigators—and students and postdoctoral fellows—in research ethics. They should ensure that investigators are fully responsible for what they do, write, and publish and should take all necessary steps to review, investigate, and manage conflicts of interest. If they want to keep conflicts to a minimum, they will follow NIH guidelines in spirit as well as in letter and encourage a research environment in which independence, integrity, and freedom from industry interference are expected cultural norms.[14]

As the *JAMA* COI issue indicated in 2017, the medical community is taking this problem more seriously, albeit more than thirty years after the *New England Journal of Medicine* first deemed disclosure of financial ties essential. Articles in that *JAMA* publication argued that high editorial standards in professional journals are critical for maintaining trust. Most medical journals follow the guidelines of the International Committee of Medical Journal Editors (ICMJE), which state that editors themselves should not be conflicted and should recuse themselves from editorial decisions that might raise conflicts.[15]

Medical journals have struggled with these issues for a long time. A former editor of the *New England Journal of Medicine* argued in 2005 that physicians with a financial interest in a product discussed in an article should not be allowed to publish it.[16] In 2013, in a sharp reversal of policy, the editors of the *BMJ* announced that they would no longer publish research sponsored by the tobacco industry. Yet only a decade earlier, the *BMJ* had opposed a ban on tobacco ads on the grounds that "the *BMJ* is passionately antitobacco, but we are also passionately prodebate and proscience. A ban would be antiscience."[17] Today, *JAMA* considers editors responsible for making sure that articles from conflicted authors accurately reflect scientific evidence and are free of bias. The Cochrane network refuses to allow conflicted individuals to participate in writing systematic reviews. So does the *New England Journal of Medicine*: "Because the essence of reviews and editorials is selection and interpretation of the literature, the *Journal* expects that authors of such articles will not have any significant financial interest in a company (or its competitor) that makes a product discussed in the article."[18]

But no nutrition journal of which I am aware refuses to publish research sponsored by food companies or articles by highly conflicted researchers. The editors of nutrition journals, many with financial conflicts of their own, act as if disclosure takes care of the problem. It is troubling that so much industry-sponsored research—especially that on single foods or ingredients—is published in leading nutrition journals. Marketing research does not belong in public health journals. I wish the editors of nutrition journals would view such articles with skepticism or at least label them as marketing research. Even better, as food-policy analyst Corinna Hawkes once suggested to me, such research should be sent to a publication that ought to be established for that precise purpose: the "*Journal of Industry-Funded Research*."

Similar considerations should apply to peer reviewers. The entire peer-review process is under increasing scrutiny over its fairness and reliability, as well as for conflicts of interest among reviewers. Despite such concerns, peer reviewers rarely reject papers on the basis of disclosure statements.[19] I frequently do peer reviews of manuscripts for medical, public health, and nutrition journals. I examine disclosure statements and, when needed, comment on conflicts of interest in my recommendations to editors. I vote to reject industry-funded studies with evident marketing objectives. Editors should encourage other peer reviewers to do the same. It would help if editors themselves had no financial conflicts, required disclosures from peer reviewers, and paid much closer attention to issues raised by such disclosures. Recognizing that a problem exists is a necessary first step.

How Should *You* Deal with These Matters?

This brings me to the question of what you—as a reader, eater, and citizen—should do about food-industry influence and its effects on your own life. As a *reader* of news accounts of nutrition science, you may have noticed that they hardly ever mention research sponsorship or financial conflicts. This adds another layer of complexity: do journalists themselves have conflicted interests? They are not supposed to. Their code of ethics requires them to avoid conflicts of interest, disclose those that are unavoidable, and "refuse gifts, favors, fees, free travel and special treatment . . . and other outside activities that may compromise integrity or impartiality, or may damage credibility."[20]

With increasing financial pressures on the media business, reporters are having a harder time adhering to these principles. Avoiding conflicts is especially difficult for science journalists who cover the drug, medical device, chemical, biotechnology, and food industries. In 2016, for example, the National Press Foundation invited journalists to attend an all-expenses-paid, four-day training workshop to explore controversial issues in food and agriculture. But the foundation was not paying for it. The funders were Monsanto, the American Farm Bureau Federation, the National Pork Board, and the Organic Trade Association—all companies or trade associations with financial interests in precisely the issues discussed at the conference and covered by the invited journalists.[21] The journalists should not have accepted the invitation, but having done so, their code of ethics required them to disclose the financial arrangements in any story they wrote about it.

Paul Thacker, writing on the debates among journalists about their relationships to the industries they cover, quotes one journalist who struggled to come up with a policy: "Don't take the honorarium. Do consider the travel money. It isn't money going into your pocket, which limits the potential COI, and you can do some good by being there, both to present your views on the panels you sit on and to bring back valuable information for your readers. And if you ever write about the conference: Disclose that money clearly."[22]

As readers, we need journalists who cover nutrition, food, and agriculture research to report who paid for the studies, their own conflicts, and the conflicts among the experts they quote. An analysis of press reports about obesity that quoted the investigators behind the GEBN found at least thirty news articles that failed to mention the scientists' financial ties to Coca-Cola.[23] The publisher of Health News Review, Gary Schwitzer, says such omissions are frequent; fewer than half of press releases merit satisfactory scores on this criterion: "Does the news release identify funding sources & disclose conflicts of interest?" For readers, he says, "it's a coin toss whether they're going to get proper disclosure or not."[24] Why this matters is demonstrated by an investigation of news articles about medical research; the study found that virtually all comments from sources with financial ties to the sponsor favored the research, whereas less than 20 percent of the independent experts did so.[25]

At least one reporter urges his colleagues to take on industry funding and financial ties whenever they write for the public: "To argue that conflicts of interest are an unavoidable evil shows a paucity of imagination and ethical ambition. Most of the world's social reforms have come about after determined people sought to challenge the 'unchangeable' status quo. Science funding isn't slavery or women's suffrage, but I think the same broad principle applies: throwing our hands in the air helps no one."[26]

Unless reporters take on this challenge, you are on your own to figure out how skeptical you need to be about news reports or expert advice. Because not all industry-funded research is necessarily skewed but much of it is, a healthy dose of skepticism is warranted whenever you see industry funding reported. Health News Review has ten criteria for deciding whether press releases are credible. Most deal with the quality of the evidence, but one addresses the independence of sources and funding: it demands that journalists quote at least one independent expert and disclose other experts' conflicted interests. It warns readers to be skeptical any time a story fails to disclose an important conflict of interest.[27]

You do not need to know a thing about science to judge whether news reports of studies make sense. There are ways to tell. Health News Review uses this criterion: "Does the story appear to rely solely or largely on a news release?" If it does, you are reading public relations, not science. I sometimes teach classes for journalists and my advice to students and practicing journalists is to read the original research whenever they can. Even if the study is difficult to understand, reading it will help them formulate better questions for the study's authors. You too can try reading original studies, and plenty of guides are available for how to do that. Some of these guides urge you to pay attention to the funding source. One, for example, summarizes the situation nicely: "Vested interests can distort research in different ways, from directly setting up research questions that are biased towards a particular outcome, to selecting only certain results for publication, to the more subtle influences on what conclusions to emphasize. So it is reasonable to 'follow the money' and know who's funded the research that you're looking at."[28]

When should you be skeptical? Any time you see a report that a single food, beverage, supplement, food product, or ingredient causes or reduces the risk for obesity, heart disease, type 2 diabetes, or cancer, it is a good idea to envision a red warning flag flying high in the air. The studies may have identified associations between the food factor and the disease, but associations can be due to any number of other causes. Dietary patterns, not single factors, are what matter to health. Look out for words like "miracle" or "breakthrough." Science tends to proceed in small increments and rarely works that way. And please be especially skeptical of "everything you thought you knew about nutrition is wrong." Science does not work that way, either. Whenever you see "may" or "might"—as in "may reduce the risk of heart disease" or "might improve cognition in the elderly"—recognize that these also mean "may not" or "might not." Overall, it is always a good idea to ask whether study results seem plausible in the light of everything else you know.

As an *eater*, you should be wary of media hype about whether fat or sugar is a more important cause of health problems. This question ignores basic principles of nutrition: we eat foods, not nutrients, and how much we eat is often just as important as what we eat. Diets of enormous variety, from Asian diets traditionally based on rice (carbohydrates that convert to sugar in the body) to Mediterranean diets rich in olive oil (fat), can all promote long and healthy lives. The basic principles of eating healthfully have remained remarkably constant over the years: eat a wide variety of relatively unprocessed foods in reasonable amounts. Note that these same dietary principles apply to prevention of the entire range of diet-related chronic diseases. If an industry-funded study claims miraculous benefits from the sponsor's products, think, "Advertising."

For those of us privileged to have access to a large and varied food supply, this advice translates to a few basic principles: eat your veggies, choose relatively unprocessed foods, keep junk foods to a minimum, and watch out for excessive calories—precepts that leave plenty of room for eating what you like and taking great pleasure in what you eat. Every time you follow these principles, you are voting with your fork for diets that will be healthier for you, your family, and the planet.

And that brings me to our roles as *citizens*—voting with our votes, as it were. This book appears at a time when corporations have taken over American society, putting democratic processes at grave risk. Democracy badly needs informed, engaged citizens to speak out against misleading and dishonest corporate practices. We need, as some have said, better rules for political participation that will level the playing field and control the political power corporations exert over legislation and policy.[29]

The public—and this means all of us—has a big influence on what food companies make and do. Food companies are in the business of selling products and have to be sensitive to what buyers want. The label of every American food product provides contact information, making it easy for you to let the company know your thoughts. Hold food companies accountable. Pick up the phone. Tell them you want them to disclose the names of the scientists, practitioners, and societies they are funding, and at what level. Tell them you do not want them involved in committees and policy decisions about nutrition and health. Make sure they know that you want them to fund research, but for the greater good of society and in ways less likely to influence study outcomes. If enough of us do this, they will have to listen.

I firmly believe that controlling the inappropriate practices of food companies is an appropriate role of government. If I may quote ethicist Marks again, "Governments, not corporations, are the guardians of public health. . . . It is time for public health agencies and regulators to 'struggle' a little more with corporations, creating structural incentives for healthier and more responsible industry practices, and calling companies to account when they fail to comply." Many governments today, our own included, appear to have been captured by corporations. If we want controls on corporate power, we, as citizens, need to make our voices heard.

Government agencies ought to be funding basic research in general and nutrition, food, and agriculture research in particular. We need to know how best to feed the world's growing population, sustainably and in ways that promote the health of people and the planet. Food companies' priorities preclude their investment in such questions except when research might lead to product development and increased sales. As a citizen, you can support efforts to increase federal spending for basic research.

In democratic societies, governments represent all citizens, and that includes us. Our leaders should not be allowing food companies to determine policies on nutrition and health. They should not be allowing advisory committees to be overrun with conflicted experts, and if they do appoint conflicted members, they need to explain why. The private National Academies of Sciences, Engineering, and Medicine, which often issues reports on nutrition at the behest of government agencies, reveals committee members' disclosures in publications and also requires disclosures from staff members.[30] We should insist that government agencies do no less.

NIH announces its guidelines for dealing with financial conflicts of interest with a quotation from its director, Francis Collins: "The public trust in what we do is just essential, and we cannot afford to take any chances with the integrity of the research process."[31] For this reason alone, the USDA should reconsider its cosponsorship of research aimed at marketing objectives and redirect its research enterprise to where it is most needed—to food, nutrition, and agricultural science.[32] As citizens, we have the right to demand that government agencies dealing with food and nutrition matters put public health first.

Just as "voting with your fork" is useful, so is voting with your vote. If you see news reports about studies that you suspect may be industry funded, write a note to the reporter and ask. If enough people question science reporters about who paid for the studies they write about, they will focus more attention on that issue. Ineffectual as such personal actions might seem against the enormity of corporate power, do not give up hope. Contact your congressional representatives. Let them know your opinions about corporate influence over matters of nutrition and health. As citizens, we need and deserve healthier, more sustainable, and more ethical food systems. If we do not demand them, who will?

Acknowledgments

SOME OF MY QUESTIONS ABOUT THE HISTORY AND PRESENT STATUS of research on funding effects could be answered relatively easily by reading the many books available on these topics. Others proved difficult for an unexpected reason: few libraries retain hard copies of archived journals. Because electronic copies rarely include instructions to authors, hard copies are the only place to find this information, as well as other useful items such as lists of industry supporters. I am grateful to the Mann Library at Cornell University for retaining full sets of nutrition journals on its shelves and in circulation, and to Patrick Stover for arranging my ongoing affiliation with Cornell's Division of Nutritional Sciences.

Unsavory Truth would have been impossible to write without this kind of generosity from colleagues and friends. I must first acknowledge my debt to Lisa Bero and her bias-in-research group—Nick Chartres, Alice Fabbri, Quinn Grundy, and Barbara Mintzes—with whom I worked at the University of Sydney's Charles Perkins Centre in early 2016, and to Stephen Simpson, the Charles Perkins Centre's director, who made it possible for me to conduct the initial research for this book under such welcoming circumstances. I am also indebted to Juan Rivera Dommarco, director of the National Institute of Public Health in Cuernavaca, and to Simón Barquera, director of its Center for Research in Nutrition and Health, for hosting my Fulbright Specialist Award fellowship from January to March 2017 while I was working on an early draft of this book.

I thank Yoni Freedhoff for spotting the tweet that launched Anahad O'Connor's *New York Times* article, which in turn triggered my interest in writing this book. O'Connor graciously provided copies of the emails he had obtained through open-records requests, as did Gary Ruskin of US Right to Know. Laura Schmidt encouraged UCSF librarian Dee Dee Kramer to copy the DC Leaks emails just before the site mysteriously disappeared, and Mimi Klausner and Rachel Taketa continue to ensure that they remain available in UCSF's food-industry documents collection.

For providing information, consultation, or documents (especially those unpublished or offered prior to publication), I thank Zara Abrams, Alberto Alemanno, Angela Amico, Lenore Arab, Andy Bellatti, Dennis Bier, Geoffrey Cannon, Arthur Caplan, John Courtney, Robert Cousins, Adam Drewnowski, Darren Early, D'Ann Finley, Stan Glantz, Fabio Gomes da Silva, Joan Gussow, Casey Hinds, Nancy Fink Huehnegarth, Michael Jacobson, Lisa Jahns, Susan Jebb, Martijn Katan, Cristin Kearns, Jim Krieger, Alexandra Lewin-Zwerdling, Bonnie Liebman, Barrie Margetts, Alfred Merrill, Linda Meyers, Mélissa Mialon, Greg Miller, Jim O'Hara, Jennifer Otten, Niyati Parekh, Juan-Pablo Peña-Rosas, Kyle Pfister, John Pierce, Kathleen Rasmussen, Susan Roberts, Marc Rodwin, Andrew Rosenberg, Gary Sacks, Sunita Sah, Ricardo Salvador, Lisa Sasson, Paulo Serôdio, Alan Shannon, Michael Siegel, James Smallbone, Robert Steinbrook, David Stuckler, Leonore Tiefer, Ann Veneman, Ralph Walton, Allison Worden, and Lisa Young. As for the many contributors who asked to remain anonymous (you know who you are), and those whom I may have inadvertently omitted, I cannot thank you enough.

I am especially grateful to Marcia Angell, Sheldon Krimsky, Naomi Oreskes, David Oshinsky, Michael Pollan, and Laura Shapiro for their wise counsel at critical moments; to my NYU colleague Domingo Piñero for his expertise and generosity in redrawing some of the figures used in this book; to Daniel Bowman Simon and Maggie Tauranac at NYU for their help with basic research points; to Ken Castronuovo, Charlotte Diamond, Muksha Jingree, Kelli Martino, Katie Robertson, Pamela Stewart, and Matt Vanzo for superb staff support; and especially to Steven Ho for his patience and skill with my almost daily needs for technical support.

At NYU's Steinhardt School, I thank Ben Vien, Lendyll Capitulo, and the rest of the Technology Services team for keeping my computers functional. To my Nutrition and Food Studies Department colleagues, chair Krishnendu Ray, and to Steinhardt dean Dominic Brewer, I offer grateful thanks for creating the remarkably supportive environment in which I am privileged to continue to work—despite my ostensible retirement.

I greatly appreciate the work of the team at Basic Books: Lara Heimert, T. J. Kelleher, Carrie Napolitano, Kathy Delfosse (the reference formatting!), Stephanie Summerhays (the endless, but endlessly enjoyable, back and forth!), Melissa Veronesi, Kelsey Odorczyk, and Connie Capone. This book is the result of your dedication.

I am the fortunate beneficiary of the tenacity and skill of my sharp-eyed friends and daughter who read the page proofs: Amy Bentley, Esther Trakinski, and Rebecca Nestle. Finally, I am everlastingly grateful to my agent Max Sinsheimer, my friend and colleague Joanne Csete, and my partner Malden Nesheim for comments and consultation on an earlier and much longer draft of the manuscript, for reading page proofs, and for support, encouragement, and invaluable advice throughout.

Abbreviations

The following abbreviations are used in more than one chapter or in the notes.

AAAS	American Association for the Advancement of Science
ABA	American Beverage Association
AEB	American Egg Board
AIN	American Institute of Nutrition
AND	Academy of Nutrition and Dietetics
AP	Associated Press
ARS	Agricultural Research Service (of the USDA)
ASN	American Society for Nutrition
CDC	US Centers for Disease Control and Prevention
COI	Conflict of interest
CRA	Corn Refiners Association
CSPI	Center for Science in the Public Interest
DFPI	Dietitians for Professional Integrity
DGAC	Dietary Guidelines Advisory Committee

DSHEA	Dietary Supplement Health and Education Act of 1994
ERS	Economic Research Service (of the USDA)
FDA	US Food and Drug Administration (of HHS)
FNCE	Food and Nutrition Conference & Expo (of the Academy of Nutrition and Dietetics)
FOIA	Freedom of Information Act of 1967
FTC	Federal Trade Commission
GEBN	Global Energy Balance Network
GRAS	Generally recognized as safe
HFCS	High-fructose corn syrup
HHS	US Department of Health and Human Services
ICMJE	International Committee of Medical Journal Editors
ILSI	International Life Sciences Institute
ISCOLE	International Study of Childhood Obesity, Lifestyle and the Environment
LSRO	Life Sciences Research Office
NGOs	Nongovernmental organizations
NHANES	National Health and Nutrition Examination Survey
NIH	National Institutes of Health
NYU	New York University
PCRM	Physicians Committee for Responsible Medicine
PhRMA	Pharmaceutical Research and Manufacturers of America
SFAs	Saturated fatty acids
SNE	Society for Nutrition Education (until 2012)
SNEB	Society for Nutrition Education and Behavior (after 2012)
UCS	Union of Concerned Scientists
UCSF	University of California, San Francisco
USDA	US Department of Agriculture
WHO	World Health Organization (of the United Nations)

Notes

Most references cited here are available online, but URLs change frequently and articles are best searched for by their titles. Journal names are indicated by standard abbreviations; if the full name is not obvious, it can be found by typing the abbreviation into a search engine.

Chapter 1. The Food Industry and Nutrition

1. "Following the links from Russian hackers to the U.S. election," *NY Times*, Jan 6, 2017; Office of the Director of National Intelligence, *Intelligence Community Assessment: Assessing Russian Activities and Intentions in Recent US Elections*, ICA 2017-01D, Jan 6, 2017. For the DC Leaks archives, see the University of California San Francisco (UCSF) Food Industry Documents Library, available online as of Nov 15, 2018. The site identifies each email by a unique code number attached to its URL, www.industrydocumentslibrary.ucsf.edu/food/docs/. See, for example, Capricia Marshall to Michael Goltzman, Subject: TCCC Invoice, May 29, 2016, www.industrydocumentslibrary.ucsf.edu/food/docs/ppcl0226.

2. Greene R, Berger R, "Hillary Clinton campaign officials helped Coca-Cola fight soda tax," *The Russells*, Oct 12, 2016; Pfister K, "Leaked: Coca-Cola's worldwide political strategy to kill soda taxes," *Medium.com*, Oct 14, 2016; Andrea Mortensen to Michelle Carfrae, Subject: Nestle presentation, Jan 28, 2016, in: Michael Goltzman to Adrian Ristow, Amanda Lin, Capricia

Penavic Marshall, et al., Subject: FW: INFORM—Marion Nestle's South Pacific tour. . . . Jan 28, 2016, UCSF ID: llcl0226; Strom M, "Coca-Cola's secret plan to monitor Sydney University academic Lisa Bero," *Sydney Morning Herald*, Oct 22, 2016.

3. Ben Sheidler to Sonya Soutus, Subject: INFORM: AP Story on RDs, Mar 13, 2015, in: Michael Goltzman to Adrian Ristow, Alexander 'Sandy' Chapman, Capricia Penavic Marshall, et al., Subject: FW: INFORM: AP Story on Registered Dieticians, Mar 13, 2015, UCSF ID: zldl0226.

4. Choi C, "Coke as a sensible snack? Coca-Cola works with dietitians who suggest cola as snack," *AP*, Mar 16, 2015.

5. Karyn Harrington to Matt Echols, Subject: INFORM: WSJ Philadelphia Tax Story, May 6, 2016, in: Michael Goltzman to Adrian Ristow, Brian Michael Frere, Capricia Penavic Marshall, et al., Subject: FW: INFORM: WSJ Philadelphia Tax Story, May 19, 2016, UCSF ID: lqcl0226.

6. Amanda Rosseter to Joanna Price, May 26, 2016. Price's reply is also dated May 26, 2016. In: Michael Goltzman to Darlene Hayes, Missy Owens, Elaine Bowers Coventry, et al., Fwd: INFORM: Pending AP Story on Corporate Funding of Nutrition Research, May 27, 2016, UCSF ID: qpcl0226.

7. Choi C, "AP Exclusive: How candy makers shape nutrition science," *AP*, Jun 2, 2016.

8. Kate Loatman to ICBA [International Council of Beverage Associations], Subject: U.S. Dietary Guidelines Advisory Committee (DGAC), Feb 19, 2015, in: Michael Goltzman to Adrian Ristow, Alexander "Sandy" Chapman, Capricia Penavic Marshall, et al., FW: U.S. Dietary Guidelines Advisory Committee (DGAC)—Report and ABA Statement, Feb 19, 2015, UCSF ID: gpdl0226.

9. Ryan Guthrie to April Jordin, Ben Deutsch, Ben Sheidler, et al., Subject: INFORM: Dietary Guidelines Article, May 28, 2015, in: Michael Goltzman to Adrian Ristow, Alexander "Sandy" Chapman, Capricia Penavic Marshall, et al., FW: INFORM: Dietary Guidelines Article, May 28, 2015, UCSF ID: qjdl0226.

10. US Department of Health and Human Services and US Department of Agriculture, *Dietary Guidelines for Americans, 2015–2020*, 8th ed., Dec 2015.

11. Huehnergarth NF, "Monsanto and the organics industry pay to train journalists: What could go wrong?" *Forbes*, May 31, 2016.

12. O'Connor A, "Coca-Cola funds scientists who shift blame for obesity away from bad diets," *NY Times*, Aug 9, 2015.

13. Nestle M, "Food company sponsorship of nutrition research and professional activities: A conflict of interest?" *Public Health Nutr.* 2001, 4(5):1015–1022.

14. Shook RP, Hand GA, Drenowatz C, et al., "Low levels of physical activity are associated with dysregulation of energy intake and fat mass gain over 1 year," *Am J Clin Nutr.* 2015, 102(6):1332–1338.

15. Lee Y, Berryman CE, West SG, et al., "Effects of dark chocolate and almonds on cardiovascular risk factors in overweight and obese individuals: A randomized controlled-feeding trial," *J Am Heart Assoc.* 2017, Nov 29, 6(12):pii:e005162.

16. Besley JC, McCright AM, Zahry NR, et al., "Perceived conflict of interest in health science partnerships," *PLoS One* 2017, 12(4):e0175643; Kroeger CM, Garza C, Lynch CJ, et al., "Scientific rigor and credibility in the nutrition research landscape" *Am J Clin Nutr.* 2018, 107(3):484–494; Miller D, Harkins C, "Corporate strategy and corporate capture: Food and alcohol industry and lobbying and public health," *Crit Soc Policy* 2010, 30:564–589.

17. US Department of Agriculture, Economic Research Service, "Food availability (per capita) data system," updated Jan 17, 2018; Mialon M, Swinburn B, Allender S, Sacks G, "'Maximising shareholder value': A detailed insight into the corporate political activity of the Australian food industry," *Aust N Z J Public Health* 2017, 41(2):165–171.

18. Pollan M, *In Defense of Food: An Eater's Manifesto*, Penguin Press, 2008.

19. Krimsky S, *Science in the Private Interest: Has the Lure of Profits Corrupted Medical Research?* Rowman and Littlefield, 2004; Lo B, Field MJ, *Conflict of Interest in Medical Research, Education, and Practice*, National Academies Press, 2009; Oreskes N, Conway EM, *Merchants of Doubt*, Bloomsbury Press, 2010; Freudenberg N, *Lethal but Legal: Corporations, Consumption, and Protecting Public Health*, Oxford University Press, 2014; Miller D, Harkins C, Schlögl M, Montague B, *Impact of Market Forces on Addictive Substances and Behaviours*, Oxford University Press, 2018.

20. Marks JH, Thompson DB, "Shifting the focus: Conflict of interest and the food industry," *Am J Bioeth.* 2011, 11(1):44–46; Marks JH, "Toward a systemic ethics of public-private partnerships related to food and health," *Kennedy Inst Ethics J.* 2014, 24(3):267–299.

21. Barnoya J, Nestle M, "The food industry and conflicts of interest in nutrition research: A Latin American perspective," *J Public Health Pol.* 2016, 37(4):552–559 [retracted]; Nestle M, "A retraction and apology," *FoodPolitics .com*, Nov 25, 2015; "Retraction published for nutrition researcher Marion Nestle," *RetractionWatch.com*, Dec 31, 2015.

22. Feed the Truth, "KIND snacks founder & CEO creates new organization to promote public health over special interests," *PRNewswire.com*, Feb 15, 2017.

23. Choi C, "Millions to fight food industry sway, from a snack bar CEO," *Wash Post*, Feb 15, 2017.

24. Wood SF, Podrasky J, McMonagle MA, et al., "Influence of pharmaceutical marketing on Medicare prescriptions in the District of Columbia," *PLoS One* 2017, 12(10):e0186060.

25. World Health Organization World Health Assembly, *International Code of Marketing of Breast-Milk Substitutes*, May 1981; Richter J, *Public-Private Partnerships and International Health Policy-Making: How Can Public Interests Be Safeguarded?* Hakapaino Oy (Finland), 2004; Nestlé Public Affairs, *Nestlé Policy and Instructions for Implementation of the WHO International Code of Marketing of Breast-Milk Substitutes*, Jul 2010; Changing Markets Foundation, *Busting the Myth of Science-Based Formula: An Investigation into Nestlé Infant Milk Products and Claims*, Feb 2018.

26. Adams PJ, *Moral Jeopardy: Risks of Accepting Money from the Alcohol, Tobacco and Gambling Industries*, Cambridge University Press, 2016; Room R, "Sources of funding as an influence on alcohol studies," *Int J Alcohol Drug Res*. 2016, 5(1):15–16.

27. Cohen PA, "The supplement paradox: Negligible benefits, robust consumption," *JAMA* 2016, 316(14):1453–1454; Kantor ED, Rehm CD, Du M, et al., "Trends in dietary supplement use among US adults from 1999–2012," *JAMA* 2016, 316(14):1464–1474.

28. Rogers PJ, Hogenkamp PS, de Graaf C, et al., "Does low-energy sweetener consumption affect energy intake and body weight? A systematic review, including meta-analyses, of the evidence from human and animal studies," *Int J Obes*. 2016, 40(3):381–394; Pase MP, Himali JJ, Beiser AS, et al., "Sugar- and artificially sweetened beverages and the risks of incident stroke and dementia: A prospective cohort study," *Stroke* 2017, 48:1139–1146.

29. Krimsky S, Gruber J, eds., *The GMO Deception: What You Need to Know about the Food, Corporations, and Government Agencies*, Skyhorse Publishing, 2014; Lipton E, "Food industry enlisted academics in G.M.O. lobbying war, emails show," *NY Times*, Sep 5, 2015; Hakim D, "Scientists loved and loathed by an agrochemical colossus," *NY Times*, Jan 2, 2017; Gilliam C, *Whitewashed: The Story of a Weed Killer, Cancer, and the Corruption of Science*, Island Press, 2017.

30. Karasu SR, "Interests conflicted: A 'wicked' problem in medical research," *Psychol Today*, Oct 12, 2016; McCoy MS, Emanuel EJ, "Why there are no 'potential' conflicts of interest," *JAMA* 2017, 317(17):1721–1722.

Chapter 2. A Cautionary Tale: Drug Company Influence

1. Gomes FS, "Conflicts of interest in food and nutrition," *Cad Saúde Pública* 2015, 31(10):2039–2046; Madureira Lima J, Galea S, "Corporate practices and health: A framework and mechanisms," *Global Health* 2018, 14(1):21.

2. Oreskes N, Conway EM, *Merchants of Doubt: How a Handful of Scientists Obscured the Truth on Issues from Tobacco Smoke to Global Warming*, Bloomsbury Press, 2010; Brownell KD, Warner KE, "The perils of ignoring history: Big Tobacco played dirty and millions died. How similar is Big Food?" *Milbank Q.* 2009, 87(1):259–294; Moodie AR, "What public health practitioners need to know about unhealthy industry tactics," *Am J Public Health* 2017, 107(7):1047–1049.

3. Thompson DF, "Understanding financial conflicts of interest," *N Engl J Med.* 1993, 329(8):573–576; White J, Bandura A, Bero LA, "Moral disengagement in the corporate world," *Account Res.* 2009, 16(1):41–74.

4. American Diabetes Association, Advance program, 65th scientific sessions, San Diego, Jun 10–14, 2005.

5. Yki-Järvinen H, "Type 2 diabetes: Remission in just a week," *Diabetologia* 2011, 54:2477–2478; Ades PA, Savage PD, Marney AM, et al., "Remission of recently diagnosed type 2 diabetes mellitus with weight loss and exercise," *J Cardiopulm Rehabil Prev.* 2015, 35(3):193–197.

6. Silverman MM, Lee PR, *Pills, Profits and Politics*, University of California Press, 1974; Angell M, *The Truth About the Drug Companies: How They Deceive Us and What to Do About It*, Random House, 2004.

7. Sah S, Fugh-Berman A, "Physicians under the influence: Social psychology and industry marketing strategies," *J Law Med Ethics* 2013, 41(3):665–672; Katz D, Caplan AL, Merz JF, "All gifts large and small: Toward an understanding of the ethics of pharmaceutical industry gift-giving," *Am J Bioeth.* 2003, 3(3):39–46; Lo B, Grady D, "Payments to physicians: Does the amount of money make a difference?" *JAMA* 2017, 317(17):1719–1720.

8. Association of American Medical Colleges and Baylor College of Medicine, *The Scientific Basis of Influence and Reciprocity: A Symposium*, Jun 12, 2007.

9. Lo B, "The future of conflicts of interest: A call for professional standards," *J Law Med Ethics* 2012, 40(3):441–451; US Department of Health and Human Services, *Medicare, Medicaid, Children's Health Insurance Programs; Transparency Reports and Reporting of Physician Ownership or Investment Interests; Final Rule*, Fed Reg. 2013, 78(27):9458–9528; Thacker PD, "Consumers deserve to know who's funding health research," *Harvard Business Rev.*, Dec 2, 2014; Centers for Medicare & Medicaid Services, "The facts about Open Payments data," for 2016, Jan 17, 2018.

10. Orlowski JP, Wateska L, "The effects of pharmaceutical firm enticements on physician prescribing patterns: There's no such thing as a free lunch," *Chest* 1992, 102:270–273; Wazana A, "Physicians and the pharmaceutical industry: Is a gift ever just a gift?" *JAMA* 2000, 283(3):373–380.

11. Tringale KR, Marshall D, Mackey TK, et al., "Types and distribution of payments from industry to physicians in 2015," JAMA 2017, 317(17):1774–1784; Yeh JS, Franklin JM, Avorn J, "Association of industry payments to physicians with the prescribing of brand-name statins in Massachusetts," JAMA Intern Med. 2016, 176(6):763–768; Hadland SE, Krieger MS, Marshall BDL, "Industry payments to physicians for opioid products, 2013–2015," Am J Public Health 2017, 107(9):1493–1495.

12. Robertson C, Rose S, Kesselheim AS, "Effect of financial relationships on the behaviors of health care professionals: A review of the evidence," J Law Med Ethics 2012, 40(3)l:452–466; Larkin I, Ang D, Steinhart J, et al., "Association between academic medical center pharmaceutical detailing policies and prescription prescribing," JAMA 2017, 317(17):1785–1795; DeJong C, Aguilar T, Tseng C-W, et al., "Pharmaceutical industry–sponsored meals and physician prescribing patterns for Medicare beneficiaries," JAMA Intern Med. 2016, 176(8):1114–1122; Ornstein C, "Public disclosure of payments to physicians from industry," JAMA 2017, 317(17):1749–1750.

13. Campbell EG, Rao SR, DesRoches CM, et al., "Physician professionalism and changes in physician-industry relationships from 2004 to 2009," Arch Intern Med. 2010, 170(20):1820–1826; Huston L, "Dollars for heart docs: 2015 edition," Cardio/Brief, Aug 24, 2016; Ornstein C, Jones RG, Tigas M, "New analysis shows relationship between drug company payments, prescription rates," ProPublica, Boston Globe, Mar 17, 2016; Miller DT, "Commentary: Psychologically naïve assumptions about the perils of conflicts of interest," in: Moore DA, Cain DM, Loewenstein G, Bazerman MH, eds., Conflicts of Interest: Challenges and Solutions in Business, Law, Medicine, and Public Policy, Cambridge University Press, 2005, 126–129.

14. Sah S, "Conflicts of interest and your physician: Psychological processes that cause unexpected changes in behavior," J Law Med Ethics 2012, 40(3):482–487; Sah S, Loewenstein G, "Effect of reminders of personal sacrifice and suggested rationalizations on residents' self-reported willingness to accept gifts," JAMA 2010, 304(11):1204–1211.

15. Krimsky S, "The ethical and legal foundations of scientific 'conflict of interest,'" in: Lemmens T, Waring DR, eds., Law and Ethics in Biomedical Research: Regulation, Conflict of Interest, and Liability, University of Toronto Press, 2006, 63–81; Steinbrook R, "Financial conflicts of interest and the Food and Drug Administration's advisory committees," N Engl J Med. 2005, 353(2):116–118.

16. US Food and Drug Administration, "Advisory committees"; US Food and Drug Administration, "Advisory committees: Financial conflicts of interest overview," undated; Steinbrook R, "Disclosing the conflicts of interest of

US Food and Drug Administration advisory committee members," *JAMA Intern Med.* 2017, 177(7):919–920.

17. Pham-Kanter G, "Revisiting financial conflicts of interest in FDA advisory committees," *Milbank Q.* 2014, 92(3):446–470; Califf RM, "FDA advisory committees: Independent, informed, essential, and evolving," *FDA Voice*, Jan 18, 2017.

18. Mitchell AP, Basch EM, Dusetzina SB, "Financial relationships with industry among National Comprehensive Cancer Network guideline authors," *JAMA Oncol.* 2016, 2(12):1628–1631; Jones DJ, Barkun AN, Lu Y, et al., "Conflicts of interest ethics: Silencing expertise in the development of international clinical practice guidelines," *Ann Intern Med.* 2012, 156(11):809–816.

19. Rose SL, Highland J, Karafa MT, et al., "Patient advocacy organizations, industry funding, and conflicts of interest," *JAMA Intern Med.* 2017, 177(3):344–350; Kopp E, Lupkin S, Lucas E, "Patient advocacy groups take in millions from drugmakers. Is there a payback?" Kaiser Health News, Apr 6, 2018.

20. US Senate Homeland Security and Government Affairs Committee, minority staff report, "Fueling an epidemic, report two: Exposing the financial ties between opioid manufacturers and third party advocacy groups." US Senate, 2018.

21. US Food and Drug Administration, "FDA approves first treatment for sexual desire disorder," press release, Aug 18, 2015.

22. Spencer PH, Cohen IG, Adashi EY, Kesselheim AS, "Influence, integrity, and the FDA: An ethical framework," *Science* 2017, 357:876–877; Moynihan R, "Evening the score on sex drugs: Feminist movement or marketing masquerade?" *BMJ* 2014, 349:g6246; Schulte B, Dennis B, "FDA approves controversial drug for women with low sex drives," *Wash Post* Aug 18, 2015.

23. Thomas K, "Loyalties split, patient groups skip drug price debate," *NY Times*, Sep 28, 2016.

24. Ross JS, Gross CP, Krumholz HM, "Promoting transparency in pharmaceutical industry–sponsored research," *Am J Public Health* 2012, 102(1):72–80.

25. Krimsky S, "Do financial conflicts of interest bias research? An inquiry into the 'funding effect' hypothesis," *Sci Tech Human Values* 2012, 38(4):566–587; Stelfox HT, Chua G, O'Rourke K, Detsky AS, "Conflict of interest in the debate over calcium-channel antagonists," *N Engl J Med.* 1998, 338(2):101–106; Bekelman JE, Li Y, Gross CP, "Scope and impact of financial conflicts of interest in biomedical research: A systematic review," *JAMA* 2003, 289(4):454–465.

26. Bero L, Oostvogel F, Bacchetti P, Lee K, "Factors associated with findings of published trials of drug-drug comparisons," *PLoS Med.* 2007, 4(6):e184; Yank V, Rennie D, Bero LA, "Financial ties and concordance between results

and conclusions in meta-analyses: Retrospective cohort study," *BMJ* 2007, 7631:1202–1205; Lundh A, Sismondo S, Lexchin J, et al., "Industry sponsorship and research outcome," *Cochrane Database Syst Rev.* 2012, 12:MR000033; Ridker PM, Torres J, "Reported outcomes in major cardiovascular clinical trials funded by for-profit and not-for-profit organizations: 2000–2005," *JAMA* 2006, 295(19):2270–2274; Cho MK, Bero LA, "The quality of drug studies published in symposium proceedings," *Ann Intern Med.* 1996, 124(5):485–489; DeAngelis CD, "Conflict of interest and the public trust," *JAMA* 2000, 284(17):2237–2238.

27. White J, Bero LA, "Corporate manipulation of research," *Stan Law and Pol Rev.* 2010, 21:105–134; Fineberg HV, "Conflict of interest: Why does it matter?" *JAMA* 2017, 317(17):1717–1718; Liu JJ, Bell CM, Matelski JJ, et al., "Payments by US pharmaceutical and medical device manufacturers to US medical journal editors: Retrospective observational study," *BMJ* 2017, 359:j4619.

28. Dana J, Loewenstein G, "A social science perspective on gifts to physicians from industry," *JAMA* 2003, 290(2):252–255.

29. Lichter AS, "Conflict of interest and the integrity of the medical profession," *JAMA* 2017, 317(17):1725–1726; Relman AS, "Dealing with conflicts of interest," *New Engl J Med.* 1984, 310(18):1192–1193, and 1985, 313(12):749–751; Council on Ethical and Judicial Affairs of the American Medical Association, "Gifts to physicians from industry," *JAMA* 1991, 265(4):501.

30. US Department of Health and Human Services, Public Health Service, "Objectivity in research," *Federal Register* 1995, 60(132):35810–35819.

31. Pharmaceutical Research and Manufacturers of America, *Code on Interactions with Healthcare Professionals*, Feb 2, 2017 (originally published in 2009).

32. Kassirer JP, "A piece of my mind: Financial indigestion," *JAMA* 2000, 284(17):2156–2157.

33. Korn D, Carlat D, "Conflicts of interest in medical education: Recommendations from the Pew Task Force on Medical Conflicts of Interest," *JAMA* 2013, 310(22):2397–2398; Steinbrook R, "Industry payments to physicians and prescribing of brand-name drugs," *JAMA Intern Med.* 2016, 176(8):1123.

34. Silverman E, "Vermont probes whether drug makers violated its gift ban," *Stat*, Nov 9, 2017; Silverman E, "Medical groups push to water down requirements for disclosing industry ties," *Stat*, Jul 21, 2016.

Chapter 3. The Unusual Complexity of Nutrition Research

1. McCollum EV, *A History of Nutrition: The Sequence of Ideas in Nutrition Investigations*, Houghton Mifflin, 1957.

2. Van Helvoort T, email to author, Jan 12, 2017; Nestlé, "Research & development," 2016, www.nestle.com/randd; Unilever, "Working in Unilever R&D," 2016, www.unilever.com/about/innovation/working-in-unilever-r-and-d/index.html.

3. Bandler DK, Holland RF, *Food Science at Cornell University . . . A Century of Excellence, 1902–2002*, Cornell eCommons, 2002.

4. Cornell University, College of Agriculture and Life Sciences, Department of Food Science, "About us," foodscience.cals.cornell.edu/about-us.

5. Nesheim MC, *The Division of Nutritional Sciences at Cornell University: A History and Personal Reflections*, Cornell eCommons, 2010; Cornell University Division of Nutritional Sciences, College of Human Ecology, www.human.cornell.edu/dns.

6. Pierce JP, Natarajan L, Caan BJ, et al., "Influence of a diet very high in vegetables, fruit, and fiber and low in fat on prognosis following treatment for breast cancer: The Women's Healthy Eating and Living (WHEL) randomized trial," *JAMA* 2007, 298(3):289–298.

7. John Pierce, emails to author, Dec 27, 2016.

8. Pierce JP, Faerber S, Wright FA, et al., "A randomized trial of the effect of a plant-based dietary pattern on additional breast cancer events and survival: The Women's Healthy Eating and Living (WHEL) Study," *Cont Clin Trials* 2002, 23:728–756; Pierce JP, Stefanick ML, Flatt SW, et al., "Greater survival after breast cancer in physically active women with high vegetable-fruit intake regardless of obesity," *J Clin Oncol.* 2007, 25(17):2345–2351; Women's Healthy Eating and Living (WHEL) Study, Bibliography, updated Jan 2016, downloadable at https://library.ucsd.edu/dc/object/bb2493244b, digital collections, University of California, San Diego, Library, Jan 2016.

9. Romano C, letter to researchers from the California Table Grape Commission, Oct 26, 2017 (author's copy).

10. Yogurt in Nutrition, "Grant application 2016: Call for research proposals," Jun 20, 2016 (author's copy).

11. California Strawberry Commission, letter to strawberry nutrition researchers, Mar 5, 2018 (author's copy).

12. Sacks G, personal communication, used with permission.

13. Wallace M, "Aspartame NutraSweet," *60 Minutes* News Segment, Dec 29, 1996, available on YouTube, Jun 9, 2011; Walton RG, "Survey of aspartame studies: Correlation of outcome and funding sources," unpublished paper, Northeastern Ohio Universities College of Medicine, 1996, summary available at www.lightenyourtoxicload.com/wp-content/uploads/2014/07/Dr-Walton-survey-of-aspartame-studies.pdf.

14. Levine J, Gussow JD, Hastings D, Eccher A, "Authors' financial relationships with the food and beverage industry and their published positions on the fat substitute Olestra," *Am J Public Health* 2003, 93(4):664–669; Nestle M, "The selling of Olestra," *Public Health Rep.* 1998, 113:508–520. See also Nestle M, "Selling the ultimate techno-food: Olestra," in: *Food Politics*, University of California Press, 2002, 338–357.

15. US Food and Drug Administration, Code of Federal Regulations Title 21: Section 172.867 "Olestra"; Gentilviso C, "The 50 worst inventions," *Time*, May 27, 2010.

16. Ludwig DS, Peterson KE, Gortmaker SL, "Relation between consumption of sugar-sweetened drinks and childhood obesity: A prospective, observational analysis," *Lancet* 2001, 357:505–508.

17. Lesser LI, Ebbeling CB, Goozner M, et al., "Relationship between funding source and conclusion among nutrition-related scientific articles," *PLoS Med.* 2007, Jan, 4(1):e5; Vartanian LR, Schwartz MB, Brownell KD, "Effects of soft drink consumption on nutrition and health: A systematic review and meta-analysis," *Am J Public Health* 2007, 97(4):667–675; Bes-Rastrollo M, Schulze MB, Ruiz-Canela M, Martinez-Gonzalez MA, "Financial conflicts of interest and reporting bias regarding the association between sugar-sweetened beverages and weight gain: A systematic review of systematic reviews," *PLoS Med.* 2013, 10(12):e1001578; Massougbodji J, Le Bodo Y, Fratu R, De Wals P, "Reviews examining sugar-sweetened beverages and body weight: Correlates of their quality and conclusions," *Am J Clin Nutr.* 2014, 99(5):1096–1104.

18. Schillinger D, Tran J, Mangurian C, Kearns C, "Do sugar-sweetened beverages cause obesity and diabetes? Industry and the manufacture of scientific controversy," *Ann Intern Med.* 2016, 165(12):895–897.

19. Litman EA, Gortmaker SL, Ebbeling CB, Ludwig DS, "Source of bias in sugar-sweetened beverage research: A systematic review," *Public Health Nutr.* 2018, 21(12):2345–2350.

20. Chartres N, Fabbri A, Bero LA, "Association of industry sponsorship with outcomes of nutrition studies: A systematic review and meta-analysis," *JAMA Intern Med.* 2016, 176(12):1769–1777.

21. Bero L, "Systematic review: A method at risk for being corrupted," *Am J Public Health* 2017, 107(1):93–96; Diels J, Cunha M, Manaia C, et al., "Association of financial or professional conflict of interest to research outcomes on health risks or nutritional assessment studies of genetically modified products," *Food Policy* 2011, 36(2):197–203.

22. Myers EF, Parrott JS, Cummins DS, Splett P, "Funding source and research report quality in nutrition practice-related research," *PLoS One* 2011, 6(12):e28437.

23. Center for Media and Democracy, SourceWatch, "International Life Sciences Institute," www.sourcewatch.org/index.php/International_Life _Sciences_Institute.

24. Kaiser KA, Cofield SS, Fontaine KR, et al., "Is funding source related to study reporting quality in obesity or nutrition randomized control trials in top-tier medical journals?" *Int J Obes.* 2012, 36(7):977–981; Thomas O, Thabane L, Douketis J, et al., "Industry funding and the reporting quality of large long-term weight trials," *Int J Obes.* 2008, 32(10):1531–1536.

25. Odierna DH, Forsyth SR, White J, Bero LA, "The cycle of bias in health research: A framework and toolbox for critical appraisal training," *Account Res.* 2013, 20(2):127–141.

26. Fabbri A, Chartres N, Scrinis G, Bero LA, "Study sponsorship and the nutrition research agenda: Analysis of randomized controlled trials included in systematic reviews of nutrition interventions to address obesity," *Public Health Nutr.* 2017, 20(7):1306–1313.

27. Bero L, "Essays on health: How food companies can sneak bias into scientific research," *The Conversation*, Nov 1, 2016.

28. Katan M, "Does industry sponsorship undermine the integrity of nutrition research?" *PLoS Med.* 2007, 4(1):e6.

29. Marks JH, "Toward a systemic ethics of public-private partnerships related to food and health," *Kennedy Inst Ethics J.* 2014, 24(3):267–299; Marks JH, "What's the big deal? The ethics of public-private partnerships related to food and health," Edmond J. Safra Working Papers, no. 11, May 23, 2013.

Chapter 4. How Sweet It Is: Sugar and Candy as Health Foods

1. Lustig R, Schmidt LA, Brindis CD, "Public health: The toxic truth about sugar," *Nature* 2012, 482:27–29; Taubes G, *The Case Against Sugar*, Knopf, 2016; Johnson RK, Appel LJ, Brands M, et al., "Dietary sugars intake and cardiovascular health: A scientific statement from the American Heart Association," *Circulation* 2009, 120(11):1011–1020; Vos MB, Kaar JL, Welsh JA, et al., "Added sugars and cardiovascular disease risk in children: A scientific statement from the American Heart Association," *Circulation* 2016, 135(19):e1017–1034; World Health Organization, *Sugars Intake for Adults and Children: Guideline*, 2015; US Department of Health and Human Services and US Department of Agriculture, *Dietary Guidelines for Americans, 2015–2020*, 8th ed., Dec 2015.

2. Gornall J, "Sugar: Spinning a web of influence," *BMJ* 2015, 350:h231; Goldman G, Carlson C, Bailin D, et al., "Added sugar, subtracted science: How industry obscures science and undermines public health policy on sugar," Union of Concerned Scientists, Jun 2014.

3. Kearns CE, Glantz SA, Schmidt LA, "Sugar industry influence on the scientific agenda of the National Institute of Dental Research's 1971 National Caries Program: A historical analysis of internal documents," *PLoS Med.* 2015, 12(3):e1001798.

4. Tenenbaum JS, Venable, Baetjer, Howard and Civiletti, LLP, letter to author, Mar 27, 2002.

5. Western Sugar Coop, et al. v. Archer-Daniels-Midland Co., et al., US District Court for the Central District of California, 2015 US dist. LEXIS 21448, Feb 13, 2015.

6. Goldman G, Carlson C, Bailin D, et al., "Added sugar, subtracted science: How industry obscures science and undermines public health policy on sugar," Union of Concerned Scientists, Jun 2014.

7. Nestle M, "Sugar v. HFCS: How I got involved in this lawsuit," *FoodPolitics.com*, Feb 12, 2014.

8. Lipton E, "A war over sweetener market share," *NY Times*, Feb 11, 2014.

9. Bocarsly ME, Powell ES, Avena NM, Hoebel BG, "High-fructose corn syrup causes characteristics of obesity in rats: Increased body weight, body fat and triglyceride levels," *Pharmacol Biochem Behav.* 2010, 97(1):101–106; Nestle M, "HFCS makes rats fat?" *FoodPolitics.com*, Mar 24, 2010; Erickson A, email exchange with J. Justin Wilson, Mar 26, 2010, p. 14, in: Lipton E, "A war over sweetener market share. Using Marion Nestle," *NY Times*, Feb 11, 2014.

10. Ventura EE, Davis JN, Goran MI, "Sugar content of popular sweetened beverages based on objective laboratory analysis: Focus on fructose content," *Obesity* 2011, 19(4):868–874.

11. Martosko D to Audrae Erickson, email, Oct 30, 2010, in: Lipton E, "A war over sweetener market share. Bury the data," p. 11, *NY Times*, Feb 11, 2014.

12. Brady B to Bonnie E. Raquet, email, Dec 8, 2008, in: Lipton E, "A war over sweetener market share. Bury the data," p. 6, *NY Times*, Feb 11, 2014; Hamburger T, "'Soft lobbying' war between sugar, corn syrup shows new tactics in Washington influence," *Wash Post*, Feb 12, 2014.

13. Erickson A to Alan Willits and Jeff Cotter at Cargill, email, Sep 25, 2009, in: Lipton E, "A war over sweetener market share. Keeping it a secret," p. 7, *NY Times*, Feb 11, 2014.

14. Rippe JM to Audrae Erickson, email, Jul 16, 2009, in: Lipton E, "A war over sweetener market share. Dr. Rippe's Work," pp. 27–29, *NY Times*, Feb 11, 2014.

15. Rippe JM, "The metabolic and endocrine response and health implications of consuming sugar-sweetened beverages: Findings from recent randomized controlled trials," *Adv Nutr.* 2013, 4(6):677–686; Angelopoulos TJ,

Lowndes J, Sinnett S, Rippe JM, "Fructose containing sugars at normal levels of consumption do not effect adversely components of the metabolic syndrome and risk factors for cardiovascular disease," *Nutrients* 2016, 8(4):179.

16. DiNicolantorio JJ, O'Keefe JH, Lucan SC, "Added fructose: A principal driver of type 2 diabetes mellitus and its consequences," *Mayo Clin Proc.* 2015, 90(3):372–381; Malik VS, Hu FB, "Fructose and cardiometabolic health," *J Am Coll Cardiol.* 2015, 66(14):1615–1624.

17. Sievenpiper JL, "Sickeningly sweet: Does sugar cause chronic disease? No," *Can J Diabetes* 2016, 40:287–295; Choo VL, Ha V, Sievenpiper JL, "Sugars and obesity: Is it the sugars or the calories?" *Nutr Bull.* 2015, 40:88–96; Kahn R, Sievenpiper J, "Dietary sugar and body weight: Have we reached a crisis in the epidemic of obesity and diabetes? We have, but the pox on sugar is overwrought and overworked," *Diabetes Care* 2014, 37:957–962.

18. Jamnik J, Rehman S, Mejia SB, et al., "Fructose intake and risk of gout and hyperuricemia: A systematic review and meta-analysis of prospective cohort studies," *BMJ Open* 2016, 6:e013191; Jayalath VH, de Souza RJ, Ha V, et al., "Sugar-sweetened beverage consumption and incident hypertension: A systematic review and meta-analysis of prospective cohorts," *Am J Clin Nutr.* 2015, 102(4):914–921.

19. Sievenpiper JL quoted in Gornell J, "Sugar's web of influence 2: Biasing the science," *BMJ* 2015, 350:h215.

20. Ioannidis JPA, "The mass production of redundant, misleading, and conflicted systematic reviews and meta-analyses," *Milbank Q.* 2016, 94(3):485–514.

21. Ohmenhaeuser M, Monakhova YB, Kuballa T, Lachenmeier DW, "Qualitative and quantitative control of honeys using NMR spectroscopy and chemometrics," *ISRN Anal Chem.* 2013:1–9; US Department of Agriculture, Agricultural Marketing Service, National Honey Board, "About the NHB," www.honey.com/about-the-nhb.

22. Raatz SK, Johnson LK, Picklo MJ, "Consumption of honey, sucrose, and high-fructose corn syrup produces similar metabolic effects in glucose-tolerant and -intolerant individuals," *J Nutr.* 2015, 145(10):2265–2272.

23. National Confectioners Association, "The economic impact and leadership of America's confectionery industry," 2018.

24. Choi C, "AP Exclusive: How candy makers shape nutrition science," AP, Jun 2, 2016.

25. O'Neil CE, Fulgoni VL, Nicklas TA, "Association of candy consumption with body weight measures, other health risk factors for cardiovascular disease, and diet quality in US children and adolescents: NHANES 1999–2004," *Food Nutr Res.* 2011, 55:10.3402/fnr.v55i0.5794.

26. National Confectioners Association, "New study shows children and adolescents who eat candy are less overweight or obese," *PR Newswire*, Jun 28, 2011.

27. Pacyniak B, "'The only thing that moves sales is health claims.' AP article claims food research more about marketing than science," *Candy Ind.*, Jun 8, 2016.

28. Victor L. Fulgoni III, Nutrition Impact, LLC, www.nutritionimpact.com.

29. O'Neil CE, Fulgoni VL, Nicklas TA, "Candy consumption was not associated with body weight measures, risk factors for cardiovascular disease, or metabolic syndrome in US adults: NHANES 1999–2004," *Nutr Res.* 2011, 31(2):122–130.

30. O'Neil CE, Nicklas TA, Liu Y, Berenson GS, "Candy consumption in childhood is not predictive of weight, adiposity measures or cardiovascular risk factors in young adults: The Bogalusa Heart Study," *J Hum Nutr Diet* 2015, 28:59–69.

31. Murphy MM, Barraj LM, Bi X, Shumow L, "Abstract: Patterns of candy consumption in the United States, WWEIA, NHANES 2009–2012," *FASEB J.* 2015, 30(1)Suppl:1154.19.

32. Murphy M, Barraj LM, Bi X, Stettler N, "Body weight status and cardiovascular risk factors in adults by frequency of candy consumption," *Nutr J.* 2013, 12:53.

33. Fattore E, Botta F, Agostoni C, Bosetti C, "Effects of free sugars on blood pressure and lipids: A systematic review and meta-analysis of nutritional isoenergetic intervention trials," *Am J Clin Nutr.* 2017, 105(1):42–56.

34. Messerli FH, "Chocolate consumption, cognitive function, and Nobel Laureates," *N Engl J Med.* 2012, 367(16):1562–64.

35. Montopoli M, Stevens LC, Smith C, et al., "The acute electrocortical and blood pressure effects of chocolate," *NeuroReg.* 2015, 2(1):3–28.

36. Pekic V, "Step aside energy drinks: Chocolate has a stimulating effect on human brains, says Hershey-backed study," *Food Navigator*, May 18, 2015.

37. Fleming N, "The dark truth about chocolate," *Guardian*, Mar 25, 2018.

38. Mars, Incorporated, "The history of CocoaVia," www.cocoavia.com /how-we-make-it/history-of-cocoavia.

39. Vlachojannis J, Erne P, Zimmermann B, Chrubasik-Hausmann S, "The impact of cocoa flavanols on cardiovascular health," *Phytother Res.* 2016, 30(10):1641–1657; Andres-LaCueva C, Monagas M, Khan N, et al., "Flavanol and flavonol contents of cocoa powder products: Influence of the manufacturing process," *J Agric Food Chem.* 2008, 56:3111–3117; Crews WD, Harrison DW, Wright JW, "A double-blind, placebo-controlled, randomized trial of the effects of dark chocolate and cocoa on variables associated with neuropsychologi-

cal functioning and cardiovascular health: Clinical findings from a sample of healthy, cognitively intact older adults," *Am J Clin Nutr.* 2008, 87(4):872–880.

40. Meek J, "Chocolate is good for you (or how Mars tried to sell us this as health food)," *Guardian*, Dec 23, 2002; Barrionuevo A, "An apple a day for health? Mars recommends two bars of chocolate," *NY Times*, Oct 31, 2005.

41. US Food and Drug Administration, Inspections, Compliance, Enforcement, and Criminal Investigations, letter to Mr. John Helferich, Masterfoods USA, May 31, 2006 (author's copy).

42. Ottaviani JI, Balz M, Kimball J, et al., "Safety and efficacy of cocoa flavanol intake in healthy adults: A randomized, controlled, double-masked trial," *Am J Clin Nutr.* 2015, 102(6):1425–1435; Necozione S, Raffaele A, Pistacchio L, et al., "Cocoa flavanol consumption improves cognitive function, blood pressure control, and metabolic profile in elderly subjects: The Cocoa, Cognition, and Aging (CoCoA) Study—a randomized controlled trial," *Am J Clin Nutr.* 2015, 101(3):538–548; Heiss C, Sansone R, Karimi H, et al., "Impact of cocoa flavanol intake on age-dependent vascular stiffness in healthy men: A randomized, controlled, double-masked trial," *Age* 2015, 37:56; Sansone R, Rodriguez-Mateos A, Heuel J, et al., "Cocoa flavanol intake improves endothelial function and Framingham Risk Score in healthy men and women: A randomised, controlled, double-masked trial: The Flaviola Health Study," *Brit J Nutr.* 2015, 114(8):1246–1255.

43. Mars Center for Cocoa Health Science, "Cocoa flavanols lower blood pressure and increase blood vessel function in healthy people," press release, Sep 9, 2015.

44. CocoaVia, "Cocoa's past and present: A new era for heart health," advertisement, *NY Times*, Sep 27, 2015.

45. Advertising Self-Regulatory Council, "NAD recommends Mars modify certain claims for CocoaVia cocoa extract," ASRCReviews.org, Aug 11, 2016.

46. Mars, Inc., "Largest nutritional intervention trial of cocoa flavanols and hearth [sic] health to be launched," MarsCocoaScience.com, Mar 17, 2014; National Institutes of Health, US National Library of Medicine, "Cocoa Supplement and Multivitamin Outcomes Study (COSMOS)," ClinicalTrials.gov.

47. Greene R, Berger R, "Does cocoa prevent cancer? Mars. [sic] Inc. pays Harvard scientists for 'research,'" *The Russells*, Sep 19, 2016; Manson JE, Sesso HD, Anderson G, letter to potential participants in the COSMOS trial, Aug 2016, https://drive.google.com/file/d/0B8wI0BJ2R7tMTW1pRTluR1 k1aTl6SG5hZ0ZYTElwNG50aTRj/view.

48. Fleming N, "The dark truth about chocolate," *Guardian*, Mar 25, 2018.

49. Belluz J, "Dark chocolate is now a health food. Here's how that happened," *Vox*, Oct 16, 2017; Nieburg O, "Mars: We have no agenda to create

chocolate health halo with cocoa flavanol studies," *Confectionary News*, Jan 17, 2018.

50. Gornall J, "Sugar's web of influence 4: Mars and company: Sweet heroes or villains?" *BMJ* 2015, 350:h220; "Dolmio and Uncle Ben's firm Mars advises limit on products," BBC broadcast, Apr 15, 2016; Choi C, "Snickers maker criticizes industry-funded paper on sugar," *Business Insider*, Dec 21, 2016; Michail N, "Breaking away from bad science? Mars to leave ILSI in transparency bid," *Food Navigator*, Feb 8, 2018.

51. Mars, Inc., Corporate Reputation Team, email to author, Sep 26, 2016.

Chapter 5. Selling Meat and Dairy Foods

1. Craig WJ, "Health effects of vegan diets," *Am J Clin Nutr*. 2009, 89(suppl):1627s–1633s; Rajaram S, Wien M, Sabaté J, eds., "Sixth International Congress on Vegetarian Nutrition: Proceedings of a symposium held in Loma Linda, CA, Feb 24–26, 2013," *Am J Clin Nutr*. 2014, 100(suppl1):303s–502s.

2. Mihrshahi S, Ding D, Gale J, et al., "Vegetarian diet and all-cause mortality: Evidence from a large population-based Australian cohort—the 45 and Up study," *Prev Med*. 2017, 97(4):1–7.

3. Pew Commission on Industrial Farm Animal Production, *Putting Meat on the Table: Industrial Farm Animal Production in America*, 2008; Greger M, Stone G, *How Not to Die: Discover the Foods Scientifically Proven to Prevent and Reverse Disease*, Flatiron Books, 2015.

4. Wilde P, *Food Policy in the United States: An Introduction*, Routledge/Earthscan, 2013.

5. National Cattlemen's Beef Association, announcement, undated, www.beefresearch.org/CMDocs/BeefResearch/Researcher's%20Hub/indirect%20cost%20statement.pdf; National Cattlemen's Beef Association, "FY 2018 call for pre-proposals: Human nutrition research," 2018.

6. Burkitt DP, "Epidemiology of cancer of the colon and rectum," *Cancer* 1971, 28(1):3–13; Cross AJ, Leitzmann MF, Gail MH, et al., "A prospective study of red and processed meat intake in relation to cancer risk," *PLoS Med*. 2007, 4(12):e325.

7. Genkinger JM, Koushik A, "Meat consumption and cancer risk," *PLoS Med*. 2007, 4(12):e345; International Agency for Research on Cancer, "IARC monographs evaluate consumption of red meat and processed meat," press release no. 240, Oct 26, 2015.

8. National Cattlemen's Beef Association, "Science does not support international agency opinion on red meat and cancer," press release, Oct 26, 2015.

9. Alexander DD, Weed DL, Miller PE, Mohamed MA, "Red meat and colorectal cancer: A quantitative update on the state of the epidemiologic science," *J Am Coll Nutr.* 2015, 34:521–543; Bylsma LC, Alexander DD, "A review and meta-analysis of prospective studies of red and processed meat, meat cooking methods, heme iron, heterocyclic amines and prostate cancer," *Nutr J.* 2015, 14:125.

10. Agarawal S, Fulgoni VL, Berg EP, "Association of lunch meat consumption with nutrient intake, diet quality and health risk factors in U.S. children and adults: NHANES 2007–2010," *Nutr J.* 2015, 14:128.

11. Slavin J, "The challenges of nutrition policymaking," *Nutr J.* 2015, 14:15.

12. O'Connor LE, Kim JE, Campbell WW, "Total red meat intake of ≥ 0.5 servings/d does not negatively influence cardiovascular disease risk factors: A systemically searched meta-analysis of randomized controlled trials," *Am J Clin Nutr.* 2017, 105(1):57–69; Phillips SM, Fulgoni VL, Heaney RP, et al., "Commonly consumed protein foods contribute to nutrient intake, diet quality, and nutrient adequacy," *Am J Clin Nutr.* 2015, 101(6):1346s–1352s.

13. Månsson HL, "Fatty acids in bovine milk fat," *Food Nutr Res.* 2008, 52:10.3402/fnr.v52i0.1821; Sacks FM, Lichtenstein AH, Wu JHY, et al., "Dietary fats and cardiovascular disease: A presidential advisory from the American Heart Association," *Circulation* 2017, 136:e1–e23.

14. Li Y, Hruby A, Bernstein AM, et al., "Saturated fats compared with unsaturated fats and sources of carbohydrates in relation to risk of coronary heart disease: A prospective cohort study," *J Am Coll Cardiol.* 2015, 66(14):1538–1548; Zong G, Li Y, Wanders AJ, et al., "Intake of individual saturated fatty acids and risk of coronary heart disease in US men and women: Two prospective longitudinal cohort studies," *BMJ* 2016, 355:i5796. Hu was senior (last) author on both.

15. Wheatley SD, Deakin T, Reeves T, Whitaker M, "Letter: Intake of individual saturated fatty acids and risk of coronary heart disease in US men and women: Two prospective longitudinal cohort studies," *BMJ* 2016, 355:i5796.

16. Faghihnia N, Mangravite LM, Chiu S, et al., "Effects of dietary saturated fat on LDL subclasses and apolipoprotein CIII in men," *Eur J Clin Nutr.* 2012, 66(11):1229–1233.

17. US Department of Agriculture, Agricultural Marketing Service, "Report to Congress on the National Dairy Promotion and Research Program and the National Fluid Milk Processor Promotion Program: 2012 Program Activities," www.ams.usda.gov.

18. Collier R, "Dairy research: 'Real' science or marketing?" *CMAJ* 2016, 188(10):715–716.

19. Simon M, *Whitewashed: How Industry and Government Promote Dairy Junk Foods,* EatDrinkPolitics.com, Jun 2014.

20. Wilde P, Morgan E, Roberts J, et al., "Relationship between funding sources and outcomes of obesity-related research," *Physiol and Behav.* 2012, 107(1):172–175.

21. National Dairy Council, "Dairy research for your business: Nutrition, product and sustainability research program overview, 2011–2016" (author's copy).

22. Lamarche B, Givens DI, Soedamah-Muthu S, et al., "Does milk consumption contribute to cardiometabolic health and overall diet quality?" *Can J Cardiol.* 2016, 32:1026–1032.

23. Guo J, Astrup A, Lovegrove JA, et al., "Milk and dairy consumption and risk of cardiovascular diseases and all-cause mortality: Dose-response, meta-analysis of prospective cohort studies," *Eur J Epidemiol.* 2017, 32(4):269–287; Atherton M, "Dairy 'does not increase heart attack or stroke risk,'" *FoodManufacture.com,* May 10, 2017.

24. Pasin G, Comerford KB, "Dairy foods and dairy proteins in the management of type 2 diabetes: A systematic review of the clinical evidence," *Adv Nutr.* 2015, 6(3):245–259; Chen G-C, Szeto IMY, Chen L-H, et al., "Dairy products consumption and metabolic syndrome in adults: Systematic review and meta-analysis of observational studies," *Sci Rep.* 2015, 5:14606; Quann EE, Fulgoni VL, Auestad N, "Consuming the daily recommended amounts of dairy products would reduce the prevalence of inadequate micronutrient intakes in the United States: Diet modeling study based on NHANES 2007–2010," *Nutr J.* 2015, 14:90; Pontes MV, Ribeiro TCM, Ribeiro H, et al., "Cow's milk–based beverage consumption in 1- to 4-year-olds and allergic manifestations: An RCT," *Nutr J.* 2016, 15:19; Seery S, Jakeman P, "A metered intake of milk following exercise and thermal dehydration restores whole-body net fluid balance better than a carbohydrate-electrolyte solution or water in healthy young men," *Brit J Nutr.* 2016, 116(6):1013–1021.

25. Drouin-Chartier J-P, Côté JA, Labonté MÈ, et al., "Comprehensive review of the impact of dairy foods and dairy fat on cardiometabolic risk," *Adv Nutr.* 2016, 7(6):1041–1051.

26. Lopez-Garcia E, Leon-Muñoz L, Guallar-Castillon P, Rodríguez-Artalejo F, "Habitual yogurt consumption and health-related quality of life: A prospective cohort study," *J Acad Nutr Diet.* 2015, 115:31–39; Bergholdt HK, Nordestgaard BG, Ellervik C, "Milk intake is not associated with low risk of diabetes or overweight-obesity: A Mendelian randomization study in 97,811 Danish individuals," *Am J Clin Nutr.* 2015, 102(2):487–496; Kim K, Wactawski-Wende J, Michels KA, et al., "Dairy food intake is associated with

reproductive hormones and sporadic anovulation among healthy premeno-pausal women," *J Nutr.* 2017, 147(2):218–226.

27. De Goede J, Geleijnse JM, Ding EL, Soedamah-Muthu SS, "Effect of cheese consumption on blood lipids: A systematic review and meta-analysis of randomized controlled trials," *Nutr Rev.* 2015, 73(5):259–275.

28. Thorning TK, Raziani F, Bendsen NT, et al., "Diets with high-fat cheese, high-fat meat, or carbohydrate on cardiovascular risk markers in over-weight postmenopausal women: A randomized crossover trial," *Am J Clin Nutr.* 2015, 102(2):573–581.

29. Marckmann P, "Letter: Misleading conclusions on health effects of cheese and meat-enriched diets in study sponsored by dairy industry," *Am J Clin Nutr.* 2016, 103(1):291–292; Thorning TK, Raziani F, Astrup A, et al., "Letter: Reply to P Marckmann," *Am J Clin Nutr.* 2016, 103(1):292.

30. Leaf A, "Every day is a gift when you are over 100," *Natl Geogr.*, Jan 1973, 93–118; Specter M, "Yogurt? Caucasus centenarians 'never eat it,'" *NY Times*, Mar 16, 1998; Babio N, Becerra-Tomás N, Martínez-González MA, et al., "Consumption of yogurt, low-fat milk, and other low-fat dairy products is associated with lower risk of metabolic syndrome incidence in an elderly Mediterranean population," *J Nutr.* 2015, 145(10):2308–2316; Laird E, Mol-loy AM, McNulty H, et al., "Greater yogurt consumption is associated with increased bone mineral density and physical function in older adults," *Oste-oporosis Int.* 2017, 28(8):2409–2419; Gijsbers L, Ding EL, Malik VS, et al., "Consumption of dairy foods and diabetes incidence: A dose-response me-ta-analysis of observational studies," *Am J Clin Nutr.* 2016, 103(4):1111–1124; Eales J, Lenoir-Wijnkoop I, King S, et al., "Is consuming yoghurt associated with weight management outcomes? Results from a systematic review," *Int J Obes.* 2016, 40(5):731–746; Brown-Riggs C, "Nutrition and health dispari-ties: The role of dairy in improving minority health outcomes," *Int J Environ Res Public Health* 2016, 13(1):28.

31. Lopez-Garcia E, Leon-Muñoz L, Guallar-Castillon P, Rodríguez-Artalejo F, "Habitual yogurt consumption and health-related quality of life: A prospective cohort study," *J Acad Nutr Diet.* 2015, 115(1):31–39.

32. Nestle M, "Industry-sponsored research: This week's collection," *Food Politics.com*, Jun 2, 2015.

33. University of Maryland, "Concussion-related measures improved in high school football players who drank new chocolate milk, UMD study shows," press release, Dec 22, 2015.

34. Bloom BM, Kinsella K, Pott J, et al., "Short-term neurocognitive and symptomatic outcomes following mild traumatic brain injury: A prospective multi-centre observational cohort study," *Brain Inj.* 2017, 31(3):304–311;

Mex J, Daneshvar DH, Kiernan PT, et al., "Clinicopathological evaluation of chronic traumatic encephalopathy in players of American football," *JAMA* 2017, 318(4):360–370; Kucera KL, Yau RK, Register-Mihalik J, et al., "Traumatic brain and spinal cord fatalities among high school and college football players—United States, 2005–2014," *MMWR* 2017, 65(52):1465–1469; Margolis LH, Canty G, Halstead M, Lantos JD, "Should school boards discontinue support for high school football?" *Pediatr.* 2017, 139(1):e20162604.

35. Swetlitz I, "Can chocolate milk speed concussion recovery? Experts cringe," *Stat News*, Jan 11, 2016.

36. Holtz A, Freedhoff Y, Stone K, "Release claiming chocolate milk improves concussion symptoms in student athletes is out-of-bounds," *Health News Review*, Jan 5, 2016.

37. Holtz A, "Why won't the University of Maryland talk about the chocolate milk / concussion study it was so eager to promote?" *Health News Review*, Jan 11, 2016.

38. Gantz S, "University of Maryland crosses ethical boundaries with chocolate milk study, experts say," *Baltimore Bus J.*, Jan 12, 2016.

39. Singal J, "The University of Maryland has a burgeoning chocolate-milk concussion scandal on its hands," *NY Mag.*, Jan 20, 2016.

40. Wylie AG, Ball GF, DeShong PR, et al., "Final report, ad hoc review committee," University of Maryland, Mar 24, 2016, (author's copy).

41. Gantz S, "University of Maryland committee finds fault in school's research, promotion of chocolate milk study," *Baltimore Bus J.*, Apr 1, 2016.

42. Belluz J, "The University of Maryland just released a report on its incredibly irresponsible chocolate milk research," *Vox*, Apr 1, 2016.

43. Lomangino K, Holland E, Holtz A, "U of Maryland review: Researcher on flawed chocolate milk / concussions study failed to disclose big dairy donations," *Health News Review*, Apr 1, 2016; Choi C, "Chocolate milk maker wanted study touted with 'Concussion,'" *Wash Post*, Apr 19, 2016; Bachynski KE, Goldberg DS, "Time out: NFL conflicts of interest with public health efforts to prevent TBI," *Inj Prev.* 2018, 24(3):180–184.

44. Caulfield T, Ogbogu U, "The commercialization of university-based research: Balancing risks and benefits," *BMC Med Ethics* 2015, 16:70.

Chapter 6. Research on Healthy Foods: Marketing, Not Necessarily Science

1. Schneeman B, "FDA's review of scientific evidence for health claims," *J Nutr.* 2007, 137(2):493–494; Royal Hawaiian Macadamia Nut, Inc., "Petition for the authorization of a qualified health claim for macadamia nuts and reduced risk of coronary heart disease," Sep 4, 2015, www.fda.gov/downloads

/Food/LabelingNutrition/UCM568057.pdf; Oriel AE, Cao Y, Bagshaw DO, et al., "A macadamia nut–rich diet reduces total and LDL-cholesterol in mildly hypercholesterolemic men and women," *J Nutr.* 2008, 138(4):761–767.

2. US Food and Drug Administration, "FDA completes review of qualified health claim petition for macadamia nuts and the risk of coronary heart disease," Jul 24, 2017.

3. Donahue L, "Go nuts, folks! FDA declares macadamia nuts heart healthy," *Hawaii News Now*, Jul 24, 2017.

4. Wild Blueberries, 2017, www.wildblueberries.com.

5. US Department of Agriculture, "Plant pigments paint a rainbow of antioxidants," *AgResearch Magazine*, Nov 1996. But see Wang H, Cao G, Prior RL, "Total antioxidant capacity of fruits," *J Agric Food Chem.* 1996, 44:701–705.

6. Conkling P, "The wild blueberry yonder," *Maine Mag.*, Dec 2015; "Amid plummeting prices, a growing fear: Fewer Maine blueberry farmers," *Portland Press Herald*, Jun 12, 2017.

7. Bjelakovic G, Nikolova D, Gluud LL, et al., "Antioxidant supplements for prevention of mortality in healthy participants and patients with various diseases," *Cochrane.org*, Mar 14, 2012.

8. US Department of Agriculture, Agricultural Research Service, "Oxygen Radical Absorbance Capacity (ORAC) of selected foods, Release 2 2010," last modified Aug 13, 2016.

9. National Center for Complementary and Integrative Health, "Antioxidants: In depth."

10. Cassidy A, Franz M, Rimm EB, "Dietary flavonoid intake and incidence of erectile dysfunction," *Am J Clin Nutr.* 2016, 103(2):534–541; University of East Anglia, "Blueberries associated with reduced risk of erectile dysfunction," press release, Jan 13, 2016.

11. Worn J, emails to author, Apr 15, 2016.

12. McKay DL, Eliasziw M, Chen C-YO, Blumberg JB, "Amelioration of cardiometabolic risk factors with a pecan-rich diet in overweight and obese adults," poster, ASN annual meeting, Experimental Biology, Boston, Apr 2016. Later, the authors aggregated data from their various measurements; the composite score indicated a clinically significant reduction in cardiometabolic risk. See McKay DL, Eliasziw M, Chen CYO, Blumberg JB, "A pecan-rich diet improves cardiometabolic risk factors in overweight and obese adults: A randomized controlled trial," *Nutrients* 2018, 10(3):339:1–17.

13. Solomon B, "Meet the Resnicks: Beverly Hills billionaire power couple behind Pom (not so) Wonderful," *Forbes*, May 22, 2012; Arax M, "A kingdom from dust," *California Sunday Mag.*, Jan 31, 2018.

14. Tupper M, email to author, Feb 20, 2008. See Kadet A, "The truth behind the pomegranate craze," *Smart Money*, Feb 4, 2008.

15. POM Wonderful lists its sponsored studies at www.wonderfulpome granateresearch.com.

16. Nestle M, "Be skeptical of food studies," *SF Chron.*, Mar 4, 2011.

17. Gillespie BK, letter to author, Apr 28, 2011.

18. US Federal Trade Commission, "FTC complaint charges deceptive advertising by POM Wonderful," Sep 27, 2010; US Federal Trade Commission, "POM Wonderful LLC and Roll Global LLC, in the matter of," Jan 16, 2013.

19. US Food and Drug Administration, "Label claims for conventional foods and dietary supplements," updated Apr 11, 2016.

20. US Food and Drug Administration, "Inspections, compliance, enforcement, and criminal investigations. Pom Wonderful. Warning letter to Matt Tupper, President," Feb 23, 2010, www.fda.gov/ICECI/EnforcementActions /WarningLetters/ucm202785.htm.

21. Pom Wonderful v. FDA, US District Court, District of Columbia, Complaint for declaratory relief, Sep 13, 2010, www.fdalawblog.net/files/pom -wonderful-complaint.pdf.

22. US Federal Trade Commission, "Administrative law judge upholds FTC's complaint that POM deceptively advertised its products as treating, preventing, or reducing the risk of heart disease, prostate cancer, and erectile dysfunction," press release, May 21, 2012.

23. Chappell DM, FTC Docket No. 9344, In the matter of Pom Wonderful, LLC, and Roll Global, LLC: Initial decision, May 17, 2012, www.ftc.gov /sites/default/files/documents/cases/2012/05/120521pomdecision.pdf.

24. Hiltzik M, "The 'science' behind Lynda Resnick's Pom Wonderful juice," *LA Times*, Oct 5, 2010.

25. POM advertisement, *Time*, Feb 27–Mar 6, 2017, 31.

26. Wu P-T, Fitschen PJ, Kistler BM, et al., "Effects of pomegranate extract supplementation on cardiovascular risk factors and physical function in hemodialysis patients," *J Med Food* 2015, 18(9):941–949.

27. Kaufman M, "FDA eases rules on touting food as healthful," *Wash Post*, Jul 11, 2003.

28. Quoted in Lee SM, "Pasta is good for you, say scientists funded by big pasta," BuzzFeed News, Apr 19, 2018.

29. MacKay D, "Guest post: These two raisin studies read like advertisements," *WeightyMatters.ca*, Dec 12, 2016.

30. Richter CK, Skulas-Ray AC, Gaugler TL, et al., "Incorporating freeze-dried strawberry powder into a high-fat meal does not alter postprandial

vascular function or blood markers of cardiovascular disease risk: A randomized controlled trial," *Am J Clin Nutr.* 2017, 105(2):313–322.

Chapter 7. Coca-Cola: A Case Study in Itself

1. Sacks G, Swinburn BA, Cameron AJ, Ruskin G, "How food companies influence evidence and opinion—straight from the horse's mouth," *Crit Public Health*, 2017, 25(2), online Sep 13; Grandjean AC, Reimers KJ, Buyckx ME, "Hydration: Issues for the 21st century," *Nutr Rev.* 2003, 61(8):261–271; Moye J, "Just the facts: 10 years in, Beverage Institute for Health and Wellness expands its reach," Coca-Cola, Dec 17, 2004; Short D, "When science met the consumer: The role of industry," *Am J Clin Nutr.* 2005, 92(suppl):256s–258s; O'Reilly CE, Freeman MC, Ravani M, et al., "The impact of a school-based safe water and hygiene programme on knowledge and practices of students and their parents in Nyanza Province, Western Kenya, 2006," *Epidemiol Infect.* 2008, 136(1):80–91.

2. Applebaum RS, "Balancing the debate," presentation to The Food Industry: Trends & Opportunities, 29th International Sweetener Symposium, Coeur d'Alene, Idaho, Aug 7, 2012, www.phaionline.org/wp-content/uploads/2015/08/Rhona-Applebaum.pdf.

3. Serôdio PM, McKee M, Stuckler D, "Coca-Cola—a model of transparency in research partnerships? A network analysis of Coca-Cola's research funding (2008–2016)," *Public Health Nutr.* 2018, 21(9):1594–1607; Shook RP, Hand GA, Drenowatz C, et al., "Low levels of physical activity are associated with dysregulation of energy intake and fat mass gain over 1 year," *Am J Clin Nutr.* 2015, 102(6):1332–1338; Choo VL, Ha V, Sievenpiper JL, "Sugars and obesity: Is it the sugars or the calories?" *Nutr Bull.* 2015, 40:88–96; Althuis MD, Weed DL, "Evidence mapping: Methodologic foundations and application to intervention and observational research on sugar-sweetened beverages and health outcomes," *Am J Clin Nutr.* 2013, 98(3):755–768; Archer E, Pavela G, Lavie CJ, "The inadmissibility of What We Eat in America and NHANES dietary data in nutrition and obesity research and the scientific formulation of national dietary guidelines," *Mayo Clin Proc.* 2015, 90(7):911–926; Menachemi N, Tajeu G, Sen B, et al., "Overstatement of results in the nutrition and obesity peer-reviewed literature," *Am J Prev Med.* 2013, 45(5):615–621.

4. Freedhoff Y, email to author, March 8, 2017.

5. "Dr. Steven Blair of Coca-Cola and ACSM's Global Energy Balance Network," video, YouTube, Sep 10, 2015.

6. Hill J to Lloyd B, Subject: Follow up, email, May 14, 2014, (author's copy).

7. Applebaum R to Blair S, Hand G, Peters J, et al., Subject: Proposal for establishment of the Global Energy Balance Network, email, Jul 9, 2014, (author's copy).

8. Freedhoff quoted in Bernhard M, "A clinician, a blogger, and now a thorn in Coca-Cola's side," *Chron Higher Educ.*, Aug 14, 2015.

9. Quint A to Freedhoff Y, email, Feb 6, 2015 (author's copy).

10. Arnold School of Public Health, University of South Carolina, "Blair connects energy balance experts world-wide with new Global Energy Balance Network (GEBN)," press release, Dec 5, 2014; Anschutz Health and Wellness Center, University of Colorado, "Energy balance experts from six continents join forces to reduce obesity," press release, Mar 31, 2015; Blair SN, Hand GA, Hill JO, "Energy balance: A crucial issue for exercise and sports medicine," *Br J Sports Med.* 2015, 49(15):970–971.

11. O'Connor A, "Coca-Cola funds effort to alter obesity battle," *NY Times*, Aug 10, 2015; Nestle M, "Coca-Cola's promotion of activity: A follow up," *FoodPolitics.com*, Aug 12, 2015.

12. DeLauro R, "DeLauro statement on Coca-Cola funding biased obesity research," press release, *DeLauro.House.gov*, Aug 10, 2015.

13. Hays E, "Setting the record straight on Coca-Cola and its scientific research," *Coca-Cola Journey*, Aug 10, 2015.

14. Kent M, "Coca-Cola: We'll do better," *Wall Street J.*, Aug 19, 2015.

15. Douglas S, "Our commitment to transparency: Our actions and way forward," *Coca-Cola Journey*, Sep 22, 2015; Douglas JAM, email to author, Mar 10, 2016. The additional countries are Australia, Belgium, Denmark, Finland, France, Ireland, the Netherlands, New Zealand, Norway, and Sweden.

16. Pfister K, "The new faces of Coke," *Medium*, Sep 28, 2015.

17. "Coca-Cola funds returned: CU School of Medicine," University of Colorado Anschutz Medical Campus, Nov 6, 2015; O'Connor A, "University returns $1 million grant to Coca-Cola," *NY Times*, Nov 6, 2015.

18. Esterl M, "Coca-Cola ends financial sponsorship of Academy of Nutrition and Dietetics," *Wall Street J.*, Sep 28, 2015; Choi C, "Excerpts from emails between Coke, anti-obesity group," *Denver Post*, Nov 24, 2015; O'Connor A, "Coke's chief scientist, who orchestrated obesity research, is leaving," *NY Times*, Nov 24, 2015; O'Connor A, "Facing criticism, a research group financed by Coca-Cola says it will disband," *NY Times*, Dec 1, 2015; "A special thank you to Rhona Applebaum," *ILSI News*, 2015, 33(2):1; Olinger D, "CU nutrition expert accepts $550,000 from Coca-Cola for obesity campaign," *Denver Post*, Dec 26, 2015; Olinger D, "CU nutrition expert who took Coca-Cola money steps down," *Denver Post*, Mar 23, 2016.

19. GEBN response, Aug 20, 2015 (author's copy).

20. GEBN response, Aug 20, 2015 (author's copy).

21. Hill JO, Blair SN, Hand G, Peters J, letter to Young L, Aug 21, 2015 (author's copy).

22. Barlow P, Serôdio P, Ruskin G, et al., "Science organisations and Coca-Cola's 'war' with the public health community: Insights from an internal industry document," *J Epidemiol Community Health* 2018, 72:761–763; Ruskin G, "Commentary: Coca-Cola's 'war' with the public health community," *Environ Health News*, Apr 3, 2018.

23. Choi C, "Emails reveal Coke's role in anti-obesity group," *Business Insider*, Nov 24, 2015.

24. "The Approval Matrix: Our deliberately oversimplified guide to who falls where on our taste hierarchies," *NY Mag.*, Nov 30–Dec 13, 2015, 96.

25. Thacker P, "Coca-Cola's secret influence on medical and science journalists," *BMJ* 2017, 357:j1638.

26. Blair S to Hill J, Subject: Procrastination is not great for your heart—Science of us, email, Mar 29, 2015 (author's copy).

27. Bottorff LC to Applebaum R, Blair S, Hand G, et al., Subject: Statement of intent, email, Aug 5, 2014 (author's copy).

28. Hill J to Layden B, Applebaum R, Hand G, et al., Subject: Draft letterhead, email, Oct 4, 2014 (author's copy).

29. Crothers B to Hill J, Subject: Brief and a few questions, email, Oct 24, 2014 (author's copy).

30. Bottorff LC to Blair S, Hill J, Hand G, et al., Subject: GEBN weekly report. "Hi team! Here's the updated work plan. Good progress this week," email, Sep 12, 2014; Sergent T to O'Connor A, Subject: Touching base. "Thank you for making time today to chat with our team regarding the story you are writing on the Global Energy Balance Network," email, May 11, 2015 (author's copies).

31. Kell J, "Coca-Cola says it spent more on health research than previously disclosed," *Fortune*, Mar 25, 2016; Douglas S, "Our commitment to transparency: Our actions and way forward," *Coca-Cola Journey*, Oct 7, 2016 and Mar 24, 2017. The site was further updated on Dec 4, 2017.

32. Katzmarzyk PT, Barreira TV, Broyles ST, et al., "The International Study of Childhood Obesity, Lifestyle and the Environment (ISCOLE): Design and methods," *BMC Public Health* 2013, 13:900; Katzmarzyk PT, Barreira TV, Broyles ST, et al., "Relationship between lifestyle behaviors and obesity in children ages 9–11: Results from a 12-country study," *Obesity* 2015, 23(8):1696–1702.

33. Applebaum R to Blair S, Katzmarzyk P, Church T, et al., Subject: A great study is published!!, email, Aug 4, 2015; Pennington Biomedical Research Center, Louisiana State University, "Pennington Biomedical Research Study shows lack of physical activity is a major predictor of childhood obesity," Aug 3, 2015 (author's copies).

34. Stuckler D, Ruskin G, McKee M, "Complexity and conflicts of interest statements: A case-study of emails exchanged between Coca-Cola and the principal investigators of the International Study of Childhood Obesity, Lifestyle and the Environment (ISCOLE)," *J Public Health Pol.* 2018, 39(1):49–56.

35. Katzmarzyk P to Pratt M at Centers for Disease Control, cc: Applebaum R and Church T, Subject: Re: ISCOLE news: Confidential, email, Apr 4, 2012 (author's copy).

36. Applebaum R to Katzmarzyk P, Subject: ISCOLE news: Confidential, email, Apr 4, 2012 (author's copy).

37. Applebaum R to Landry L and Buyckx M, cc: Katzmarzyk P and Church T, Subject: ISCOLE meeting, email, Nov 5, 2013 (author's copy).

38. Katzmarzyk P to Applebaum R, Subject: ISCOLE meeting, email, Nov 5, 2013 (author's copy).

39. Rowe S, Alexander N, Clydesdale FM, et al., "Funding food science and nutrition research: Financial conflicts and scientific integrity," *J Nutr.* 2009, 139(6):1051–1053.

40. Applebaum R to Hill J and Peters J, Subject: This may help, email, Nov 8, 2012 (author's copy).

41. Serôdio PM, McKee M, Stuckler D, "Coca-Cola—a model of transparency in research partnerships? A network analysis of Coca-Cola's research funding (2008–2016)," *Public Health Nutr.* 2018, 21(9):1594–1607; Tseng M, Barnoya J, Kruger S, et al., "Disclosures of Coca-Cola funding: Transparent or opaque?," editorial, *Public Health Nutr.* 2018, 21(9):1591–1593.

42. McGrath M, "Coca-Cola CEO Muhtar Kent stepping down in 2017," *Forbes*, Dec 9, 2016; Coca-Cola, "Guiding principles for well-being scientific research and third party engagement," *Coca-Cola Journey*, Mar 24, 2017.

43. "Coca-Cola's funding of health research and partnerships," editorial, *Lancet* 2015, 386:1312

Chapter 8. Conflicted Advisory Committees: Then and Now

1. UK Health Forum, "Public health and the food and drinks industry: The governance and ethics of interaction; Lessons from research, policy and practice," 2018, www.ukhealthforum.org.uk/prevention/pie/?entryid43=58305.

2. Proxmire W, "Conflict of interest on vitamin Recommended Dietary Allowances," Congr Rec.—Senate 18477, Jun 10, 1974.

3. Federal Food, Drug, and Cosmetic Act Amendments, Publ L. 94-278, 90 Stat. 410, Title V, Sec 411, Apr 22, 1976.

4. Reported in Jukes T, "Letter: Fleecing the public," *Scientist*, Mar 20, 1989; McNeill L, "The woman who stood between America and a generation of 'thalidomide babies,'" *Smithsonian*, May 8, 2017.

5. Wade N, "Food board's fat report hits fire," *Science* 1980, 209: 248–250.

6. Fisher KD, "A successful peer review program for regulatory decisions," *Reg Toxicol Pharmacol.* 1982, 2:331–334; Fisher quotations are from emails to author, Jul 31, Aug 5, and Aug 10, 2016.

7. Taubes, G, *The Case Against Sugar*, Knopf, 2016; US Food and Drug Administration, Select Committee on GRAS Substances (SCOGS), "Opinion: Sucrose," SCOGS Report no 69, 1976, www.accessdata.fda.gov/scripts/fdcc/?set=scogs&sort=Sortsubstance&order=ASC&startrow=1&type=basic&search=sucrose.

8. Neltner TG, Alger HM, O'Reilly JT, et al., "Conflicts of interest in approvals of additives to food determined to be Generally Recognized as Safe: Out of balance," *JAMA Intern Med.* 2013, 173(22):2032–2036; Nestle M, "Conflict of interest in the regulation of food safety: A threat to scientific integrity," *JAMA Intern Med.* 2013, 173(22):2036–2038.

9. Jacobson MJ, emails to author, Jul 15, 2016, and Jan 6, 2017.

10. Rosenthal B, "Feeding at the company trough," Congr Rec. 1976, 122(Pt 21, Aug 24):27526–27527.

11. Center for Science in the Public Interest, "Integrity in science database: Corporate funding of scientists," Nov 4, 2016.

12. Activist Facts, "Center for Science in the Public Interest," www.activistfacts.com/organizations/13-center-for-science-in-the-public-interest/.

13. Van Horn L, Carson AS, Appel LJ, et al., "Recommended dietary pattern to achieve adherence to the American Heart Association / American College of Cardiology (AHA/ACC) guidelines: A scientific statement from the American Heart Association," *Circulation* 2016, 134:e505–e529.

14. Marchione M, "Cholesterol guidelines become a morality play," *The Dispatch*, Oct 19, 2004.

15. "Petition to the National Institutes of Health seeking an independent review panel to re-evaluate the National Cholesterol Education Program Guidelines," Center for Science in the Public Interest, Sep 23, 2004, https://cspinet.org/sites/default/files/attachment/finalnihltr.pdf; Redberg RF, Katz MH, "Statins for primary prevention: The debate is intense but the data are weak," *JAMA Intern Med.* 2017, 117(1):21–23.

16. For this history, see Nestle M, *Food Politics*, rev. and exp. ed., University of California Press, 2013.

17. McGahn quoted in Kotch A, "Corn syrup lobbyist is helping set USDA dietary guidelines," *Intl Business Times*, Feb 2, 2018.

18. Herman J, "Saving U.S. dietary advice from conflicts of interest," *Food Drug Law J.* 2010, 65(2):285–316.

19. Abrams Z, "The food industry and the U.S. dietary guidelines: Investigating nutrition's most powerful players," *Medium*, Dec 17, 2016.

20. Teicholz N, *The Big Fat Surprise*, Simon and Schuster, 2014; Teicholz N, "The scientific report guiding the US dietary guidelines: Is it scientific?" *BMJ* 2015, 351:h4962.

21. Abrams S, Adams-Campbell LL, Akabas S, et al., letter requesting BMJ to retract "investigation," Center for Science in the Public Interest, Nov 5, 2015, https://cspinet.org/letter-requesting-bmj-retract-investigation.

22. The Arnold Foundation, New initiatives, BMJ Publishing Group, Ltd., www.arnoldfoundation.org/grants/#grant-16454; "Independent experts find no grounds for retraction of the *BMJ* article on dietary guidelines," press release, *BMJ*, Dec 2, 2016, www.bmj.com/company/wp-content/uploads/2016/12/the-bmj-US-dietary-correction.pdf; "The scientific report guiding the US dietary guidelines: Is it scientific? Corrections," *BMJ* 2015, 351:h5686; "Correction," *BMJ* 2016, 355:i6061. The reports from Bero and Helfand are available in the second "Correction."

23. Purdy C, Evich HB, "The money behind the fight over healthy eating," *Politico*, Oct 7, 2015.

24. House of Representatives, "Division A—Agriculture, Rural Development, Food and Drug Administration, and Related Agencies Appropriations Act, 2016. Congressional Directives," "Title 1: Agricultural Programs," http://docs.house.gov/meetings/RU/RU00/20151216/104298/HMTG-114-RU00-20151216-SD002.pdf.

25. National Academies of Sciences, Engineering, and Medicine, *Optimizing the Process for Establishing the Dietary Guidelines for Americans: The Selection Process*, National Academies Press, 2017; National Academies of Sciences, Engineering, and Medicine, *Redesigning the Process for Establishing the Dietary Guidelines for Americans*, National Academies Press, 2017.

26. US Department of Agriculture, Dietary Guidelines Advisory Committee, *Scientific report of the 2015 Dietary Guidelines Advisory Committee*, USDA, Feb 2015.

27. Eckel RH, Jakicic JM, Ard JD, et al., "2013 AHA/ACC guideline on lifestyle management to reduce cardiovascular risk: A report of the American College of Cardiology/American Heart Association Task Force on Practice

Guidelines," *Circulation* 2014, 129(25Suppl2):s76–s99; Shin JY, Xun P, Nakamura Y, He K, "Egg consumption in relation to risk of cardiovascular disease and diabetes: A systematic review and meta-analysis," *Am J Clin Nutr.* 2013, 98(1):146–159.

28. Physicians Committee for Responsible Medicine, McDougall J, Agarwal U, et al. v. Vilsack T, Burwell SM, Complaint for declaratory and injunctive relief, US District Court, Northern District of California, Jan 6, 2016.

29. Griffin JD, Lichtenstein AH, "Dietary cholesterol and plasma lipoprotein profiles: Randomized-controlled trials," *Curr Nutr Rep.* 2013, 2(4):274–282.

30. Lichtenstein A, email to author, Feb 14, 2018.

31. Bittman M, "How should we eat?," *NY Times*, Feb 25, 2016; Hamblin J, "Eggs are back: The earnest simplicity of the new nutrition guidelines," *Atlantic*, Feb 19, 2015.

32. Kim JE, Ferruzzi MG, Campbell WW, "Egg consumption increases vitamin E absorption from co-consumed raw mixed vegetables in healthy young men," *J Nutr.* 2016, 146(11):2199–2205.

33. US Department of Health and Human Services and US Department of Agriculture, *Dietary Guidelines for Americans, 2015–2020*, 8th ed., Dec 2015.

34. Beeler L, Order dismissing case, Physicians Committee for Responsible Medicine, et al. v. Thomas V. Vilsack, et al., US District Court, Northern District of California, Oct 12, 2016.

35. Brodwin E, "A single line in an obscure court case reveals how the food industry decides what we're told is healthy," *Business Insider*, Oct 21, 2016.

36. World Health Organization, *Sugars Intake for Adults and Children: Guideline*, 2015.

37. Sugar Association, "Sugar Association statement on WHO guideline on sugars: It's misleading for 'strong' guidelines to be backed by only 'moderate,' 'low' and 'very low' evidence," Mar 4, 2015; Sugar Association, "2015 Dietary Guidelines for Americans recommendation for added sugars intake: Agenda based, not science based," Jan 7, 2016.

38. Erickson J, Sadeghirad B, Lytvyn L, et al., "The scientific basis of guideline recommendations on sugar intake: A systematic review," *Ann Intern Med.* 2017, 166(4):257–267.

39. Schillinger D, Kearns C, "Guidelines to limit added sugar intake: Junk science or junk food?" *Ann Intern Med.* 2017, 166(4):305–306.

40. O'Connor A, "Study tied to food industry tries to discredit sugar guidelines," *NY Times*, Dec 19, 2016; Choi C, "Snickers maker criticizes industry-funded paper on sugar," *AP*, Dec 21, 2016.

41. Rowe S, Alexander N, Weaver CM, et al., "How experts are chosen to inform public policy: Can the process be improved?" *Health Policy* 2013, 112:172–178.

Chapter 9. Co-opted? The American Society for Nutrition

1. Freedhoff Y, Hébert PC, "Partnerships between health organizations and the food industry risk derailing public health nutrition," *CMAJ* 2011, 183(3):291–292; Integrity in Science Project, "Lifting the veil of secrecy: Corporate support for health and environmental professional associations, charities, and industry front groups," Center for Science in the Public Interest, 2003, https://cspinet.org/sites/default/files/attachment/lift_the_veil_intro.pdf.

2. Aaron DG, Siegel MB, "Sponsorship of national health organizations by two major soda companies," *Am J Prev Med.* 2017, 52(1):20–30; Canella DS, Martins AP, Silva HF, et al., "Food and beverage industries' participation in health scientific events: Considerations on conflicts of interest," *Rev Panam Salud Pública* 2015, 38(4):339–343; Oshaug A, "What is the food and drink industry doing in nutrition conferences?" *Public Health Nutr.* 2009, 12(7):1019–1020; Flint SW, "Are we selling our souls? Novel aspects of the presence in academic conferences of brands linked to ill health," *J Epidemiol Community Health* 2016, 70(8):739–740; Margetts B, "Time to agree guidelines and apply an ethical framework for public health nutrition," *Public Health Nutr.* 2009, 12(7):885–886.

3. American Society for Nutrition, "About ASN," www.nutrition.org /about-asn/.

4. Swan PB, "The American Society for Nutritional Sciences (1979–2003): Years of action and change," *J Nutr.* 2003, 133(3):646–656; Hill FW, ed., *The American Institute of Nutrition: A History of the First 50 Years 1928–1978 and the Proceedings of a Symposium Commemorating the 50th Anniversary of the* Journal of Nutrition, American Institute of Nutrition, 1978.

5. Nestle M, Baron RB, "Nutrition in medical education: From counting hours to measuring competence," *JAMA Intern Med.* 2014, 174(6):843–844.

6. American Society for Nutrition, "ASN Advisory Committee on Ensuring Trust in Nutrition Science: Talking points [for committee members]," Feb 9, 2016 (author's copy).

7. John Courtney's quotations are from emails to author, Jul 10 and 11, 2017.

8. The awards went to James Hill (Class of 2017 Fellow), John Peters (McCormick Science Institute Research Award), and Coca-Cola's Beate Lloyd (Sustaining Partner Roundtable Award of Distinction).

9. These problems are typical. See Boothby A, Wang R, Cetnar J, Prasad V, "Effect of the American Society of Clinical Oncology's conflict of interest policy on information overload," *JAMA Oncol.* 2016, 2(12):1653–1654.

10. Global Stevia Institute, "Stevia leaf to Stevia sweetener: Exploring its science, benefits and future potential," ASN Scientific Sessions, Chicago, Apr 22, 2017; Tey SL, Salleh NB, Henry J, Forde CG, "Effects of aspartame-, monk fruit-, stevia- and sucrose-sweetened beverages on postprandial glucose, insulin and energy intake," *Int J Obes.* 2017, 41(3):450–457.

11. American Society for Nutrition, "Have you heard about the pre-meeting activities?," email to members, Mar 27, 2018. Also see American Society for Nutrition, "Nutrition 2018: Full schedule," www.eventscribe.com/2018/Nutrition2018/agenda.asp?pfp=FullSchedule.

12. Nestle M, "Open letter to nutrition colleagues," *FoodPolitics.com*, May 11, 2009.

13. Lupton JR, Balentine DA, Black RM, et al., "The Smart Choices front-of-package nutrition labeling program: Rationale and development of the nutrition criteria," *Am J Clin Nutr.* 2010, 91(4):1078s–1089s; Nestle M, "Reply from the American Society of Nutrition," *FoodPolitics.com*, May 18, 2009.

14. Neuman W, "For your health, Froot Loops," *NY Times*, Sep 4, 2009.

15. "The popularity of 'natural' food spawns an unnatural response," *Economist*, Sep 24, 2009.

16. The US Food and Drug Administration letter is at Nestle M, "Smart Choices: 44% sugar calories!" *FoodPolitics.com*, Aug 24, 2009; other relevant blog posts at *FoodPolitics.com* include "You don't like Smart Choices? Act now!" Sep 16, 2009; "Update on not-so-Smart Choice labels," Sept 23, 2009; and "Connecticut takes on Smart Choices!," Oct 15, 2009.

17. Smart Choices Program, "Smart Choices Program™ postpones active operations," press release, Oct 23, 2009.

18. Ruiz R, "Smart Choices fails," *Forbes*, Oct 23, 2009.

19. Nestle M, "Smart Choices suspended! May it rest in peace," *FoodPolitics.com*, Oct 23, 2009.

20. Eicher-Miller HA, Fulgoni VL, Keast DR, "Contributions of processed foods to dietary intake in the US from 2003–2008: A report of the Food and Nutrition Science Solutions Joint Task Force of the Academy of Nutrition and Dietetics, American Society for Nutrition, Institute of Food Technologists, and International Food Information Council," *J Nutr.* 2012, 142(11):2065s–2072s.

21. Monteiro CA, Cannon G, Moubarac J-C, et al., "The UN decade of nutrition, the NOVA food classification and the trouble with ultra-processing," *Public Health Nutr.* 2018, 21(1):5–17.

22. US Food and Drug Administration, "Food labeling: Revision of the nutrition and supplement facts labels; extension of comment period," May 27, 2014.

23. American Society for Nutrition, "Comment from American Society for Nutrition," www.regulations.gov/document?D=FDA-2012-N-1210-0268.

24. US Food and Drug Administration, "Changes to the Nutrition Facts label," www.fda.gov/Food/GuidanceRegulation/GuidanceDocumentsRegulatory Information/LabelingNutrition/ucm385663.htm.

25. US Food and Drug Administration, "Use of the term 'natural' in the labeling of human food products; Request for information and comments: Proposed rule. 80 FR 69905," Nov 12, 2015; Rock A, "Peeling back the 'natural' food label," *Consumer Rep.*, Jan 29, 2016.

26. US Food and Drug Administration, "What is the meaning of 'natural' on the label of food?," www.fda.gov/AboutFDA/Transparency/Basics /ucm214868.htm.

27. Brown A, "Let industry fund science," *Slate*, Sep 21, 2016.

28. American Society for Nutrition, @nutritionorg, Twitter, Sep 21, 2016.

29. Gomes F, "Words for our sponsors," *World Nutr.* 2013, 4(8):618–644.

30. Greene R, Berger R, "Malaysian government official personally profited from soda-government partnership," *The Russells*, Jan 5, 2018.

31. Fuller T, O'Connor A, Richtel M, "In Asia's fattest country, nutritionists take money from food giants," *NY Times*, Dec 23, 2017.

32. Hamid J, Mohamed J, Soy SL, et al., "Characteristics associated with the consumption of malted drinks among Malaysian primary school children: Findings from the MyBreakfast study," BMC *Public Health* 2015, 15:1322.

33. A Malaysian Scientist, "Improper attack on study," *Star Online*, Dec 25, 2017; Ludwig D, "Comment on BMC Public Health. 2015, 15:1322," *PubMed Commons*, Jan 6, 2018 (author's copy).

Chapter 10. Nutrition Education and Dietetics Societies: Industry Influence

1. Ullrich HD, *The SNE Story: 25 Years of Advancing Nutrition Education*, Nutrition Communications Associates, 1992, 5; Ullrich HD, *The Nutritionists: Scientists and Practitioners*, Helen Denning Ullrich, 2004.

2. Joan Dye Gussow, interview by author, Aug 24, 2016.

3. Gussow J, "Can industry afford a healthy America?" *CNI Weekly Rep.* 1979, 9(22):4–7.

4. Gussow JD, "Who pays the piper?" *Teach Coll Rec.* 1980, 81(4):448–466.

5. "Defending the honor of the potato chip," *CNI Weekly Rep.* 1978, 8(31):2.

6. Society for Nutrition Education and Behavior, "External funding policy," Jun 27, 2014, www.sneb.org/clientuploads/directory/Documents/External_Funding_Policy_2014.pdf.

7. Society for Nutrition Education and Behavior, *Program: 2017 Annual Conference, July 20–24, Washington DC*, www.sneb.org/clientuploads/directory/Documents/2017_Onsite_Program_Final.pdf.

8. Pfister K, "The new faces of Coke," *Medium.com*, Sep 28, 2015; Choi C, "Coke as a sensible snack? Coca-Cola works with dietitians who suggest cola as snack," *AP*, Mar 16, 2015; Choi C, "Coke ending sponsorship of dietitians group," *AP*, Sep 29, 2015.

9. Choi C, "Soda group suspends payments to dietitians opposing new tax," *AP*, Oct 6, 2016.

10. Choi C, "How Kellogg worked with 'independent experts' to tout cereal," *AP*, Nov 21, 2016.

11. Academy of Nutrition and Dietetics, "About us," www.eatrightpro.org/about-us.

12. Stein K, "Advancing health through sustained collaboration: How the history of corporate relations extended the academy's reach," *J Acad Nutr Diet*. 2015, 115:131–142.

13. See, for example, Burros M, "Additives in advice on food," *NY Times*, Nov 15, 1995.

14. Academy of Nutrition and Dietetics, "Academy guidelines for corporate sponsors," www.eatrightpro.org/about-us/advertising-and-sponsorship/about-sponsorship/academy-guidelines-for-corporate-sponsors.

15. Bratskeir K, "Kraft American Cheese Singles have been labeled a health food by professional nutritionists (not as a joke)," *Huff Post*, Mar 18, 2015; Nestle M, "Dietitians put seal on Kraft Singles (you can't make this stuff up)," *FoodPolitics.com*, Mar 13, 2015.

16. Strom S, "A cheese 'product' gets kids' nutrition seal," *NY Times*, Mar 12, 2015.

17. Academy of Nutrition and Dietetics Foundation, "Statement from Academy of Nutrition and Dietetics Foundation on new 'Kids Eat Right' nutrition education campaign," *PR Newswire*, Mar 13, 2015.

18. Lupkin S, "Kraft Singles is 1st food allowed to display 'Kids Eat Right' logo," *ABC News*, Mar 13, 2015.

19. Stewart J, "The snacks of life," *The Daily Show*, Mar 17, 2015, YouTube segment at 4:30 min, www.youtube.com/watch?v=jCG_i9lnBFc.

20. Bellatti A, "Dietitians fight Kraft Singles' 'Kids Eat Right' seal," *Civil Eats*, Mar 13, 2015; Best J, "Kraft drops dubious 'Kids Eat Right' logo from its processed 'cheese' singles," *Take Part*, Mar 31, 2015.

21. Kaplan S, "Nutritionists built close ties with the food industry. Now they're seeking some distance," *Stat News*, Oct 31, 2016.

22. Choi C, "Sugar Association's tips for pleasing picky eaters—sprinkle a little sugar on vegetables before cooking," @candicechoi, Twitter, Oct 23, 2016.

23. Choi C, "Do candy and soda makers belong at a dietitians' conference?" *AP*, Oct 31, 2016.

24. Bellatti A, "Corporate sponsorship influence is not about 'weak-mindedness,'" DFPI, Oct 15, 2016, https://integritydietitians.org/2016/10/15/corporate-sponsorship-influence-not-weak-mindedness/.

25. Bellatti A, "Academy of Nutrition and Dietetics sponsorship update," DFPI, Sep 7, 2016, https://integritydietitians.org/2016/09/07/academy-nutrition-dietetics-sponsorship-update-2; Sifferlin A, "Soda and snack food companies welcomed at nutrition conference," *Time*, Oct 14, 2016.

26. Simon M, "And now a word from our sponsors: Are America's nutrition professionals in the pocket of Big Food?," *Eat Drink Politics*, Jan 2013, www.eatdrinkpolitics.com/wp-content/uploads/AND_Corporate_Sponsorship_Report.pdf.

27. Strom S, "Report faults food group's sponsor ties," *NY Times*, Jan 22, 2013; Bergman E, quoted in Nestle M, "An open letter to Registered Dietitians and RDs in training: Response to yesterday's comments," *FoodPolitics.com*, Jan 24, 2013.

28. Bellatti A, email to author, Jul 30, 2016.

29. Bellatti A, "The food ties that bind: The Academy of Nutrition & Dietetics' 2013 Conference & Expo," DFPI, Nov 2013.

30. Bellatti A, email to author, Nov 17, 2016.

31. Bellatti A, letter to DFPI supporters, Jul 10, 2018 (author's copy).

32. Freeland-Graves J, Nitzke S, "Position of the American Dietetic Association: Total diet approach to communicating food and nutrition information," *J Am Diet Assoc.* 2002, 102(7):100–108.

33. American Dietetic Association, "Code of ethics for the profession of dietetics," *J Am Diet Assoc.* 1999, 99(1):109–113.

34. O'Sullivan Maillet J, "Conflicting priorities, questions without easy answers: Ethics and ADA," *J Am Diet Assoc.* 2002, 102(9):1208.

35. Woteki CE, "Ethics opinion: Conflicts of interest in presentations and publications and dietetics research," *J Am Diet Assoc.* 2006, 106(1):27–31.

36. Miles A, Speaker, House of Delegates, "Letter to AND House of Delegates regarding the 2015 Sponsorship Summit," Sep 10, 2015 (author's copy); Academy of Nutrition and Dietetics Sponsorship Advisory Task Force, "Summary report to the House of Delegates," Fall 2015 House of Delegates meeting, Nashville, TN (author's copy).

37. Tappenden KA, "A unifying vision for scientific decision making: The Academy of Nutrition and Dietetics' Scientific Integrity Principles," *J Acad Nutr Diet*. 2015, 115:1486–1490.

38. Crayton EF, Academy of Nutrition and Dietetics President, "Letter to members," AND, Jan 19, 2016 (author's copy).

Chapter 11. Justifications, Rationales, Excuses: Isn't Everyone Conflicted?

1. Purdy S, Little M, Mayes C, et al., "Debates about conflict of interest in medicine: Deconstructing a divided discourse," *J Bioeth Inq*. 2017, 14(1):135–149.

2. Anonymous (by request), email to author, Apr 18, 2017.

3. Clancy M, Fuglie K, Heisey P, "U.S. Agricultural R&D in an era of falling public funding," *Amber Waves*, Nov 10, 2016; Hourihan M, "Science and technology funding under Obama: A look back," *AAAS*, Jan 19, 2017; Hourihan M, "The Trump administration's science budget: Toughest since Apollo?" *AAAS*, Mar 29, 2017.

4. New York University Office of Industrial Liaison, "Technology transfer at New York University," https://med.nyu.edu/oil/frontpage.

5. University of Colorado Boulder, "Federal and industry research partnerships," https://www.colorado.edu/research/federal-industry-research-partnerships.

6. Spence M, email to all staff, University of Sydney, Mar 2, 2016 (author's copy).

7. Hourihan M, Parkes D, "Federal R&D budget trends: A summary," *AAAS*, Dec 20, 2016.

8. Kuchler F, Toole A, "Federal support for nutrition research trends upward as USDA share declines," *Amber Waves*, Jun 1, 2015; US Congress, *Agricultural Act of 2014*, HR 2642, 113th Cong., sec. 7601, www.agriculture.senate.gov/imo/media/doc/Farm_Bill_Final.pdf; Foundation for Food and Agriculture Research, https://foundationfar.org.

9. US Department of Agriculture, Agricultural Research Service, "Forming partnerships," Sep 8, 2016, www.ars.usda.gov/office-of-technology-transfer/forming-partnerships/.

10. US Department of Agriculture, Agricultural Research Service, "Specific cooperative agreements with the Agricultural Research Service," Feb 2005.

11. US Department of Agriculture, Agricultural Research Service, "Research projects," Aug 25, 2016, www.ars.usda.gov/research/projects/?slicetype=keyword; US Department of Agriculture, Agricultural Research Service, "National Program 107: Human Nutrition Annual Reports," www.ars.usda.gov/nutrition-food-safetyquality/human-nutrition/docs/annual-reports.

12. Victor L. Fulgoni III, Nutrition Impact, LLC, www.nutritionimpact .com.

13. Stanford History Education Group, "Evaluating information: The cornerstone of civic online reasoning," 2016, https://sheg.stanford.edu/upload /V3LessonPlans/Executive%20Summary%2011.21.16.pdf; Besley JC, Mc-Cright AM, Zahry NR, et al., "Perceived conflict of interest in health science partnerships," *PLoS One* 2017, 12(4):e0175643.

14. Raatz SK, Johnson LK, Picklo MJ, "Consumption of honey, sucrose, and high-fructose corn syrup produces similar metabolic effects in glucose-tolerant and -intolerant individuals," *J Nutr.* 2015, 145(10):2265–2272; Chiu S, Williams PT, Krauss RM, "Effects of a very high saturated fat diet on LDL particles in adults with atherogenic dyslipidemia: A randomized controlled trial," *PLoS One* 2017, 12(2):e0170664.

15. Song F, Parekh-Bhurke S, Hooper L, et al., "Extent of publication bias in different categories of research cohorts: A meta-analysis of empirical studies," *BMC Med Res Methodol.* 2009, 9:79.

16. Katz D, emails to author, Dec 1, 2015, and Jan 5, 2016.

17. Oransky I, Marcus A, "Keep negativity out of politics. We need more of it in journals," *Stat News*, Oct 14, 2016.

18. Goldberg DS, "COI bingo," *BMJ* 2015, 351:h6577.

19. Goldberg D, @prof_goldberg, Twitter, Aug 10, 2015; Goldberg D, "Are nutrition conflicts of interest less worrisome?" *Weighty Matters*, Oct 24, 2016; Goldberg DS, "COI bingo," *BMJ Opinion*, Aug 24, 2015, http://blogs.bmj.com/ bmj/2015/08/24/daniel-s-goldberg-coi-bingo.

20. Lipton S, Boyd EA, Bero LA, "Conflicts of interest in academic research: Policies, processes, and attitudes," *Account Res.* 2004, 11(2):83–102.

21. Haddock CK, Poston WS, Lagrotte C, et al., "Findings from an online behavioural weight management programme provided with or without a fortified diet beverage," *Brit J Nutr.* 2014, 111(2):372–379.

22. Gornall J, "Sugar: Spinning a web of influence," *BMJ* 2015, 350:h231.

23. Jebb S, "Yes, I work with the food industry, but I doubt they see me as a friend," *Guardian*, Feb 13, 2015.

24. Zachwieja J, Hentges E, Hill JO, et al., "Public-private partnerships: The evolving role of industry funding in nutrition research," *Adv Nutr.* 2013, 4(5):570–572.

25. Coppola AR, FitzGerald GA, "Confluence, not conflict of interest: Name change necessary," *JAMA* 2015, 314(17):1791–1792.

26. Katz D, "Industry-funded research: Conflict or confluence?" *Huff Post*, Aug 20, 2015.

27. Aveyard P, Yach D, Gilmore AB, Capewell S, "Head to head: Should we welcome food industry funding of public health research?" *BMJ* 2016, 353:i2161; Ludwig DS, Nestle M, "Can the food industry play a constructive role in the obesity epidemic?" *JAMA* 2008, 300(15):1808–1811.

28. Rothman KJ, "Conflict of interest: The new McCarthyism in science," *JAMA* 1993, 269(21):2782–2784.

29. Ombudsman, comment on Nestle M, "Five more industry-funded studies with expected results. Score 70:5," *FoodPolitics.com*, Oct 8, 2015.

30. Allison quoted in Karasu SR, "Interests conflicted: A 'wicked problem' in medical research," *Psychol Today*, Oct 12, 2016.

31. Sagner M, Binks M, Yapijakis C, et al., "Overcoming potential threats to scientific advancements: Conflict of interest, ulterior motives, false innuendos and harassment," *Prog Cardiovasc Dis*. 2017, 59(5):522–524.

32. Drazen JM, "The quality of medical research, not its source of funding, is what matters," *NY Times*, Sep 20, 2016.

33. Brown T, "It's silly to assume all research funded by corporations is bent," *Guardian*, May 14, 2016.

34. Caulfield T, Ogbobu U, "The commercialization of university-based research: Balancing risks and benefits," *BMC Med Ethics* 2015, 16:70.

35. Cope MB, Allison DB, "White hat bias: Examples of its presence in obesity research and a call for renewed commitment to faithfulness in research reporting," *Int J Obes*. 2010, 34(1):84–88.

36. Galea S, "A typology of nonfinancial conflict in population health research," *Am J Public Health* 2018, 108(5):631–632.

37. Ioannidis J, "Why most published research findings are false," *PLoS Med*. 2005:2(8):e124.

38. Ioannidis JPA, Trepanowski JF, "Disclosures in nutrition research: Why it is different," *JAMA* 2018, 319(6):547–548.

39. "*Nature* journals tighten rules on non-financial conflicts," editorial, *Nature* 2018, 554:6.

40. Krimsky S, "The ethical and legal foundations of scientific 'conflict of interest,'" in: Lemmens T, Waring DR, *Law and Ethics in Biomedical Research: Regulation, Conflict of Interest, and Liability*, University of Toronto Press, 2006, 63–81; Levinsky NG, "Sounding board: Nonfinancial conflicts of interest in research," *N Engl J Med*. 2002, 347(10):759–761; Krimsky S, "Autonomy, disinterest, and entrepreneurial science," *Society* 2006, 43(4):22–29.

41. Bero LA, Grundy Q, "Why having a (nonfinancial) interest is not a conflict of interest," *PLoS Biol*. 2016, 14(12):e2001221; Bero L, "Addressing bias and conflict of interest among biomedical researchers," *JAMA* 2017,

317(17):1723–1724; Bero LA, Grundy Q, "Not all influences on science are conflicts of interest," *Am J Public Health* 2018, 108(5):632–633; PLoS Medicine Editors, "Making sense of non-financial competing interests," *PLoS Med.* 2008, 5(9):e199.

42. Rodwin MA, "Attempts to redefine conflicts of interest," research paper no. 17–18, Suffolk University Law School, Dec 7, 2017; Rodwin MA, "Should we try to manage non-financial interests? No," *BMJ* 2018, 361:k1240; Schwab T, "Dietary disclosures: How important are non-financial disclosures?," *BMJ* 2018, 361:k1451; Bero L, "What is in a name? Nonfinancial influences on the outcomes of systematic reviews and guidelines," *J Clin Epidemiol.* 2014, 67:1239–1241.

43. Anonymous (by request), email to author, Nov 30, 2015.

44. Korn D, "Conflicts of interest in biomedical research," *JAMA* 2000, 284(17):2234–2237.

Chapter 12. Disclosure—and Its Discontents

1. Nestle M, ed., "Mediterranean diets: Science and policy implications," *Am J Clin Nutr.* 1995, 61(suppl):1313s–1427s.

2. International Committee of Medical Journal Editors, "Conflicts of interest. ICMJE Form for disclosure of potential conflicts of interest," http://icmje.org/conflicts-of-interest/.

3. JAMA Network, "Conflicts of interest and financial disclosures," http://jamanetwork.com/journals/jama/pages/instructions-for-authors#Sec ConflictsofInterestandFinancialDisclosures.

4. Editor, *JAMA Intern Med.*, email to author, Jul 15, 2016.

5. American Society for Nutrition, "Conflict of interest guidelines," https://nutrition.org/publications/guidelines-and-policies/conflict-of-interest/.

6. Kesselheim AS, Robertson CT, Myers JA, et al., "A randomized study of how physicians interpret research funding disclosures," *N Engl J Med.* 2012, 367(12):1119–1127.

7. Goozner M, "Unrevealed: Non-disclosure of conflicts of interest in four leading medical and scientific journals," Center for Science in the Public Interest, Jul 12, 2004; Mandrioli D, Kearns CE, Bero LA, "Relationship between research outcomes and risk of bias, study sponsorship, and author financial conflicts of interest in reviews of the effects of artificially sweetened beverages on weight outcomes: A systematic review of reviews," *PLoS One* 2016, 11(9):e0162198; Serôdio PM, McKee M, Stuckler D, "Coca-Cola—a model of transparency in research partnerships? A network analy-

sis of Coca-Cola's research funding (2008–2016)," *Public Health Nutr.* 2018, 21(9):1594–1607.

8. Archer E, Hand GA, Blair SN, "Validity of U.S. nutritional surveillance: National Health and Nutrition Examination Survey caloric energy intake data, 1971–2010," *PLoS One* 2013, 8(10):e76632; "Correction," *PLoS One* 2013, 8(10):10.1371/annotation.

9. Chiavaroli L, de Souza RJ, Ha V, et al., "Effect of fructose on established lipid targets: A systematic review and meta-analysis of controlled feeding trials," *J Am Heart Assoc.* 2015, 4:e001700.

10. London B, email to author, Sep 17, 2015.

11. Nestle M, "Another five industry-funded nutrition studies with industry-favorable results. Score: 60:3," *FoodPolitics.com*, Sep 17, 2015.

12. Freedhoff Y, "Is this epic study disclosure statement the world's greatest or most absurd?" *Weighty Matters*, Sep 17, 2015.

13. Sievenpiper JL, "Sickeningly sweet: Does sugar cause chronic disease? No," *Can J Diabetes* 2016, 40:287–295; "Correction," *Can J Diabetes* 2016, 40:603.

14. Barnoya J, Nestle M, "The food industry and conflicts of interest in nutrition research: A Latin American perspective," *J Public Health Pol.* 2016, 37(4):552–559 [retracted]; Nestle M, "A retraction and apology," *FoodPolitics .com*, Nov 25, 2015; "Retraction published for nutrition researcher Marion Nestle," *RetractionWatch.com*, Dec 31, 2015.

15. Sackett DL, "List of DLS's potential conflicts," www.bmj.com/content /suppl/2002/02/28/324.7336.539.DC1; "David Sackett," obituary, *BMJ* 2015, 350:h2639.

16. Loewenstein G, Sah S, Cain DM, "The unintended consequences of conflict of interest disclosure," *JAMA* 2012, 307(7):669–670; Sah S, "Conflicts of interest and your physician: Psychological processes that cause unexpected changes in behavior," *J Law Med Ethics* 2012, 40(3):482–487; Sah S, Loewenstein G, Cain DM, "The burden of disclosure: Increased compliance with distrusted advice," *J Pers Soc Psychol.* 2013, 104(2):289–304.

17. Bero LA, "Disclosure policies for gifts from industry to academic faculty," *JAMA* 1998, 279(13):1031; Cornell University, Office of Research Integrity and Assurance, "Sanctions for non-compliance with the financial conflict of interest related to research policy," 2017.

18. Cain DM, Loewenstein G, Moore DA, "Coming clean but playing dirtier: The shortcomings of disclosure as a solution to conflicts of interest," in: Moore DA, Cain DM, Loewenstein G, Bazerman MH, eds., *Conflicts of Interest: Challenges and Solutions in Business, Law, Medicine, and Public Policy*, Cambridge

University Press, 2005, 104–125; Dana J, Loewenstein G, "A social science perspective on gifts to physicians from industry," *JAMA* 2003, 290(2):252–255; Bero L, "Accepting commercial sponsorship: Disclosure helps—but is not a panacea," *BMJ* 1999, 319:653–654.

19. "PubMed urged to include funding info, conflicts of interest with study abstracts," Center for Science in the Public Interest, Mar 30, 2016; Blumenthal R, "Blumenthal, colleagues urge clear disclosure of conflicts of interest in scientific papers," press release, Mar 30, 2016; Collins M, "PubMed updates March 2017," *NLM Tech Bull.* Mar–Apr 2017, 415:e2.

20. Center for Science in the Public Interest, "PubMed to include conflict-of-interest statements with study abstracts," Apr 18, 2017.

21. Freedom of Information Act Advocates, "State public record laws," www.foiadvocates.com/records.html; Judicial Watch, "Open records laws and resources," www.judicialwatch.org/open-records-laws-and-resources.

22. US House of Representatives Committee on Oversight and Government Reform, "FOIA is broken: A report," staff report to 114th Cong., Jan 2016.

23. Lewandowsky S, Bishop D, "Don't let transparency damage science," *Nature* 2016, 529:459–461.

24. Halpern M, "Freedom to bully: How laws intended to free information are used to harass researchers," Union of Concerned Scientists, Feb 2015; Abel D, "How public must science be? Union of Concerned Scientists would limit disclosures," *Boston Globe*, Mar 19, 2016.

25. Union of Concerned Scientists, "Science in an age of scrutiny: How scientists can respond to criticism and personal attacks," Sep 2012.

26. Thacker PD, Seife C, "Post removed by *PLoS*—The fight over transparency: Round two," *PLoS Biologue*, Aug 13, 2015.

27. Thacker PD, "Scientists, give up your emails," *NY Times*, Jan 9, 2016.

28. For examples, see Branch J, "N.F.L. tried to influence concussion research, Congressional study finds," *NY Times*, May 23, 2016; Lala E, "Emails between Coca-Cola industry advocate and CDC director point to possible political sway," *Philly Voice*, Jun 30, 2016; Waters R, "Trump's pick to head CDC partnered with Coke, boosting agency's longstanding ties to soda giant," *Forbes*, Jul 10, 2017; Waters R, "The Coca-Cola network: Soda giant mines connections with officials and scientists to wield influence," *Forbes*, Jul 11, 2017.

29. Lipton E, "Food industry enlisted academics in G.M.O. war, emails show," *NY Times*, Sep 5, 2015; Thacker PD, "Why scientific transparency is so tricky: People love transparency in science, until they don't," *Pacific Standard*, Mar 21, 2017.

30. Leschin-Hoar C, "Fisheries scientist under fire for undisclosed seafood industry funding," *NPR*, *The Salt*, May 12, 2016.

31. U.S. House of Representatives, "Agriculture, rural development, Food and Drug Administration, and related agencies appropriations bill, 2017," Rep. 114-531, p. 34, Apr 26, 2016.

32. Jalonick MC, "From eggs to trees, USDA promotional programs controversial," *US News*, Sep 4, 2015.

33. Watson E, "American Egg Board denies claims it 'went way beyond its mandate' as Hampton Creek calls for Congressional investigation," *Food Navigator*, Sep 15, 2015; Watson E, "American Egg board to get 'ethics training' after USDA uncovers 'inappropriate behavior' over Hampton Creek," *Food Navigator*, Oct 7, 2016; Monke J, Greene JL, Dabrowska A, et al., "FY2017 Agriculture and related agencies appropriations: In brief," Congressional Research Service, Dec 20, 2016; Watson E, "Hampton Creek smells a rat in ag appropriations bill over FOIA requests," *Food Navigator*, Apr 29, 2016. The status of checkoff FOIA was still pending in August 2018.

Chapter 13. Managing Conflicts: Early Attempts

1. "The Nutrition Foundation, Inc.," *Science* 1942, 95:64.

2. King CG, A Good Idea: The History of the Nutrition Foundation, Nutrition Foundation, 1976. The quotations in the next several paragraphs are from pages 10, 11, 25, 163, and 118, respectively.

3. "62 institutions get $1,810,730 in grants for research," *NY Times*, Nov 19, 1948.

4. "Rachel Carson book is called one-sided," *NY Times*, Sep 14, 1962.

5. Klemesrud J, "'The martyred meal': Some skip it, some skim it, some splurge," *NY Times*, Jan 21, 1967; Neuman W, "For your health, Froot Loops," *NY Times*, Sep 4, 2009.

6. Hess JL, "Dining in the laboratory," *NY Times*, Aug 14, 1974.

7. Hodgson M, "Taking the fat out of eating," *NY Times*, Mar 17, 1982.

8. Marshall E, "Diet advice, with a grain of salt and a large helping of pepper," *Science* 1986, 231:537–539; Center for Media and Democracy, Source-Watch, "International Life Sciences Institute," www.sourcewatch.org/index.php/International_Life_Sciences_Institute.

9. Stare FJ, *Adventures in Nutrition*, Christopher Publishing House, 1991. The quotation comes from statements on pages 155 and 158.

10. Stare FJ, *Harvard's Department of Nutrition, 1942–86*, Christopher Publishing House, 1987. The quotations appear on page xxvii.

11. "Frederick J. Stare, defender of the American diet, died on April 4th, aged 91," *Economist*, Apr 18, 2002; Rosenthal B, Jacobson M, Bohm M, "Feeding at the company trough," Congr Rec. 1976, 122 (part 21, Aug 24):27527–27531.

12. Kearns CE, Schmidt LA, Glantz SA, "Sugar industry efforts to steer science on coronary heart disease: An historical analysis of internal industry documents," *JAMA Intern Med.* 2016, 176(11):1680–1685; Hegsted archives at Harvard Library, http://oasis.lib.harvard.edu/oasis/deliver/findingAidDisplay?_collection=oasis&inoid=1501&histno=0; McGandy RB, Hegsted DM, Stare FJ, "Dietary fats, carbohydrates and atherosclerotic vascular disease," part I, *N Engl J Med.* 1967, 277(4):186–192 and part II, *N Engl J Med.* 1967, 277(5):242–247; Kearns CE, Apollonio D, Glantz SA, "Sugar industry sponsorship of germ-free rodent studies linking sucrose to hyperlipidemia and cancer: An historical analysis of internal documents," *PLoS Biol.* 2017, 15(11):e2003460.

13. Nestle M, "Food industry funding of nutrition research: The relevance of history for current debates," *JAMA Intern Med.* 2016, 176(11):1685–1686.

14. Hegsted DM, "Serum-cholesterol response to dietary cholesterol: A re-evaluation," *Am J Clin Nutr.* 1986, 44(2):299–305; Nestle M, "In memoriam: Mark Hegsted, 1914–2009," *FoodPolitics.com*, Aug 18, 2009.

15. Hegsted DM, "Statement," in: US Senate, Select Committee on Nutrition and Human Needs, *Dietary Goals for the United States*, Feb 1977:xv.

16. Glinsmann WH, Irausquin H, Park YK, "Report from FDA's Sugars Task Force, 1986: Evaluation of health aspects of sugars contained in carbohydrate sweeteners," *J Nutr.* 1986, 116(11 Suppl):s1–s216; Johns DM, Oppenheimer GM, "Was there ever really a 'sugar conspiracy'?" *Science* 2018, 359:747–750.

17. World Health Organization, *Sugars Intake for Adults and Children: Guideline*, 2015; Shilhavy B, "We were wrong about saturated fats," *Time*, Jul 7, 2016; Lustig R, *Fat Chance: Beating the Odds Against Sugar, Processed Food, Obesity, and Disease*, Hudson Street Press, 2012; Taubes G, *The Case Against Sugar*, Knopf, 2016.

18. Kowitt B, "These ubiquitous food industry ingredients are now on the decline," *Fortune*, Mar 14, 2017; Scrinis G, *Nutritionism: The Science and Politics of Dietary Advice*, Columbia University Press, 2013; Pollan M, "Unhappy meals," *NY Times Mag.*, Jan 28, 2007.

19. "Instructions for authors," *J Nutr.* 1960, 70(1):127–128.

20. Nestle M, Roberts WK, "Separation of ribonucleosides and ribonucleotides by a one-dimensional paper chromatographic system," *Anal Biochem.* 1968, 22:349–351; Nestle M, Roberts WK, "An extracellular nuclease from *Serratia marcescens*. I. Purification and some properties of the enzyme," *J Biol Chem.* 1969, 244:5213–5218; Nestle M, Roberts WK, "An extracellular nuclease from *Serratia marcescens*. II. Specificity of the enzyme," *J Biol Chem.* 1969, 244:5219–5225.

21. "Instructions for authors," *J Nutr.* 1990, 120(1):5–11.

22. Cousins RJ, email to author, July 27, 2016.

23. Council of Science Editors, "Guidance for journals developing or revising policies on conflict of interest, disclosure, or competing financial interests," Feb 2005; Relman AS, "Dealing with conflicts of interest," *New Engl J Med.* 1984, 310:1192–1193; .

24. Merrill A, email to author, July 27, 2016.

25. Humane Society, "U.S. per capita egg consumption, 1950–2008," data from US Department of Agriculture, Educational Research Service, 2010, www.humanesociety.org/assets/pdfs/farm/Per-Cap-Cons-Eggs-1.pdf; Garwin JL, Morgan JM, Stowell RL, et al., "Modified eggs are compatible with a diet that reduces serum cholesterol concentrations in humans," *J Nutr.* 1992, 122(11):2153–2160.

26. Donaldson WE, Garlich JD, Hill CH, "Comments on the paper by Garwin et al. (1992)," *J Nutr.* 1993, 123(9):1601.

27. Merrill AH, "Comment by A.H. Merrill, Associate Editor," *J Nutr.* 1993, 123(9):1605.

28. "Guidelines for authors: Acknowledgment," *Am J Clin Nutr.* 1981, 34(1):133–140; "Guidelines for authors: Conflict of interest," *Am J Clin Nutr.* 2002, 75(1):171–175.

29. Finley D, email to author, Jul 28, 2016.

30. "Guidelines for authors," *J Am Diet Assoc.* 1992, 92(1):14–16; "Guidelines for authors," *J Am Diet Assoc.* 1995, 95(1):18–21; "Guidelines for authors," *J Am Diet Assoc.* 2001, 101(1):19; "Guidelines for authors," *J Am Diet Assoc.* 2002, 102(1):27.

Chapter 14. Beyond Disclosure: What to Do?

1. "In this issue of JAMA," JAMA 2017, 317(17):1705–1812.

2. Nestlé, "Nestlé policy on public-private science & research partnerships," Nestlé Research and Development, Sep 2016.

3. Anonymous (by request), email to author, Jan 26, 2016.

4. Sah S, Fugh-Berman A, "Physicians under the influence: Social psychology and industry marketing strategies," *J Law Med Ethics* 2013, 41(3):665–672.

5. Mozaffarian D, "Conflict of interest and the role of the food industry in nutrition research," JAMA 2017, 317(17):1755–1756.

6. National Academies of Sciences, Engineering, and Medicine, *Fostering Integrity in Research*, National Academies Press, 2017; Thornton JP, "Conflict of interest and legal issues for investigators and authors," JAMA 2017, 317(17):1761–1762.

7. Alberts B, Cicerone RJ, Fienberg SE, et al., "Self-correction in science at work," *Science* 2015, 348:1420–1422; Cornell University, "Sanctions for

non-compliance with the Financial Conflict of Interest Related to Research policy," 2017.

8. World Health Organization, "Sixty-Ninth World Health Assembly (WHA) agenda item 11.3: Framework of Engagement with Non-State Actors," May 28, 2016, http://apps.who.int/gb/ebwha/pdf_files/WHA69/A69 _R10-en.pdf?ua=1.

9. O'Donnell P, "NGOs protest industry influence at WHO," *Politico*, Jan 26, 2016.

10. "Civil Society Statement on the World Health Organization's proposed Framework of Engagement with Non-State Actors (FENSA), 69th World Health Assembly," May 2016, www.ghwatch.org/sites/www.ghwatch .org/files/Civil%20Society%20Statement%2060.pdf.

11. Brown K, Rundall P, Lobstein T, et al., "On behalf of sixty-one signatories. Open letter to WHO DG candidates: Keep policy and priority setting free of commercial influence," *Lancet* 2017, 389:1879.

12. World Health Organization, *Technical Report: Addressing and Managing Conflicts of Interest in the Planning and Delivery of Nutrition Programmes at Country Level: Report of a Technical Consultation Convened in Geneva, Switzerland, on 8–9 October 2015*, 2016; World Health Organization, "Safeguarding against possible conflicts of interest in nutrition programmes: Approach for the prevention and management of conflicts of interest in the policy development and implementation of nutrition programmes at country level; Feedback on the WHO consultation," final version, Dec 2017.

13. World Health Organization, "Guidance on ending the inappropriate promotion of foods for infants and young children: Mandate from the World Health Assembly," May 28, 2016.

14. Rowe S, Alexander N, Clydesdale FM, et al., "Funding food science and nutrition research: financial conflicts and scientific integrity," *Nutr Rev.* 2009, 67(5):264–272. Also *J Nutr.* 2009, 139(6):1051–1053; *Am J Clin Nutr.* 2009, 89(5):1285–1291; *J Acad Nutr Diet.* 2009, 109(5):929–936.

15. Rowe S, Alexander N, Kretser A, et al., "Principles for building public-private partnerships to benefit food safety, nutrition, and health research," *Nutr Rev.* 2013, 71(10):682–691.

16. Alexander N, Rowe S, Brackett RE, et al., "Achieving a transparent, actionable framework for public-private partnerships for food and nutrition research," *Am J Clin Nutr.* 2015, 101(6):1359–1363.

17. Charles Perkins Centre, *Engagement with Industry Guidelines*, University of Sydney, 2016.

18. Ludwig D, Nestle M, "Can the food industry play a constructive role in the obesity epidemic?," *JAMA* 2008, 300(15):1808–1811; Richter J,

Public-Private Partnerships and International Health Policy-Making: How Can Public Interests Be Safeguarded? Hakapaino Oy (Finland), 2004; Hawkes C, Buse K, "Public health sector and food industry interaction: It's time to clarify the term 'partnership' and be honest about underlying interests," *Eur J Public Health* 2011, 21(4):400–403.

19. Bero LA, "Accepting commercial sponsorship," *BMJ* 1999, 319:653–654; Monteiro CA, Cannon G, "The impact of transnational 'Big Food' companies on the South: A view from Brazil," *PLoS Med.* 2012, 9(7):e1001252; Centre for Diet and Activity Research (CEDAR), "Dietary public health research and the food industry: Towards a consensus," Robinson College (Cambridge), Dec 11, 2015.

20. Bellatti A, "Ethical sponsorship," DFPI, 2017, https://integritydietitians.org/practice-area/sponsorship-rubric.

21. Monteiro CA, Cannon G, Moubarac J-C, et al., "The UN Decade of Nutrition, the NOVA food classification and the trouble with ultra-processing," *Public Health Nutr.* 2018, 21(1):5–17.

22. Kassirer JP, Angell M, "Financial conflicts of interest in biomedical research," *N Engl J Med.* 1993, 329(8):570–571; National Institutes of Health, "Financial conflict of interest: 2011 revised regulations," Nov 2, 2016.

23. New York University, "Academic conflict of interest and conflict of commitment," Sep, 2013.

24. Boyd EA, Lipton S, Bero LA, "Implementation of financial disclosure politics to manage conflicts of interest," *Health Aff.* 2004, 23(2):206–214.

25. University of California, Berkeley, Compliance Services, "Conflict of interest," https://compliance.berkeley/conflict-of-interest.

26. Cornell University, Office of Research Integrity and Assurance, "Financial conflicts of interest related to research," 2017, www.oria.cornell.edu/COI/requestinfo/.

27. Nipp RD, Moy B, "No conflict, no interest," *JAMA Oncol.* 2016, 2(12):1631–1632; Bero L, "Essays on health: How food companies can sneak bias into scientific research," *The Conversation*, Nov 1, 2016.

Chapter 15. Stakeholders: Take Action

1. Marks JH, "Caveat partner: Sharing responsibility for health with the food industry," *Am J Public Health* 2017, 107(3):360–361.

2. Tempels T, Verweij M, Blok V, "Big Food's ambivalence: Seeking profit and responsibility for health," *Am J Public Health* 2017, 107(3):402–406.

3. Unilever, "Science with objectivity and integrity"; Nestlé Regulatory and Scientific Affairs, "Nestlé policy on public-private science & research

partnerships," Sep 2016; Douglas S, "Our commitment to transparency: Our actions and way forward," *Coca-Cola Journey*, Mar 24, 2017.

4. Kaplan S, "New C.D.C. chief saw Coca-Cola as ally in obesity fight," *NY Times*, Jul 22, 2017.

5. Dixon Hughes Goodman LLP, "Foundation for the National Institutes of Health, Inc.: Financial statements and supplementary information years ended December 31, 2016 and 2015," https://fnih.org/sites/default/files/final /pdf/2016%20Audited%20Financial%20Statements.pdf; Foundation for the National Institutes of Health, "Celebrating 20 years: 2016 Annual Report," http://2016-annual-report.fnih.org/wp-content/uploads/2016-fnih-annual -report-web.pdf.

6. Rabin RC, "Is alcohol good for you? An industry-backed study seeks answers," *NY Times*, Jul 3, 2017.

7. Begley S, "NIH rejected a study of alcohol advertising while pursuing industry funding for other research," *Stat News*, Apr 2, 2018; Siegel M, "Congressional investigation needed into scientific and ethical corruption at the NIAAA," *Tobacco Analysis*, Mar 26, 2018, http://tobaccoanalysis.blogspot .com/2018/03/congressional-investigation-needed-into.html; Rabin RC, "Major study of drinking will be shut down," *NY Times*, Jun 15, 2018.

8. Schafer A, "Biomedical conflicts of interest: A defense of the sequestration thesis," *J Med Ethics* 2004, 30(1):8–24; Marks JH, "Toward a systemic ethics of public-private partnerships related to food and health," *Kennedy Inst Ethics J.* 2014, 24(3):267–299; Agostoni C, "Sponsors and investigators in food science: Vicious circle or virtuous circle?," *Pediatr Res.* 2009, 65(4):369.

9. Centre for Diet and Activity Research (CEDAR), "Dietary public health research and the food industry: Towards a consensus," Robinson College (Cambridge), Dec 11, 2015; Curzer HJ, Santillanes G, "Managing conflict of interest in research: Some suggestions for investigators," *Account Res.* 2012, 19(3):143–155.

10. Zachwieja J, Hentges E, Hill JO, et al., "Public-private partnerships: The evolving role of industry funding in nutrition research," *Adv Nutr.* 2013, 4(5):570–572.

11. Katan MB, "Does industry sponsorship undermine the integrity of nutrition research?" *PLoS Med.* 2007, 1(4):e6.

12. World Obesity, "World Obesity's terms of engagement," www .worldobesity.org/who-we-are/what-we-stand-for/financial-engagement-policy/.

13. Rothman DJ, McDonald WJ, Berkowitz CD, et al., "Professional medical associations and their relationships with industry: A proposal for controlling conflict of interest," *JAMA* 2009, 301(13):1367–1372.

14. Alberts B, Cicerone RJ, Fienberg SE, et al., "Self-correction in science at work," *Science* 2015, 348:1420–1422.

15. Gottlieb JD, Bressler NM, "How should journals handle the conflict of interest of their editors? Who watches the 'watchers'?" *JAMA* 2017, 317(17):1757–1758; Easley TJ, "Medical journals, publishers, and conflict of interest," *JAMA* 2017, 317(17):1759–1760; International Committee of Medical Journal Editors, "Recommendations for the conduct, reporting, editing, and publication of scholarly work in medical journals," updated Dec 2017, www.icmje.org/icmje-recommendations.pdf.

16. Kassirer JP, "Physicians' financial ties with the pharmaceutical industry: A critical element of a formidable marketing network," in: Moore DA, Cain DM, Loewenstein G, Bazerman MH, eds., *Conflicts of Interest: Challenges and Solutions in Business, Law, Medicine, and Public Policy*, Cambridge University Press, 2005, 133–141.

17. Godlee F, Malone R, Timmis A, et al., "Journal policy on research funded by the tobacco industry," *BMJ* 2013, 347:f5193; Smith R, "Comment from the editor," *BMJ* 2003, 327:505.

18. Fontanarosa P, Bauchner H, "Conflict of interest and medical journals," *JAMA* 2017, 317(17):1768–1771; Tovey D, "Cochrane and conflict of interest," Cochrane Community, Apr 18, 2016, http://community.cochrane.org/news/cochrane-and-conflict-interest; *New England Journal of Medicine*, Author Center, "New manuscripts," www.nejm.org/author-center/new-manuscripts.

19. Daniel H-D, *Guardians of Science: Fairness and Reliability of Peer Review*, Wiley Online Library, 2004; Smith R, "Peer review: A flawed process at the heart of science and journals," *JR Soc Med.* 2006, 99(4):178–182; Shawwa K, Kallas R, Koujanian S, et al., "Requirements of clinical journals for authors' disclosure of financial and non-financial conflicts of interest: A cross sectional study," *PLoS One* 2016, 11(3):e0152301.

20. Society of Professional Journalists, "SPJ Code of Ethics," revised Sep 6, 2014.

21. Huehnergarth NF, "Monsanto and the organics industry pay to train journalists: What could go wrong?" *Forbes*, May 31, 2016.

22. Thacker PD, "Where do science journalists draw the line?" *Columbia Journal Rev.*, Nov 23, 2015.

23. Ruskin G, "Journalists fail to reveal sources funded by Coca-Cola: A short report," US Right to Know, Dec 14, 2015.

24. Schwitzer quoted in Holtz A, "Conflict of interest/funding disclosure missing from half of news releases we've reviewed—a case study on why that's important," HealthNewsRev.org, Aug 18, 2016.

25. Wang MTM, Grey A, Bolland MJ, "Conflicts of interest and expertise of independent commenters in news stories about medical research," CMAJ, 2017, 189(15):e553–559.

26. Wilner T, "How to talk about conflict of interest," Center for Skeptical Inquiry, Oct 5, 2016.

27. HealthNewsReview.org, "Our review criteria," www.healthnewsreview .org/about-us/review-criteria/.

28. Raff J, "How to read and understand a scientific paper: A step-by-step guide for non-scientists," Huff Post, June 18, 2014; Ask for Evidence, "Working out what's reliable evidence," Sense About Science, undated.

29. Miller D, Harkins C, Schlögl M, Montague B, Impact of Market Forces on Addictive Substances and Behaviours, Oxford University Press, 2018.

30. Taylor AP, "National Academies revise conflict of interest policy," Scientist, May 3, 2017.

31. National Institutes of Health, "Financial conflict of interest: 2011 revised regulations," Nov 2, 2016.

32. Association of Public and Land-Grant Universities, The Challenge of Change: Harnessing University Discovery, Engagement, and Learning to Achieve Food and Nutrition Security, 2017.

Notes to Tables

Table 3.1. Studies Examining Food-Industry Influence on Nutritional Health Research, 2003–2018 (page 38)

1. Levine J, Gussow JD, Hastings D, Eccher A, "Authors' financial relationships with the food and beverage industry and their published positions on the fat substitute Olestra," *Am J Public Health* 2003, 93(4):664–669.

2. Lesser LI, Ebbeling CB, Goozner M, et al., "Relationship between funding source and conclusion among nutrition-related scientific articles," *PLoS Med.* 2007, Jan 4(1):e5.

3. Vartanian LR, Schwartz MB, Brownell KD, "Effects of soft drink consumption on nutrition and health: A systematic review and meta-analysis," *Am J Public Health* 2007, 97(4):667–675.

4. Nkansah N, Nguyen T, Iraninezhad H, Bero L, "Randomized trials assessing calcium supplementation in healthy children: Relationship between industry sponsorship and study outcomes," *Public Health Nutr.* 2009, 12(10):1931–1937.

5. Wilde P, Morgan E, Roberts J, et al., "Relationship between funding sources and outcomes of obesity-related research," *Physiol & Behav.* 2012, 107:172–175.

6. Bes-Rastrollo M, Schulze MB, Ruiz-Canela M, Martinez-Gonzalez MA, "Financial conflicts of interest and reporting bias regarding the association between sugar-sweetened beverages and weight gain: A systematic review of systematic reviews," *PLoS Med.* 2013, 10(12):e1001578.

7. Mugambi MN, Musekiwa A, Lombard M, et al., "Association between funding source, methodological quality and research outcomes in randomized controlled trials of synbiotics, probiotics and prebiotics added to infant formula: A systematic review," *BMC Med Res Methodol.* 2013, 13:137.

8. Massougbodji J, Le Bodo Y, Fratu R, De Wals P, "Reviews examining sugar-sweetened beverages and body weight: Correlates of their quality and conclusions," *Am J Clin Nutr.* 2014, 99:1096–1104.

9. Schillinger D, Tran J, Mangurian C, Kearns C, "Do sugar-sweetened beverages cause obesity and diabetes? Industry and the manufacture of scientific controversy," *Ann Intern Med.* 2016, 165(12):895–897.

10. Mandrioli D, Kearns CE, Bero LA, "Relationship between research outcomes and risk of bias, study sponsorship, and author financial conflicts of interest in reviews of the effects of artificially sweetened beverages on weight outcomes: A systematic review of reviews," *PLoS One* 2016, 11(9):e0162198.

11. Litman EA, Gortmaker SL, Ebbeling CB, Ludwig DS, "Source of bias in sugar-sweetened beverage research: A systematic review," *Public Health Nutr.* 2018, Mar 26:1–6 (epub ahead of print).

Table 6.2. Industry-Funded Studies of Food Plants with Results Useful for Health Claims (Selected Examples), 2015–2018 (page 88)

1. Dhillon J, Tan S-Y, Mattes RD, "Almond consumption during energy restriction lowers truncal fat and blood pressure in compliant overweight or obese adults," *J Nutr.* 2016, 146(12):2513–2519.

2. Scott TM, Rasmussen HM, Chen O, Johnson EJ, "Avocado consumption increases macular pigment density in older adults: A randomized, controlled trial," *Nutrients* 2017, 9(9):919.

3. Nieman DC, Gillitt ND, Sha W, et al., "Metabolic recovery from heavy exertion following banana compared to sugar beverage or water only ingestion: A randomized, crossover trial," *PLoS One* 2018, 13(3):e0194843.

4. Mah E, Schulz JA, Kaden VN, et al., "Cashew consumption reduces total and LDL cholesterol: A randomized, crossover, controlled-feeding trial," *Am J Clin Nutr.* 2017, 105:1070–1078.

5. Fu Z, Liska D, Talan D, Chung M, "Cranberry reduces the risk of urinary tract infection recurrence in otherwise healthy women: A systematic review and meta-analysis," *J Nutr*. 2017, 147:2282–2288.

6. Percival SS, "Aged garlic extract modifies human immunity," *J Nutr*. 2016, 146:433s–436s.

7. Lamport DJ, Lawton CL, Merat CL, et al., "Concord grape juice, cognitive function, and driving performance: A 12-wk, placebo-controlled, randomized crossover trial in mothers of preteen children," *Am J Clin Nutr*. 2016, 103(3):775–783.

8. Ojo B, El-Rassi DG, Payton ME, et al., "Mango supplementation modulates gut microbial dysbiosis and short-chain fatty acid production independent of body weight reduction in C57BL/6 mice fed a high-fat diet," *J Nutr*. 2016, 146:1483–1491.

9. Liu X, Hill Am, West SG, et al., "Acute peanut consumption alters postprandial lipids and vascular responses in healthy overweight or obese men," *J Nutr*. 2017, 147:835–840.

10. Akilen R, Deljoomanesh N, Hunschede S, et al., "The effects of potatoes and other carbohydrate side dishes consumed with meat on food intake, glycemia and satiety response in children," *Nutr Diet*. 2016, 6:e195.

11. Bays H, Weiter K, Anderson J, "A randomized study of raisins versus alternative snacks on glycemic control and other cardiovascular risk factors in patients with type 2 diabetes mellitus," *Phys Sportsmed*. 2015, 43(1):37–43.

12. Burton-Freeman BM, Sandhu AK, Edirisinghe I, "Red raspberries and their bioactive polyphenols: Cardiometabolic and neuronal health links," *Adv Nutr*. 2016, 7:44–65.

13. Leidy HJ, Todd CB, Zino AZ, et al., "Consuming high-protein soy snacks affects appetite control, satiety, and diet quality in young people and influences select aspects of mood and cognition," *J Nutr*. 2015, 145:1614–1622.

14. Freedman MR, Fulgoni VL, "Canned vegetable and fruit consumption is associated with changes in nutrient intake and higher diet quality in children and adults: National Health and Nutrition Examination Survey 2001–2010," *J Acad Nutr Diet*. 2016, 116(6):940–948.

15. Njike VY, Ayettey R, Petraro P, et al., "Walnut ingestion in adults at risk for diabetes: Effects on body composition, diet quality, and cardiac risk measures," *BMJ Open Diabetes Res Care* 2015, 3:e000115.

16. Albertson AM, Reicks M, Joshi N, Gugger CK, "Whole grain consumption trends and associations with body weight measures in the United States: Results from the cross sectional National Health and Nutrition Examination Survey 2001–2012," *Nutr J*. 2016, 15:8.

Table 11.1. Examples of Studies with Favorable Results Funded through Cooperative Agreements with the USDA's Agricultural Research Service, 2014–2018 (page 161)

1. O'Neil CE, Nicklas TA, Fulgoni VL, "Avocado consumption by adults is associated with better nutrient intake, diet quality, and some measures of adiposity: National Health and Nutrition Examination Survey, 2001–2002," *Int Med Rev.* 2017, 3(4):1–23.

2. Miller MG, Hamilton DA, Joseph JA, Shukitt-Hale B, "Dietary blueberry improves cognition among older adults in a randomized, double-blind, placebo-controlled trial," *Eur J Nutr.* 2018, 57(3):1169–1180.

3. Berger S, Ramen G, Vishwanathan R, et al., "Dietary cholesterol and cardiovascular disease: A systematic review and meta-analysis," *Am J Clin Nutr.* 2015, 102(2):276–294.

4. O'Neil CE, Nicklas TA, Fulgoni VL, "Fresh pear consumption is associated with better nutrient intake, diet quality, and weight parameters in adults: National Health and Nutrition Examination Survey 2001–2010," *J Nutr Food Sci.* 2015, 5:377.

5. Nicklas TA, O'Neil CE, Fulgoni VL, "Rice consumption is associated with better nutrient intake and diet quality in adults: National Health and Nutrition Examination Survey (NHANES) 2005–2010," *Food Nutr Sci.* 2014, 5:525–532.

6. Raatz SK, Johnson LK, Rosenberger TA, "Twice weekly intake of farmed Atlantic salmon (*Salmo salar*) positively influences lipoprotein concentration and particle size in overweight men and women," *Nutr Res.* 2016, 36(9):899–906.

7. Baer DJ, Gebauer SK, Novotny JA, "Walnuts consumed by healthy adults provide less available energy than predicted by the Atwater factors," *J Nutr.* 2016, 146(1):9–13.

Index

Bill Hayes Photo

MARION NESTLE is Paulette Goddard Professor of Nutrition, Food Studies, and Public Health, Emerita, at New York University in the department she chaired from 1988 to 2003. She is also professor of sociology at New York University and visiting professor of nutritional sciences at Cornell University. She earned a PhD in molecular biology and an MPH in public health nutrition from the University of California, Berkeley. She holds honorary degrees from Transylvania University in Kentucky (2012) and from the City University of New York's Macaulay Honors College (2016). She lives in New York City.